RECIPE JUBILEE

A unique phenomenon occurs on the eastern shore of Mobile Bay. Natives of the area know the signs to watch for—in the moon, the tide, and the winds.

Shrimps, crabs, and fish
race to the water's edge
and the cry of *JUBILEE!*
rings up and down the
beach. With buckets, bas-
kets and nets in tow,
visitors and natives alike
gather a bounty of fresh
sea food.

RECIPE JUBILEE COMMITTEE

Chairman—Mrs. Selwyn Turner, Jr.

Editor	Mrs. Frank B. Frazer
Business Manager	Mrs. John M. Morrissette, Jr.
Art Editors	Mrs. John D. McCown
	Mrs. Robert A. Guthans
Recipe Chairman	Mrs. Jere Austill, Jr.
Promotion	Mrs. Edward B. Baumhauer
Publicity	Mrs. Gillette Burton
Typist	Mrs. Wallace S. Clark, III
Secretary	Mrs. John Brady

Many others have aided and abetted these chairmen in compiling this cookbook. Without the wholehearted efforts of the League membership, we would have no book. Our many thanks to all who have given their time so generously.

Recipe Jubilee

published by

THE JUNIOR LEAGUE OF MOBILE, INC.

1964

"The purpose of the Junior League is to foster interest among its members in the social, economic, educational, cultural and civic conditions of the community, and to make efficient their volunteer service."

COPYRIGHT

JUNIOR LEAGUE OF MOBILE, INC.

1964

First Printing	September, 1964	7,000 copies
Second Printing	December, 1964	10,000 copies
Third Printing	September, 1967	10,000 copies
Fourth Printing	January, 1969	20,000 copies
Fifth Printing	January, 1972	20,000 copies
Sixth Printing	October, 1975	20,000 copies
Seventh Printing	June, 1977	20,000 copies
Eighth Printing	December, 1979	20,000 copies
Ninth Printing	October, 1983	10,000 copies
Tenth Printing	January, 1987	5,000 copies
Eleventh Printing	June, 1988	5,000 copies

ISBN # 0-9603054-1-6

Additional copies may be ordered from:

Mobile Junior League Publications
P.O. Box 7091
Mobile, Alabama 36607

WIMMER BROTHERS
Memphis   Dallas

INTRODUCTION

There is much about Mobile that is unique. When the Spanish explorers came in 1519, they found the Indians living in the vicinity were highly civilized. They farmed, lived in wooden houses and their women were beautiful.

Mobile was founded by the French in 1702, a few miles up the river from its present location. The gay French soldiers celebrated Mardi Gras there in the wilderness. Ours is the only city in America established under the direct auspices of fabulous Louis XIV.

This area has a singular history in the struggle between the Teutonic and Latin nations. It is the only territory, later to become part of the United States, which actually lived under France, Great Britain, and Spain. Throughout Mobile's history, as one flag was lowered to be replaced by the next, some inhabitants moved out and some remained. Streets were often renamed and old customs adopted and adapted to the new culture.

Rapid change of flags make colorful history, but it is not conducive to growth. Not until 1813, when the Stars and Stripes was raised and there was a large influx of Americans, did Mobile begin to develop into a real city with a promising future. During the 1850's it was an important port—a social, business and cultural center. This period is known as the "Golden Fifties." It was also the threshold of the War Between the States and the reign of the Battle Flag of the Confederacy.

And so from an Indian habitat through five flags and more than 250 years, Mobile has developed a unique personality. She has great natural beauty in her rivers and bay; her ancient, powerful oaks laced with Spanish moss; and her famous flaming azaleas. Indeed singular are her gracious hospitality and festive Mardi Gras. The houses and buildings, over 100 years old, are reminiscent of France, have a suggestion of Spain, with gardens as beautiful as England's. But, more than any of these, they are distinctly Mobile.

This is so of Mobile in its entirety. Perhaps you will find some evidence of her history reflected in these recipes; a delightful delicacy of the French, a specialty of Spain, an old Southern recipe. You will discover that what is good from the past has been skillfully adapted to today. So we give to you a "RECIPE JUBILEE."

All recipes in this book have been compiled, tested, or approved for publication by the membership of the Junior League of Mobile, Inc. We acknowledge and appreciate contributions from friends of the members and our sustaining members.

Proceeds from the sale of *Recipe Jubilee* are used to finance the Junior League's educational, cultural and welfare projects in our community.

TABLE OF CONTENTS

Appetizers and Beverages

MARDI GRAS FAVORITES

APPETIZERS AND BEVERAGES

COCKTAIL MEAT BALLS

Season ground meat (about 3 pounds beef and pork) with onions, Worcestershire, salt, pepper and a little wet bread. Shape into small balls and refrigerate. Brown meat balls and add to sauce made of a bottle of chili sauce, a bottle of water, eight mashed ginger snaps, simmer gently. Serves 12 generously.

Mrs. T. Potter Yeend

HAM ROUND

1 cup baked ham, ground	mayonnaise
½ cup chopped hazel nuts	rye rounds
½ cup chopped olives	a few capers

Mix ham, nuts and olives well with mayonnaise. Pile on rye rounds, sprinkle center with a few capers.

Mrs. Frank J. Sauer

BELLE FONTAINE CRAB DIP

1 pound crabmeat	1-2 dashes Louisiana hot sauce
2 small packages cream cheese	salt and pepper to taste
one very small onion, grated fine	4 tablespoons mayonnaise
few dashes Worcestershire sauce	

Mix cream cheese and seasonings. Add crabmeat. Serve as hors d'oeuvre or in stuffed tomato.

Mrs. Scranton Dunlap

13

CRAB BALLS

7-8 slices fresh bread	1 egg
1 pound crabmeat	¼ teaspoon red pepper
3 heaping tablespoons	¼ teaspoon celery seed
mayonnaise	

Crumble bread in blender. Combine all ingredients, make into balls about the size of a fifty cent piece. Refrigerate three to four hours, fry in deep fat about five minutes.

Mrs. Paul Thompson

HOT CRABMEAT PUFFS

2 egg whites	toast beds
1 cup mayonnaise	paprika
1 cup crabmeat	

Beat eggs until stiff, fold in mayonnaise and crabmeat. Season and pile on toast beds. Sprinkle with paprika. Broil about three minutes until puffy and lightly browned.

Mrs. Potter Yeend

PARTY DIP

½ pound butter	salt to taste
1 cup flour	2 pounds crabmeat
1 small can Pet milk	1 pound cooked shrimp,
2 cups sweet milk	chopped
1 tablespoon sherry	1 can chopped mushrooms
1 teaspoon paprika	1 bunch green onions, chopped
1 teaspoon pepper	2 cups chopped parsley

In double boiler melt butter, add flour gradually. Add Pet milk, sweet milk, sherry and seasonings. Add remaining ingredients when sauce is smooth. Serve from chafing dish.

Mrs. Paul E. Sheldon

SHRIMP COCKTAIL FRITTERS

1 cup flour	1 small onion, minced
1 teaspoon baking powder	1 tablespoon parsley, minced
½ teaspoon salt	dash of Tabasco
pepper to taste	1 pound raw shrimp, cleaned,
2 eggs, beaten well	de-veined, and minced
milk	

Sift together dry ingredients; add eggs and enough milk to make a thick batter. Add onion, parsley, Tabasco and shrimp. Beat well, drop by teaspoonsful into deep fat (hot), brown until golden. Serve hot on toothpicks. These fritters may be served as hors d'oeuvres or made into layers and served as an entree. As an entree, substitute one cup mashed potatoes for flour and add a tablespoon melted butter. Then roll into marble sized balls and fry.

Mrs. Leon McVay, Jr.

SHRIMP PASTE

¾ pound cooked shrimp,	½ teaspoon lemon juice
peeled and de-veined	dash dry mustard
1 stick butter	salt to taste
1 teaspoon horseradish	red pepper to taste

Grind shrimp, blend into soft butter and add other ingredients. Turn into seafood mold and refrigerate for several hours. If too thick, add a little mayonnaise. Serve with crackers.

Mrs. Russell Terry

SHRIMP DIP

½ pound boiled shrimp, finely	salt
chopped	Beau Monde
1 large cream cheese	Tabasco
onion juice	

Soften cream cheese with mayonnaise and add seasonings to taste. Yields about 2 cups.

Mrs. Randall Hollinger

15

HOT PICKLED SHRIMP

Clean and de-vein shrimp. In large saucepan blend with one large sliced onion enough pure cider vinegar (red) to cover shrimp. Add one-half can crushed red pepper. Boil mixture about ten to fifteen minutes, add shrimp and cook ten minutes longer. Cool in liquid, drain and chill. Good with cocktails.

Mrs. Richard Cunningham

PICKLED SHRIMP

3 pounds fresh shrimp in shells	2½ cups sliced onion
¾ cup celery tops	10 bay leaves
½ cup mixed pickling spices	1 recipe of pickling marinade
1 tablespoon salt	

Cover shrimp with boiling water, add celery tops, spices, and salt. Cover and simmer five minutes. Drain, peel and de-vein shrimp under cold water. Alternate cleaned shrimp, onions and bay leaves in shallow baking dish. Marinade.

2 cups salad oil	3 teaspoons celery seed
1 cup white vinegar	2 teaspoons salt
4 tablespoons capers with juice	few drops Tabasco

Combine ingredients, mix well, pour over shrimp and cover. Chill at least twenty-four hours, spooning marinade over shrimp occasionally. Keeps about a week in refrigerator. 8 servings. May be served as hors d'oeuvres or salad.

Mrs. O. H. Delchamps, Jr.

SMOKED OYSTER AND OLIVE CANAPÉ

Large green pitted olives   smoked oysters

Stuff olives with smoked oysters. Refrigerate overnight and serve cold.

Mrs. James Pollard

OYSTER CANAPÉ

Use small oysters. Soak in onion and lemon juice (about ¼ cup lemon juice for 1 quart oysters) for two hours. Place oysters on toast and cover with grated cheese, perferably sharp cheddar, and brown under broiler.

Mrs. Frank Terrell

COCKTAIL OYSTERS

Cut bacon slices in half. Lay one drained raw oyster on each half. Sprinkle with salt and pepper, minced green onion and a little grated lemon peel. Fold bacon over oyster, secure with toothpick and place on rack in broiler pan. Place in preheated 450° oven and cook until crisp on one side, turn and cook until crisp.

Mrs. T. B. Snevely

LOBSTER ROUNDS

2 cups lobster
1 hard boiled egg, chopped
1 tomato, peeled, drained
    and chopped

salt and pepper
mayonnaise
cracked wheat rounds
cucumber slices

Mix lobster, egg, tomato, salt and pepper. Bind with mayonnaise. Pile on wheat rounds and garnish center with cucumber slices.

Mrs. Frank Sauer

CREAMED CLAMS

½ clove garlic
8 ounce package cream cheese
2 teaspoons lemon juice
1½ teaspoons Worcestershire
½ teaspoon salt

dash red pepper
1 can minced clams, drained
¼ cup clam juice
1 tablespoon grated onion juice

Rub bowl with garlic. Blend cream cheese with remaining ingredients. Serve warm from a chafing dish with Melba toast rounds or cold as a spread on crackers or as a dip.

Mrs. Robert Clark

MINCED CLAM DIP

1 (8 ounce) package cream cheese
1 carton cottage cheese
1 can (flat) minced clams, drained

2 tablespoons minced onion
1 small can pimentos, chopped fine

Cream above ingredients and season with parsley flakes, Worcestershire, cayenne pepper, salt, lemon juice and enough mayonnaise to obtain desired consistency for dip.

Mrs. James Duffy, Jr.

17

SALMON EGG SPREAD

1 pint sour cream	2 small jars red salmon eggs
1 tablespoon grated onion	(or caviar)
ground pepper and pinch of salt	

Mix well, adding salmon last so as not to break eggs. Serve with crackers.

Mrs. Ernest Brown

SARDINE SPREAD

½ pound cream cheese	2 cans (3¾ ounce size) sardines
¼ cup cream	4 tablespoons parsley, chopped
2 tablespoons lemon juice	1 teaspoon paprika
1 teaspoon Worcestershire	4 tablespoons pimentos, chopped

Soften cream cheese with cream. Add lemon juice and Worcestershire. Mash sardines or put in blender, add to cream cheese mixture and mix well. Add parsley, paprika and pimentos. Form into a mound, sprinkle with paprika and decorate with pimento strips. Serve with crackers.

Mrs. Marion S. Adams, Jr.

SARDINE PATÉ

1 can Portuguese boneless, skinless sardines	1 teaspoon mayonnaise
1 tablespoon grated onion juice	1 teaspoon lemon juice
1 heaping teaspoon horseradish	few drops Tabasco
1 teaspoon mustard	few drops Worcestershire
	Cayenne pepper to taste

Put all ingredients in blender and blend until a good consistency to spread on saltine crackers.

Mrs. Robert Clark

ROQUEFORT CANAPÉS

Cream 1 (3 ounces) Roquefort cheese, blend with 2 stiffly beaten egg whites. Spread on bread rounds or crackers and toast until cheese is puffed and brown. Serve at once. About 30 cracker canapes.

Mrs. Leon McVay, Jr.

BLUE CHEESE DIP I

Into blender place:

1 cup cottage cheese
4 ounces blue cheese, crumbled
⅓ cup cream or homogenized
   milk

6 sprigs (or more) parsley
¼ small onion
1 teaspoon Worcestershire sauce
⅛ teaspoon or dash Tabasco

Cover and blend on high until smooth. Season to taste.

Mrs. Vernon Dukes

BLUE CHEESE DIP II

2 (3 ounce) packages cream
   cheese
1 (4 ounce) package blue cheese

1 small package Roquefort cheese
milk (or sour cream)
mayonnaise

Let cheeses stand at room temperature until softened. Mix cheeses together. Add equal amounts of milk and mayonnaise until mixture reaches dip consistency. Serve with Fritos and potato chips. Sour cream may be substituted for milk.

Mrs. H. C. Slaton, Jr.

CAULIFLOWER DIP

1 cup mayonnaise
6 ounces blue cheese

1 clove garlic, crushed
1 teaspoon Worcestershire sauce

Mix together and refrigerate for several hours before serving with raw cauliflower or other raw vegetables.

Mrs. Everett Sapp

CHEESE STRAWS I

1¼ pounds extra sharp cheese
1 stick butter
1¾ cups flour

⅓ teaspoon salt
¼ teaspoon red pepper
pinch of Cayenne

Grate cheese or run through meat grinder. Cream butter and cheese together. Mix all ingredients thoroughly and put in cookie press. Bake in 350° oven until brown, about thirty minutes.

Mrs. John Pitman

19

CHEESE STRAWS II

1½ cups flour	¼ teaspoon dry mustard
½ teaspoon baking powder	4 tablespoons butter
dash of salt	1½ cups grated cheese
Cayenne	5 tablespoons cold water

Sift flour, baking powder, salt, Cayenne and mustard. Cut in butter, add grated cheese and cold water. Roll out and cut into quarter inch strips three inches long. Bake for twenty minutes in 400° oven, until golden.

Mrs. Frank Sauer

CHEESE PUFFS

1 loaf unsliced bread	garlic to taste
1 stick butter	paprika
1 jar sharp cheese	

Remove crust from loaf, cut bread into one and a half inch cubes. Combine cheese, butter, and garlic. Cover bread with cheese mixture, sprinkle with paprika and heat before serving.

Mrs. Carl Hixon

CHEESE CANAPÉS

Grate finely 1 pound rat trap or similar cheese. Add 5 finely sliced green onions, using part of the green and ½ to ¾ cup finely sliced pimento stuffed green olives. Add about ½ cup mayonnaise or just enough to hold the above ingredients together, season with a dash of salt and pepper. Spread on Holland Rusk or bread, etc. and place in broiler until mixture has melted.

Mrs. V. L. Oberkirch

CHEESE DIP

1 pound New York State cheese	½ cup mayonnaise
1 large onion, grated	1 tablespoon Worcestershire
½ small jar mustard	2 teaspoons Tabasco

Beat and heat dip. Serve with assorted crackers or celery sticks.

Mrs. W. B. Taylor, Jr.

DIP FOR CAULIFLOWER AND CARROTS

2 cups chive cheese
1 pint mayonnaise
1 teaspoon Worcestershire
½ teaspoon Tabasco

5 or 6 cloves garlic, crushed
¼ onion, grated
chopped parsley (optional)

Mix all ingredients together.

Mrs. Randall Hollinger

CHEESE ROLL I

1 pound yellow cheese
2 packages cream cheese
(3 ounces each)

1 cup cashew nuts
2 cloves garlic, minced
paprika

Soften cheese at room temperature. Alternate yellow cheese and cashews through food grinder using finest blade. Soften and whip cream cheese. Mix ingredients. Shape into a roll 1½ inches in diameter. Roll generously in paprika. Wrap in wax paper. Refrigerate. Slice thin and serve on round crackers. Keeps well. 16 to 20 servings.

Mrs. George McNally

CHEESE ROLL II

¼ pound New York cheese
¼ pound cream cheese
¼ pound pimento cheese
1 cup pecans

1 garlic clove, crushed
salt to taste
paprika or chili powder

Allow cheeses to soften. Grind cheeses and pecans. Add other ingredients and mix well. Shape into three rolls and roll in paprika or chili powder. Refrigerate. Serve with crackers.

Mrs. M. L. Screven

CHEESE BALLS

1 egg white
1 cup grated sharp cheese
cracker crumbs

Cayenne pepper
garlic salt

Mix egg white and cheese well, make into ten balls. Season cracker crumbs with pepper and salt, roll balls in crumbs and fry in very hot deep fat.

Mrs. Ernest L. Brown

21

HOT APPETIZERS

1 cup grated sharp New York cheese	¼ cup melted butter
½ cup sifted flour	½ teaspoon paprika
	pinch of salt

Mix in electric mixer. Dip hands in flour and shape into individual small balls, using a drained stuffed olive in the center of each. Refrigerate an hour or two. Bake on cookie sheet in 350° oven about fifteen minutes.

Mrs. W. B. Erickson, Jr.

PARTY MOLD

2 (8 ounce) packages cream cheese	2 tablespoons Worcestershire
½ pound sharp cheese, grated	1 teaspoon paprika
1 small wedge Roquefort cheese	1 tablespoon mayonnaise
1 teaspoon garlic salt	1 tablespoon lemon juice
½ teaspoon curry powder	1 can lobster, crabmeat or shrimp

Have all ingredients at room temperature. Mix, adding cream if necessary to bind. Grease cold one quart mold with salad oil. Turn mixture into mold and refrigerate, overnight if possible. Unmold by shaking. Garnish with chopped parsley, pimentos and stuffed olives. Serve with crackers.

Mrs. Theo Middleton

LIPTAUER CHEESE

6 ounces cream cheese	2 anchovies, finely chopped
¼ cup soft butter	1 green onion, minced
1 teaspoon bell pepper, minced	½ teaspoon salt
1 teaspoon capers	½ teaspoon caraway seeds

Work cream cheese smooth, blend in butter. Add bell pepper, capers, anchovies, onion, salt and caraway seeds. Mix well. Refrigerate overnight in pint jar.

Mrs. T. B. Snevely

CHILI CON QUESO

⅔ cup chopped onion	3 tablespoons flour
3 tablespoons cooking oil	¼ cup cold water
1 can El Paso tomatoes and green chilis (10 ounces)	1 pound hoop cheese
4 teaspoons paprika	⅓ cup sharp cheese
4 teaspoons chili powder	salt to taste
½ garlic clove, chopped fine	red pepper to taste

Sauté onion in oil until soft, but not brown. Add, breaking up well, tomatoes and green chilis, paprika, chili powder and garlic. Stir in paste made of flour and cold water. Simmer, stirring, ten minutes or so. Add crumbled cheeses, salt and red pepper. When cheese is melted, keep warm and serve from chafing dish.

Pat Martin

ALMOND CHEESE BALLS

¼ cup chopped almonds	¼ cup butter
¼ cup flour	1 cup grated American cheese
¼ teaspoon salt	2 tablespoons cold water
dash of paprika	

Chop almonds, sift flour, salt and paprika together. Blend butter and cheese, add nuts and flour mixture, sprinkle water over mixture and mix well. Make balls about three-fourths inch in diameter, bake in 350° oven about fifteen minutes. Makes 24.

Mrs. Paul Sheldon

WALNUT BALLS

Mix equal parts of cream cheese and blue cheese. Chill and stuff between walnut halves.

Mrs. W. Buck Taylor

CHEESE WAFERS WITH PECANS

1 stick butter minus a portion equal to a pat served in restaurants (Do not substitute margarine)	½ teaspoon salt
	¼ teaspoon red pepper
	1 cup flour
1 pound New York State cheese	pecans

23

Set butter out to soften. Grate cheese into large bowl. Cream cheese and butter together by hand. Add salt and pepper and cream well. Add flour to mixture a little at a time. Work mixture by hand until it is smooth and can be rolled into a ball. Divide the dough into three portions. Roll each portion of the dough back and forth on a piece of waxed paper until you have a long slender roll about the diameter of a fifty cent piece. Wrap in waxed paper. Store in refrigerator until hard or overnight. Preheat oven to 225° or 250°. With a sharp knife slice the cheese into thin wafers. Place on aluminum foil covered cookie sheet. Place a pecan half in center of each wafer. Remove from oven when only a few bubbles remain on tops, about thirty minutes. Yields 15 dozen wafers. Mixture keeps well in refrigerator for at least two weeks.

Mrs. Manson Murray

MUSHROOM CANAPÉS

Cut bread into desired shapes. Chop either fresh or canned mushrooms fine, sauté in butter, add minced onion to taste. Spread on toast, cover with grated Parmesan cheese, toast in oven one minute. Sprinkle with paprika. Serve hot.

Mrs. Leon McVay, Jr.

MUSHROOM SANDWICHES

2 tablespoons flour	1 can mushroom soup
¼ to ⅓ cup sherry	salt, pepper, onion salt, garlic salt,
4 (3 ounce) cans chopped	Worcestershire sauce and
mushrooms	Tabasco to taste

Dissolve flour in sherry and add to mushroom soup mixed with mushrooms. Add seasonings. Simmer slowly for about ten minutes, stirring constantly. Refrigerate until mixture is thick enough to spread. Make sandwiches, buttering top and bottom of bread. Heat until golden brown. Serve hot. Makes 8 to 10 sandwiches. May be made ahead and kept in freezer.

Mrs. Thomas Taul, Jr.

PICKLED MUSHROOMS

1 teaspoon oregano	⅓ cup wine vinegar
1 teaspoon peppercorns	½ cup olive oil
1 garlic pod, whole	2 small cans button mushrooms
1 teaspoon salt	

Mix first six ingredients in a jar and shake well. Add mushrooms. Marinate, shaking occasionally, for several hours before serving. These may be kept two to three weeks in refrigerator, but become stronger with age. Remove from refrigerator in plenty of time for oil to become liquefied again. Strain and serve on toothpicks or on small crackers.

Mrs. John McClelland

STUFFED HARD BOILED EGGS

Half eggs lengthwise, mash hot yolks. Add a little olive oil, mayonnaise. Add to taste, minced green onion, bell pepper, celery and parsley. Add a dash of Worcestershire and Cayenne or pepperoni, garlic salt, salt and pepper. Mold into creamy mixture and stuff egg whites. In center put a few capers, anchovy bit or sliced stuffed olive. Chill.

Mrs. Frank Sauer

BRAUNSCHWEIGER IN GELATIN

1 tablespoon gelatin	1 tablespoon wine vinegar
½ cup water	3½ tablespoons mayonnaise
1 can condensed consomme	1 teaspoon poppy seed
½ pound Braunschweiger	¼ teaspoon dry mustard

Soften gelatin in cold water. Heat consomme to boiling. Remove from heat, add gelatin and stir until dissolved. Pour into a lightly greased two cup mold. Chill until firm. Mix remaining ingredients. Take top off gelatin mixture and scoop out enough to put Braunschweiger mixture in mold. Be sure to leave enough gelatin on the sides. Fill center with Braunschweiger mixture. Heat the gelatin that has been scooped out until melted. Pour melted gelatin over top of mold. Chill until firm. Unmold and serve with crackers.

Mrs. John Pitman

25

CUCUMBER CASES

6 three-inch cucumbers
½ cup finely chopped cooked
  spinach
3 small green onions, minced
⅓ cup mayonnaise

salt and freshly ground pepper
few drops lemon juice
sieved yolk of one hard cooked
  egg

Peel and cut the cucumber into eighteen one-inch pieces and scoop out the seeds from one end of each cucumber piece, leaving the other end closed to form a little case. Chill and dry the cucumber cases. Fill with spinach mixed with remaining ingredients. And chill again after filling.

Mrs. W. B. Taylor, Jr.

CURRY RIPE OLIVE SANDWICH

2 cups chopped ripe olives
  (2—7 ounce cans)
1 cup thinly sliced green onions
  and tops
3 cups grated American cheese
  (about 1½ pounds)

1 cup mayonnaise
½ teaspoon salt
½ teaspoon curry powder
  (1 teaspoon if desired)
6 English muffins

Mix thoroughly in a bowl all ingredients except muffins. Toast backs of muffins, split in half lengthwise. Pile mixture high on other side. Mixture is piled high because it flattens as cheese melts. Place under broiler until puffy and brown. This is an excellent main dish for lunch. Serves 6. Makes 3-4 dozen canapés on melba toast rounds.

Mrs. Leonard McGowin

SPICY CEREAL BITS

¼ pound butter
1½ tablespoon Worcestershire
1¼ teaspoon chili powder
¾ teaspoon garlic salt
½ teaspoon salt

1 cup shelled pecans
2 cups each of four cereals
  (bite size shredded rice, bite
  size shredded wheat, corn
  puffs, Cheerios)

Preheat over to 300°. Melt butter in large pan, stir in Worcestershire, chili powder, garlic salt and salt. Add pecans and cereals, stirring well to combine. Bake one hour, stirring every fifteen minutes. Store in tightly covered container.

Mrs. Robert L. Meador

26

COCKTAIL CREAM PUFFS

½ cup butter or margarine	¼ teaspoon salt
1 cup boiling water	4 eggs
1 cup sifted flour	

Heat oven to 425°. Combine butter and boiling water in saucepan; keep over low heat until butter is melted. Add flour and salt all at once and stir vigorously over low heat until mixture forms a ball and leaves sides of pan. This will take about two minutes. Remove from heat. Add eggs, one at a time, beating well after each addition. Continue beating until smooth and satiny. Drop level teaspoonsful of mixture onto greased baking sheet, bake twenty to twenty-two minutes. Cool on racks. Cut slice off top of puffs. Fill with Nutted Chicken Filling. Serve warm. Makes about 6 dozen.

NUTTED CHICKEN FILLING

2 tablespoons butter or margarine	1 (3 ounces) package cream cheese
1 cup finely chopped pecans	¼ teaspoon salt
1⅓ cups finely minced chicken	½ teaspoon ground nutmeg
¼ cup mayonnaise	½ teaspoon grated lemon rind

Melt butter in skillet, add pecans and cook over low heat until lightly browned. Cool. Combine with remaining ingredients. Makes two cups, enough to fill about three and a half dozen puffs.

Mrs. Potter Yeend

BEVERAGES

SPICED TOMATO JUICE

1 quart tomato juice	¼ teaspoon celery seed
1 teaspoon onion juice	¼ teaspoon fresh ground black
1 teaspoon salt	pepper
½ teaspoon minced marjoram	1 garlic clove, crushed
½ teaspoon sweet basil	

Mix all together, shake well and chill at least four hours, preferably over-night. Strain before serving.

Mrs. T. B. Snevely

BASIC PUNCH

Make a base of one quart boiling water and ¼ cup of tea. Let stand until cool, then add:

6 oranges, thinly sliced	1 No. 5 can pineapple juice
6 lemons, grated rind of 2 lemons	2 cups sugar

Pour into gallon jars or a crock until serving time. Pour over ice and add sparkling water (about 4 pints). Add cherries or orange slices to garnish, if desired, for fruit punch. Add rum, bourbon or sauterne for a spiked punch. Forty servings.

Mrs. E. Ward Faulk

COFFEE PUNCH

1 gallon slightly sweetened, strong coffee	2-3 quarts milk
	1 gallon vanilla ice cream

Let coffee cool. Add milk and chopped up ice cream. Serves 50-60.

Mrs. Russell Terry

VIENNESE (SPICY) ICED COFFEE

¼ cup instant coffee	Crushed ice
2½ tablespoons sugar	1 pint vanilla ice cream
8 whole cloves	½ cup heavy cream, whipped
3 inch stick cinnamon	ground cinnamon
3 cups water	

Combine coffee, sugar, cloves, stick cinnamon and water. Cover, bring to a boil. Remove from heat and let stand, covered, five minutes to steep.

Strain. Chill well. Fill four chilled tall glasses one-fourth full with crushed ice. Add a scoop of ice cream to each. Pour in coffee and mix with ice cream. Top each with whipped cream and a dash of cinnamon.

Mrs. B. F. King

ICED TEA

2¼ cups sugar
4 tablespoons tea or 8 tea bags

2 cups orange juice
1 cup lemon juice

Combine 2 cups water and sugar, boil for five minutes. Steep tea in one quart boiling hot water for five minutes; put into two quarts cold water. Add remaining ingredients. Serves 12-24 depending on size of glasses.

Mrs. Richard Overby

SPICED TEA

½ pound tea
4 tablespoons grated orange peel, dried
2 tablespoons grated lemon peel, dried
¼ cup whole cloves

2 four inch cinnamon sticks, crushed
1 tablespoon grated nutmeg
1 cup (¼ pound) candied orange peel

Mix together and store in glass jar or tea cannister. This makes a lot, but it will keep all winter.

Mrs. Frank B. Frazer

CAFÉ BRÛLOT

1 orange peel
4 cinnamon sticks
10 lumps sugar rubbed with cut orange or lemon

10 whole cloves
½ cup cognac
3 cups freshly made coffee

Place the orange peel, spices and sugar in a silver lined chafing dish. Pour cognac over all. Set a lighted match to mixture for flame. Ladle mixture until sugar is dissolved, add coffee, mix. Ladle into demitasse cups. Serves 6.

Mrs. Mac Greer

EGG NOG

6 eggs, separated	1 pint bourbon
¾ cup sugar	2 ounces golden rum
1 pint cream	grated nutmeg
1 pint milk	

Beat egg yolks lightly, add one-half cup sugar and continue beating. Beat egg whites stiff, add one-fourth cup sugar. Fold whites into yolks, stir in cream and milk. Add whiskey and rum. Serve very cold, topped with grated nutmeg. Fills 16 punch cups.

Mrs. Comer Train

CONFEDERATE EGG NOG

5 egg yolks	½ pint whipping cream
6 teaspoons sugar	6 egg whites
6 jiggers rum	

Beat egg yolks with sugar until very light in color. Add rum, fold in whipped cream. Fold in stiffly beaten egg whites. Additional rum may be used to taste.

Mrs. Cowan Butler

KENTUCKY MINT JULEPS

A silver mint julep cup is preferable for making this famous old drink, but an iced tea glass is all right.

Chill glass thoroughly. Allow one to two ounces of Kentucky Bourbon for each drink. Into the bottom of the glass or cup place one tablespoon sugar and one tablespoon chopped mint leaves. Bruise the mint leaves well, using the back of a spoon and pressing as much juice as possible into sugar. Add one tablespoon water to dissolve the sugar. When sugar is dissolved, add the whiskey. Mix well and fill each glass with shaved ice. Place a sprig of mint in each glass. Let stand a few minutes before serving. These are even better if the sugar, mint leaves and water are fixed and then allowed to sit in the refrigerator for a couple of hours before adding whiskey and serving.

Mrs. Robert D. Hays

MARTINI

6 jiggers gin	1 dash Scotch
1 jigger dry vermouth	½ teaspoon olive juice

For best results, make enough for twelve martinis six to eight hours before serving and place in glass container in freezer. Dip martini glasses in water and place in freezer. Just before serving, run a split olive around rim of martini glass. Place olive, onion, or twist of lemon peel in glass before serving.

John Brady

MRS. BESTOR'S RUM PUNCH

6 dozen lemons	1 cup plus 2 tablespoons green tea
3 pounds sugar	6 quarts rum
6 quarts and 6 cups boiling water	6 wine glasses cognac
1 cup plus 2 tablespoons black tea	

Put strained juice of lemons in bowl. Add sugar. Put rinds in another bowl. Pour boiling water over black and green tea, steep five minutes. Strain over lemon rinds, let stand one-half hour. Strain into lemon juice and sugar. Add rum and cognac. Serves about 100.

Mrs. Frank Sauer

RUM PUNCH

1 quart dark rum	1 quart lemon juice
1 quart light rum	1 quart pineapple juice
1 quart brandy	1 quart tea
1 pint Cointreau	1 quart hot water to dilute
added to:	1 pound brown sugar

Pour over block of ice in punch bowl and serve. The number of guests this serves is a questionable subject because—well—I haven't met your guests.

Mrs. J. R. Macpherson

RAMOS GIN FIZZ

white of 1 egg
1 teaspoon lime juice
1 teaspoon lemon juice
2 teaspoons powdered sugar
1 tablespoon carbonated water

1 tablespoon cream
few drops orange flower water
1 jigger gin
Finely crushed ice

Place all ingredients in blender and blend well.

Marion R. Vickers

NORTHERN MICHIGAN COCKTAIL

3 fifths of port wine
8 ounces light rum
juice of 4 lemons

maraschino cherries or fresh
strawberries

Chill port, add rum and lemon juice. Mix and refrigerate. Chill wine or martini glasses. When ready to serve, place cherry or strawberry in each chilled glass. Stir cocktail well before pouring. 16 to 24 cocktails.

Mrs. George McNally

SUMMER BOOSTER

1 can gin, vodka or rum or
bourbon

1 can frozen lemonade
1 tray of ice cubes

Put all ingredients into blender, mix until thick with pulverized ice. Garnish with cherries or mint. Can be made a short while ahead and kept in freezer. Serves 4.

Mrs. John McGehee

PINK DELIGHT

1 jigger undiluted frozen pink
lemonade

1 jigger Rosé wine
crushed ice

Place all in blender with enough ice to make it very frothy. A pretty luncheon cocktail served in champagne glasses.

Mrs. Robert A. Guthans

32

GRASSHOPPER

Put in blender:

4 jiggers Crème de Menthe   **4 small scoops vanilla ice cream**
4 jiggers brandy

Swirl. Serves 6.

Mrs. Clarence Partridge

OLD FASHIONED COCKTAIL

1 teaspoon orange marmalade   **5 drops bitters**
2 teaspoons orange juice

Stir and add:
2 ounces bourbon and cracked ice. Decorate with a slice of orange and marachino cherry.

Wallace S. Clark, II

MY FAVORITES

MY FAVORITES

SOUPS

TOMATO BISQUE

1 can chilled cream of tomato
    soup
1 soup can milk (1⅓ cups)
2 tablespoons tarragon vinegar
1 cup juice from canned beets
Salt and pepper to taste

3-4 drops Tabasco
1 unpeeled cucumber
1 green pepper
minced parsley, chives or chopped
    green onion tops

Blend in electric blender one minute: soup, milk, vinegar, beet juice, salt, pepper and Tabasco. Add cucumber, cut in three or four pieces, and green pepper, cut in pieces. Blend fifteen seconds. Serve in chilled bowls and sprinkle with parsley, chives or onion tops. Serves 6-8.

Mrs. Robert Meador

JELLIED BORSCH

1 can (10½ ounces) condensed
    consommé
1 can (1 pound) julienne beets
½ cup beet juice
2 tablespoons chopped parsley

1 tablespoon minced onion
1 tablespoon lemon juice
dash of salt
sour cream

Empty consommé into medium bowl. Drain beets, reserving liquid. Cut beets in half and add to consommé with beet juice, parsley, onion, lemon juice and salt. Chill four hours or longer. Stir mixture once during chilling period (when partially jelled) to distribute vegetables evenly. Serve in chilled consommé cups with a dessert spoon of sour cream in center for extra flavor and garnish. Serves 4.

Mrs. Marion H. Lyons

35

VICHYSSOISE I

2 small onions, cut up	1 cup milk
2 tablespoons butter	1½ cups cream
2 cups chicken broth	⅛ teaspoon pepper
4 cups thinly sliced potatoes	1 teaspoon salt
½ teaspoon salt	½ teaspoon nutmeg

Brown onions lightly in butter. Add chicken broth, potatoes and salt. Simmer about forty minutes. Press the potato mixture through a fine sieve and add milk, one cup of cream, salt, pepper and nutmeg. Bring to a boil. Strain and add the other ½ cup of cream, scalded. Cool and chill several hours. Serve cold, garnished with chopped chives. Serves 6.

Mrs. B. F. King

VICHYSSOISE II

3½ cups diced raw potatoes	2 bunches green onions, chopped
¼ cup butter	2 cups light cream
3-4 cups chicken broth	¾ teaspoon salt, pinch of pepper
chopped chives	

Add potatoes and butter to chicken broth. Cover and simmer fifteen to twenty minutes. Add green onions. Cook five minutes more. Add cream and seasonings. Pour into blender and blend. Chill. Stir well before serving. Garnish with chopped chives.

Mrs. J. W. Hartman

SENATOR'S SOUP

1 large, very meaty, ham bone	1 teaspoon freshly ground pepper
1 package navy beans	salt to taste
1 large onion, peeled	

Strip ham of all fat and gristle, leaving only chunks of meat on bone. Place in deep kettle with cold water to cover. Add beans, onion and pepper. Bring to a boil, uncovered. Reduce heat immediately. Cover and cook very slowly six to eight hours. After four or five hours season with salt, to taste.

Mrs. N. Q. Adams

36

BLACK BEAN SOUP

1 pound black beans	½ cup olive oil
1 pound salt pork	salt
3 large onions, chopped	fresh ground black pepper
3 garlic pods, chopped	1 tablespoon basil wine vinegar
3 green peppers, chopped	

Wash beans well. Place in large pot and cover with cold water. Add salt pork and allow to come to a good boil. Reduce heat to simmer. In skillet, cook vegetables in olive oil until limp and add all to beans. Cook until beans are tender. Remove salt pork. Drain about one cup of beans from soup and put in blender. Blend until it forms a paste. Return to soup. Add salt, pepper and wine vinegar.

Mrs. Dewitt King
Mobile Country Club

ROCKEFELLER STEW

4 rounded tablespoons flour	1 small can mushrooms
3 tablespoons half-and-half cream	1 teaspoon Worcestershire
liquor from oysters	¼ teaspoon salt
1 tablespoon chopped parsley	⅛ teaspoon pepper
1 tablespoon shallots	dash of Tabasco
(or green onions)	1 pint large oysters

Brown flour. Add half-and-half. Gradually add two cups oyster liquor (supplement with water if necessary) and cook slowly until mixture thickens. Add all seasonings. Add oysters and cook in double boiler about fifteen minutes. For small servings.

Mrs. T. G. St. John, Jr.

OYSTER SOUP

4 tablespoons flour	2 tablespoons margarine
4 tablespoons onion, finely	oyster liquor
chopped	1 quart chicken broth
4 tablespoons celery, finely	1 quart oysters
chopped	2 tablespoons parsley

Make a roux using flour and margarine. When light brown, add onion and celery, stirring constantly. Cook until vegetables are transparent. Strain oyster liquor into roux and add chicken broth. Heat in double boiler top. When hot, add oysters and parsley. Water in double boiler bottom should simmer, not boil. Leave an hour to an hour and a half, then add salt and pepper to taste, and serve.

Mrs. C. D. Wilson

ESCAMBIA FISH CHOWDER

2 tablespoons shortening	2 medium Idaho potatoes,
2 tablespoons flour	sliced in rounds
1 large onion	10 whole cloves
1 can tomatoes (No. 2)	salt and pepper
3 quarts water	Worcester
1 can salmon (No. 2)	Tabasco
½ lemon, sliced in rounds	Beau Monde

Brown roux, add onions and soften. Add tomatoes and water. Remove bones and skin from salmon and add to soup. Add potatoes and cloves. Add seasonings to taste. Cook soup for approximately two hours or make the day before.

Mrs. J. R. Druhan

OYSTER STEW

1 pint fresh oysters and liquor	¼ teaspoon Tabasco
½ stick butter	2 cups milk, cream or
1 medium green onion, chopped	half-and-half
1 teaspoon parsley flakes	salt and pepper to taste
½ teaspoon Worcestershire	

In a saucepan, combine all ingredients, except milk. Heat and simmer until edges of oysters curl. (About ten minutes.) In another saucepan, scald milk. Add milk to other ingredients and serve. Sprinkle paprika over each serving. Makes 4 small servings.

Mrs. John Brady

TURKEY AND OYSTER GUMBO

2 tablespoons flour	salt and pepper to taste
2 tablespoons bacon grease	2 quarts water
1 medium onion, diced	at least 2 cups de-boned,
1 small bell pepper, diced	cooked turkey
¼ cup celery, diced	1 pint oysters
¼ cup chopped parsley	1 tablespoon Creole gumbo filé
1 small can tomatoes	1 teaspoon thyme

In skillet, brown flour in grease until very, very dark brown, stirring constantly. Add onion, bell pepper, celery, parsley, and thyme. Cook until tender. Add tomatoes and seasoning. Cover and simmer ten minutes. In a large pot bring two quarts water to a boil; add turkey and first mixture. Simmer two hours. Ten minutes before serving, add oysters. Five minutes before serving add filé. Add salt and pepper to taste. Serve over fluffy rice in individual soup bowls. (Eight cleaned, fresh crabs or one pound crabmeat may be substituted for turkey.) Serves 6.

Mrs. William Rowell

TURTLE SOUP

2 pounds turtle meat	1 tablespoon tomato paste
¾ cup chopped ham or	salt and pepper
smoked butt	⅛ teaspoon thyme
⅔ cup flour	⅛ teaspoon ground allspice
⅓ cup salad oil	1 teaspoon Kitchen Bouquet
1 large onion, chopped	2 bay leaves
½ green pepper, chopped	1 tablespoon Worcestershire
1 small can whole tomatoes,	¼ teaspoon crushed red pepper
chopped	1 small lemon, chopped
1 garlic clove, cut very fine	

Clean turtle meat and remove fat and gristle. Parboil in three pints of water for twenty minutes. Drain meat in colander. Add water to stock to make seven pints. Brown flour in oil, being careful not to burn. Add peppers, onion, ham, turtle meat. Cook for 15 minutes until brown. Add boiling liquid and all other ingredients except lemon. Simmer for 1½ to 2 hours. Add lemon, seasoning and continue to cook until soup is of a good, thick consistency. Remove turtle meat. Cut in small pieces, discarding bones. Return meat to soup and continue cooking. Serve boiling hot with 1 to 3 teaspoons Madeira wine and 1 tablespoon chopped hard boiled egg in each bowl. Serves ten.

Mrs. Jack Friend

NANNY'S NEVER FAIL CRAB GUMBO

2 tablespoons lard	1 pound raw shrimp, cleaned
2 tablespoons flour	and de-veined
2 medium onions, finely chopped	8-12 crabs, cleaned
4 celery stalks, finely chopped	1 pound crabmeat (optional)
1 green pepper, finely chopped	1 teaspoon salt
2 (No. 2) cans tomatoes	black and red pepper to taste
1 pound okra, sliced round	Tabasco

Make a golden roux in heavy skillet of lard and flour. Stir in onions, celery, green pepper and simmer a few minutes, stirring constantly. Add undrained tomatoes, and okra. Simmer until okra is tender. Place in large soup pot, add shrimp, crabs and three quarts of water. Add seasonings and cook slowly over low fire for several hours. (The longer the better.) Serve in soup bowls over steaming hot rice. (Gumbo is much tastier if crabmeat is added. More red pepper makes a hotter soup.)

Mrs. Jere Austill, Jr.

MRS. EDWARD SLEDGE, SR'S. GUMBO

5 tablespoons bacon drippings	5-6 cups water
6 tablespoons flour	3 teaspoons salt
2 onions, chopped fine	1 teaspoon pepper
1½ cups finely chopped celery	2 pounds shrimp (or crab)
1 garlic pod	1 package frozen okra cut up
1 large can tomatoes	1 pint oysters
1 can tomato sauce	3 tablespoons Worcestershire

Brown flour in bacon drippings to make roux. Add onions, celery and garlic, and brown for five minutes. Add tomatoes, tomato sauce, water, salt and pepper, and boil for one hour over medium fire. Add shrimp (or crab) and okra and cook twenty minutes longer. Add Worcestershire, stir well and serve with steamed rice.

Mrs. Horace Spottswood

MISS AMY'S CRAB SOUP

5 tablespoons flour
2 heaping teaspoons butter
1½ quarts milk
1 pound crabmeat

½ glass sherry (about ¼ cup)
½ teaspoon Tabasco
1½ tablespoons Worcestershire
salt to taste

Make thin cream sauce with flour, butter and milk. When sauce is slightly thickened add crabmeat, sherry, Tabasco, Worcestershire and salt. Serves 12.

Mrs. John van Aken

FISH CHOWDER

3 tablespoons flour
bacon fat
1 large onion, chopped
½ cup chopped celery
1 small can tomatoes

water
2-3 cups diced potatoes
boneless fish
salt and pepper to taste
Worcestershire to taste

Brown flour in bacon fat, add onion and celery. Stir and add tomatoes and enough water to make gravy. Add potatoes and simmer. When almost done, add fish. Add salt, pepper, Worcestershire.

Mrs. Dupree Hays

VEGETABLE SOUP

1 large soup bone
2 quarts water
1 pound lean stew meat
1 Irish potato, chopped coarsely
1 onion, chopped
1 celery stalk, chopped
5 carrots, sliced across
1 small can of corn

1 can tomatoes
1 small can English peas
½ pint butter beans
small amount of okra
left over vegetables from refrigerator
salt and pepper to taste

Boil soup bone in water until done. Remove meat from bone. Add stew meat. Add remaining ingredients and cook slowly for several hours. If thick soup is preferred, this is fine. If thinner soup desired, add more water. A small amount of noodles or spaghetti may be added fifteen minutes before serving, if desired.

Mrs. Marshall J. DeMouy

41

SPLIT PEA SOUP

1 pound split green peas	2 celery stalks, chopped
1 tablespoon salt	1 large onion, chopped
1½ teaspoons pepper	1 "meaty" ham bone
3 tablespoons butter	

Boil two quarts water. Rinse and drain split peas. Add peas, salt, pepper, butter, celery, onion and ham to boiling water. (Make sure water is boiling.) Cover and cook slowly for two hours, stirring occasionally to keep peas from sticking to bottom of the pan. If soup cooks down a lot and seems too thick (it is supposed to be thick), add more boiling water. Serve generously with a dash of grated carrot on top. Serves 6.

Mrs. Manning McPhillips

GASPACHO

1 (1 pound) can tomatoes, chopped	¼ cup green onions, finely chopped
1 No. 2 can tomato juice	¼ cup celery, finely chopped
juice of one lemon	2 tablespoons parsley, finely chopped
1 tablespoon Worcestershire	salt and freshly ground pepper, to taste
¼ cup cucumber, finely chopped	
¼ cup green pepper, finely chopped	1 bud garlic, crushed

Combine chopped vegetables. Add to liquids and seasonings. (If only slight garlic taste is preferred, add one whole clove garlic, peeled and pierced with a toothpick. Remove after one hour.) Chill at least five or six hours and serve in small soup plates with a cube of ice and a slice of fresh lime. Serves 10.

Mrs. Jack Friend

ICED CUCUMBER SOUP

3 cucumbers, peeled and sliced thin	2 tablespoons flour
½ cup chopped green onions	2 cups hot water
½ teaspoon salt	pinch of Cayenne
pinch of pepper	½ teaspoon chopped mint
1 cup water	½ cup heavy cream

In a saucepan, bring to a boil cucumbers, onions, salt, pepper and cold water. Simmer about fifteen minutes or until cucumbers are soft. Stir in

42

flour mixed with a little cold water to a smooth paste. Add hot water.
Continue to stir until soup boils. Simmer ten minutes. Add a pinch of
Cayenne and more salt if needed. Pour soup through a fine sieve, pressing
through as much pulp as possible. Add mint and stir in cream. Chill.
Serve cold, garnished with a cucumber slice and a dash of paprika.

Mrs. Paul E. Sheldon

CREAM POTATO SOUP

2 cups raw diced potatoes	4 cups water
⅓ cup diced celery	3 tablespoons flour
¼ cup chopped onion	2 tablespoons butter
2 tablespoons chopped parsley	2 cups milk
½ tablespoon salt	¼ teaspoon pepper

Cook vegetables and salt in water for twenty minutes in a covered pan.
Press through food strainer. Add butter, melted and mixed with flour. Add
milk and season to taste with more salt and pepper and a little Worcestershire.

Mrs. Marion Adams, Sr.

AVOCADO SOUP

3 large avocados	¾ teaspoon salt
1 can clear chicken broth	½ cup light cream
1 tablespoon lemon juice	3 bacon slices, cooked and
1½ cups water	crumbled
pepper	

Place first six ingredients in blender, blend until smooth. Chill about two
hours. Just before serving stir in cream. Top each serving with crumbled
bacon.

Mrs. John Morrissette, Jr.

CRAB BISQUE

2 cans condensed cream of celery soup	1 soup can water
1 soup can milk	1 pound white crabmeat
	⅔ cup celery, finely chopped

Blend soup, milk and water until well mixed. Add picked over crabmeat
and celery to mixture and chill thoroughly before serving.

Mrs. John Morrissette, Jr.

SAUCES

STEAK MARINADE

⅓ cup wine vinegar
3 tablespoons salad oil
1 tablespoon minced onion or
⅓ cup chopped onion
⅛ teaspoon garlic powder or
1 clove garlic, crushed
¼ teaspoon rosemary

¼ teaspoon oregano
¼ teaspoon dried dill weed
½ teaspoon salt
¼ teaspoon paprika
2 tablespoons honey or brown
sugar

Combine ingredients. Pour over steak. Marinate several hours or overnight. Turn meat several times.

Mrs. Wallace S. Clark, II

MARCHAND DE VIN

½ stick butter
2 garlic pods, chopped fine
3 green onions, chopped
¼ teaspoon fresh ground black
pepper
pinch of dried marjoram
½ cup red wine

1 tablespoon flour
3 cups beef stock
½ pound mushrooms broiled in
butter
2 tablespoons sherry
2 tablespoons brandy
salt to taste

Braise in butter: garlic, green onion, pepper and marjoram. Add red wine. Cook to a paste. Add flour and beef stock. Simmer. Add broiled mushrooms, sherry, brandy. Season to taste with salt.

Mrs. Dewitt King
Mobile Country Club

MARCHAND DE VIN SAUCE

4 garlic cloves, diced
1 large onion, diced
¼ pound butter
2 (3-ounce) cans chopped
mushrooms
1 cup beef bouillon

½ teaspoon salt
ground black pepper
Bouquet Garni
1 tablespoon brown gravy sauce
1 teaspoon flour
¾ cup white wine

Sauté diced garlic and diced onion in butter until golden. Add mushrooms and sauté five minutes longer. Add bouillon, salt, pepper, a pinch of Bouquet Garni and brown gravy sauce. Mix flour with a little water to

44

allow pouring. Add flour to sauce slowly and stir to thicken. Stir in white wine and simmer fifteen to twenty minutes. Allow to stand. Heat before serving, adding a little more wine if necessary.

Dr. Jack Hyman

RAISIN SAUCE

1½ cups liquid—bouillon
½ cup cider vinegar
½ cup raisins
1½ teaspoon dry mustard
½ cup brown sugar
1 tablespoon butter
1 tablespoon corn starch

Heat all ingredients, except corn starch, together in a saucepan. Simmer about three minutes. Add corn starch.

Mrs. Richard Bounds

FRESH CRANBERRY SAUCE

1 pounds (4 cups or more) fresh cranberries
1 cup boiling water
2 cups sugar
pinch of salt

Wash, sort and drain cranberries. Cook slowly, covered, in water until berries pop. Stir and break with a wooden spoon. Cook out all water. Remove from heat. Add sugar and salt, barely stirring in. Replace on fairly high flame, stirring occasionally. When mixture bubbles once or twice, remove from heat and pour into mold. Cool and then refrigerate.

Mrs. Mac B. Greer

ORANGE SAUCE FOR BAKED HAM OR LAMB

¾ cup apple jelly
½ cup fresh orange juice
3 tablespoons fresh lemon juice
1 tablespoon dry mustard
¾ teaspoon ginger
2 large, unpeeled oranges, cut in cartwheels, halved

Combine jelly, juices, mustard and ginger in saucepan. Bring to a boil. Add the orange slices and simmer for five minutes. Serve warm. This sauce can be refrigerated for several days.

Mrs. Mac B. Greer

SAUCE FOR CANADIAN BACON

1 glass apple or currant jelly	1 teaspoon prepared mustard
1 tablespoon vinegar	½ teaspoon ground cloves

Heat together until jelly melts. Also good with apple or banana fritters.

Mrs. J. Manson Murray

BARBECUE SAUCE I

1 stick butter	⅔ cup vinegar
2 medium onions, diced	2 tablespoons dry mustard
juice of two lemons	1 bottle chili sauce
1 can tomato paste	½ cup water
½ cup Worcestershire	1 teaspoon salt

Melt butter, add onions and cook until tender. Add other ingredients. Simmer covered for ten minutes. Hot sauce may be added if desired.

Mrs. John B. Flynn

BARBECUE SAUCE II

4 cups catsup	3 sticks butter
4 cups white vinegar	½ cup Worcestershire
2 cups sherry	Tabasco to taste
¾ bottle A-1 sauce	salt and pepper to taste
½ bottle 57 sauce	onion salt to taste
⅓ cup tarragon vinegar	garlic salt to taste

Simmer combined ingredients until butter has melted. May be kept in freezer indefinitely or for several weeks in refrigerator.

Mrs. Thomas M. Taul, Jr.

MUSTARD SAUCE FOR HAM I

1 egg	½ cup beef bouillon
½ cup sugar	½ cup prepared mustard
1 tablespoon flour	¼ cup butter
½ cup vinegar	

Beat egg until light. Add sugar and flour mixed together. Add vinegar and bouillon to mustard. Mix well and add other mixture. Cook in double boiler until thick. Add butter. Makes one pint.

Mrs. Edward Converse

46

MUSTARD SAUCE FOR HAM II

5 tablespoons dry mustard	1 cup milk
½ cup sugar	1 egg yolk
½ teaspoon salt	½ cup vinegar
2 tablespoons flour	

Sift dry ingredients together. Add remaining ingredients and cook in double boiler about five minutes or until thick. Really hot! Delicious with ham.

Mrs. J. C. Sutherland

BARBECUE SAUCE FOR FRESH PORK

1 quart vinegar	juice of ½ lemon
¼ bottle Worcestershire sauce	scant ¼ pound butter or margarine
¼ bottle catsup	salt, pepper and Tabasco to taste

Simmer in glass or enamel container for one hour. Baste five pound pork roast with this sauce during baking. Do not serve as sauce.

Mrs. W. R. Carter

SMOOTH BARBECUE SAUCE FOR RIBS

3 teaspoons salt	3½ cups catsup
3 teaspoons chili powder	4 cups water
3 teaspoons celery seeds	½ teaspoon Tabasco
½ cup brown sugar	1 cup Worcestershire
¾ cup vinegar	

Mrs. Tom Horst, Jr.

HOT DOG SAUCE

1 bunch celery, chopped	1 (No. 1) can solid pack tomatoes
2 large green peppers, chopped	2 tablespoons fat
3 large onions, chopped	1½ bottles catsup
3 small garlic buds, minced	2 large cans chili without beans
salt and pepper	1 tablespoon Worcestershire
chili powder to taste	1 (No. 2½) can sauerkraut
1 tablespoon barbecue sauce	
1 tablespoon vinegar	

Simmer celery, pepper, onions and garlic with salt, pepper and chili powder

47

in fat until tender. Add tomatoes and cook to sauce consistency (10 minutes under pressure). Add remaining ingredients. Mix well and simmer five or ten minutes. This sauce freezes well. Yields a little over a half gallon.

Mrs. Robert Whiting

CHILI SAUCE I

4 dozen ripe tomatoes	½ cup prepared mustard
4 small red hot peppers	2 teaspoons cinnamon
6 green bell peppers	2 teaspoons ground cloves
5 large onions	2 teaspoons ginger
1 quart vinegar	2 teaspoons nutmeg
4 tablespoons salt	2 teaspoons allspice
1¾ cups sugar	

Put tomatoes, peppers (red and bell) and onions through meat grinder. Add other ingredients and boil together slowly until very thick. Put in jars and seal while hot. Makes about 6 pints.

Mrs. C. D. Wilson

CHILI SAUCE II

1 gallon ripe tomatoes	1 tablespoon pickling spice
1 quart vinegar	6-8 bell peppers, chopped
1 quart sugar	6 large onions, chopped, or
2 tablespoons salt	2 packages chopped onions

Boil slowly, cooking until thick. Stir constantly at the last. This cooks down to about a quart and a half of sauce and is worth doubling as it is delicious on roast beef and hamburgers.

Mrs. A. P. Ogburn, Jr.

TARTAR SAUCE

1 dill pickle, chopped	1 tablespoon minced onion
4 tablespoons parsley, chopped	1 tablespoon vinegar
2 tablespoons capers	salt and pepper
6 stuffed olives, sliced and chopped	1½ cups mayonnaise

Mix all together.

Mrs. Leon McVay, Jr.

48

SAUCE FOR COLD BOILED SALMON

1 pint thick sour cream
1 pint mayonnaise
1 clove garlic, crushed
2 tablespoons white wine vinegar
1 tablespoon grated onion
3 level teaspoons salt
¼ teaspoon paprika

½ teaspoon fresh ground black
   pepper
¼ cup chopped parsley
2 teaspoons prepared mustard
fresh drained horseradish to taste
   (at least ½ cup and more if
   you like)

Mrs. J. H. Friend

MUSHROOM SAUCE

4 tablespoons fat
5 tablespoons flour
salt to taste
2 cups chicken stock
2 egg yolks, beaten
¼ cup thick cream

½ pound fresh mushrooms,
   sautéed in butter
1 tablespoon lemon juice
2 tablespoons chopped parsley
salt and pepper

Melt fat, add flour and salt to taste. Add stock. Mix egg yolks and cream. Add to the other mixture and cook gently until egg yolks are cooked. Add mushrooms, lemon juice and parsley. Serve over salmon loaf.

Mrs. Thomas G. Greaves, Jr.

SAUCE FOR BOILED SHRIMP

2 parts mayonnaise
1 part chili sauce

1 garlic clove, mashed
Tabasco to taste

Delicious with shrimp boiled in beer.

Mrs. John Howard Wilson

HOT SHRIMP SAUCE

1 stick butter
6 tablespoons Worcestershire
6 tablespoons tomato catsup

juice of 1 lemon
dash of Tabasco
salt and pepper

Mix and bring to a boil. Serve hot over cold shrimp. Serves 6.

Mrs. Robert T. King

49

GULF SHORES SPECIAL (SEAFOOD SAUCE)

2 tablespoons chili sauce   ½ teaspoon anchovy paste
1 tablespoon mayonnaise   few drops Tabasco
1 teaspoon tarragon vinegar

Combine all ingredients and chill thoroughly. Sauce may be poured over seafood and then refrigerated, allowing sauce to permeate seafood. (Above is for individual serving for shellfish cocktail.)

Mrs. Jere Austill, Jr.

SHRIMP ARNAUD

3 pounds shrimp   2 teaspoons vinegar
thyme   4 teaspoons salad oil (or more)
garlic   1 teaspoon prepared Creole
bay leaves   mustard
onion   2 green onions, with tops,
2 lemons, quartered   minced fine
celery   ¼ stalk celery, minced
salt and pepper   salt and pepper to taste

Boil shrimp in water to which thyme, garlic, bay leaves, onion, lemons, celery, salt and pepper have been added. Cook about fifteen minutes. Cool and clean shrimp. Prepare sauce using vinegar, oil, Creole mustard, onions, celery, salt and pepper. Mix shrimp with sauce and refrigerate (set in ice) for at least two hours. Mix again just before serving.

Mrs. E. Ward Faulk

SHRIMP "GREEN GODDESS"

½ tube anchovy paste   2 tablespoons lemon juice
2 tablespoons mayonnaise   1 tablespoon tarragon vinegar
3 green onions, minced   1 teaspoon grated black pepper
½ cup sour cream   1 pint small shrimp
2 tablespoons minced parsley

All ingredients should be mixed together and served on lettuce over small shrimp.

Mrs. Robert Bacon

SHRIMP REMOULADE I

⅓ cup horseradish mustard
¾ teaspoon Cayenne pepper
⅓ cup tarragon vinegar
2 cloves garlic, finely chopped
3 tablespoons catsup
2 tablespoons paprika

1 teaspoon salt
½ cup olive oil or salad oil
½ cup chopped green onions
  and tops
1 pound peeled, cooked shrimp

Combine all ingredients except shrimp and shake well. Marinate the shrimp in the sauce for several hours in refrigerator. Serve on chilled lettuce. 8 generous servings.

Mrs. Kenneth Granger

SHRIMP REMOULADE II

¾ cup mayonnaise
1 teaspoon salt
2 teaspoons dry mustard
6 scallions (or green onions)
  (greens and all)
2 celery stalks

3 parsley sprigs
1 teaspoon paprika
2 drops Tabasco
1½-2 pounds cooked and
  cleaned shrimp

Put all ingredients except shrimp in blender and mix. Refrigerate this sauce for at least four hours. Shrimp may be added whole, chopped or sauce may be poured over shrimp for luncheon dish.

Mrs. C. M. A. Rogers, III

CHIVE SAUCE

1 (8 ounce) package cream
  cheese
⅓ cup light cream

2 tablespoons snipped chives
1½ teaspoon lemon juice
dash of garlic salt

Beat cream cheese with cream until fluffy. Add remaining ingredients and spoon on baked potatoes.

Mrs. Robert L. Byrd, Jr.

ABSOLUTELY PERFECT HOLLANDAISE SAUCE

4 egg yolks
juice of ½ lemon
  (or more to taste)

½ cup butter
dash of Cayenne
¼ teaspoon salt

Beat egg yolks until very, very thick. (Just turn on mixer and forget them for a while). Melt butter in double boiler top. Remove from heat and add to egg yolks all at once, stirring swiftly with a wooden spoon until well blended. Blend in lemon juice, salt and Cayenne. Place back over hot (water but not boiling) and continue stirring. If eggs were beaten properly, sauce is now desired thickness. If overcooked, slowly add three table-spoonfuls cream, stirring constantly.

Mrs. John M. Scott, Jr.

HOLLANDAISE SAUCE

4 egg yolks	1 stick of butter, melted
1 teaspoon salt	⅓ cup hot water
½ teaspoon dry mustard	¼ cup lemon juice
1 tablespoon mayonnaise	(or to taste)

In large cup, sitting in a pot of boiling water, mix egg yolks, salt, mustard and mayonnaise. Beating constantly, drip butter over this, then add hot water. Cook until thick. Add lemon juice. This may be reheated and be-comes smooth simply by beating again with egg beater. Will keep for several days in refrigerator.

Mrs. Marshall J. DeMouy

ALMOND CHEESE SAUCE

2 tablespoons margarine	1 teaspoon salt
2 tablespoons flour	1 cup sharp cheese, grated
1 cup milk	¼ teaspoon almond extract

Melt margarine, stir in flour, add milk and salt. Cook and stir until thick. Add grated cheese, and extract just before pouring over vegetable. Use over broccoli, Brussel sprouts or asparagus. Garnish with slivered almonds.

Mrs. John McGehee

52

MY FAVORITES

MY FAVORITES

Salad

Jamboree

SALAD JAMBOREE

CRABMEAT SALAD I

1 pound lump crabmeat	1 small garlic clove, mashed
2 tablespoons fresh parsley, finely snipped	fresh ground pepper to taste salt to taste
2 spring onions, sliced thin (tops and all)	enough mayonnaise to make quite moist

Mix all ingredients together and refrigerate several hours. Serve on lettuce, crackers or in avocado halves. Top with Roquefort dressing, if desired. If used for shrimp salad I add chopped hard boiled eggs and small amount of celery.

Mrs. Ernest L. Brown

CRABMEAT SALAD II

1 pound white lump crabmeat	few drops Tabasco
1 hard cooked egg, chopped fine	2 teaspoons olive oil
1 green onion, chopped	¾ cup mayonnaise
2 celery stalks, chopped fine	

In large bowl, separate crabmeat, add egg, onion, celery, Tabasco and salt and pepper. Mix well. Add oil and mayonnaise, mix well. Serve with avocado, tomato wedges or lettuce, topped with paprika.

Mrs. John D. Brady

55

SEAFOOD CANAPÉ

1 Holland Rusk per serving	1 teaspoon vinegar
cream cheese	1 teaspoon Worcestershire
Worcestershire	1 tablespoon grated onion
sliced tomato	3 teaspoons anchovy paste
sliced avocado	Tabasco to taste
sliced hard cooked egg(s)	1 pound shrimp or crabmeat
1 cup mayonnaise	(or both)
1 cup chili sauce	

Spread Holland rusk with cream cheese seasoned with Worcestershire. Place a tomato slice on top, then an avocado slice topped with sliced egg. Combine remaining ingredients and pour sauce over rusk. Delicious summer salad or first course. Some may prefer to put crab meat on top of egg and pour sauce over.

Mrs. B. Franklin King

EGG AND SHRIMP SALAD

12 hard boiled eggs	1 cup mayonnaise
1 cup whipped cream	½ cup chili sauce
1 cup mayonnaise	2 tablespoons lemon juice
1 envelope gelatin	2½ pounds cold, cooked
½ cup boiling water	shrimp
salt	

Slice egg whites and yolks separately. Soak gelatin in a minimum amount of water and then dissolve in boiling water. Mix whipped cream, mayonnaise, salt and gelatin together. In individual molds or one large mold, place yolks on bottom, mixture in middle and whites on top. Chill overnight. Turn out on salad greens, garnish with avocado slices, if desired and serve with dressing of mayonnaise, chili sauce, lemon juice and shrimp combined. Serves 10-12.

Mrs. M. J. Berg

CONGEALED SHRIMP SALAD I

1½ envelopes gelatin
2 tablespoons lemon juice
1⅓ cups hot water
½ teaspoon salt
½ onion, grated
¼ cup chili sauce
⅓ cup mayonnaise

2 pounds boiled shrimp,
    cleaned (1¼ cups)
2 hard cooked eggs, diced
¾ cup finely chopped celery
2 tablespoons finely chopped
    green pepper

Soften gelatin in lemon juice, dissolve in hot water. Blend in salt, onion and chili—cool to consistency of unbeaten egg whites. Blend in mayonnaise, shrimp, eggs, celery and pepper to first mixture. Turn into greased molds. Serve with mayonnaise dressing. Serves 8 generously.

Mrs. Randall Hollinger

CONGEALED SHRIMP SALAD II

1 can cream of tomato soup
3 small packages cream cheese
2 envelopes gelatin
½ cup boiling water
1 pound shrimp, cooked and
    de-veined (or canned)

½ cup finely chopped celery
½ cup green pepper, chopped fine
½ teaspoon onion salt or onion
    juice
1 cup mayonnaise

Bring soup to boil, dissolve cream cheese in soup. Melt gelatin in boiling water and add to mixture. Mince shrimp. Add remaining ingredients and pour into flat mold. Refrigerate until congealed. Slices well. Serves 6–8.

Mrs. C. D. Garrison, Jr.

JELLIED ARTICHOKES

2 cooked artichokes or
    1 can artichoke hearts
    in brine
2 cans undiluted beef
    consommé

2 envelopes gelatin
⅓ cup lemon juice
Tabasco to taste
salt and pepper to taste

Cut hearts into small pieces. If fresh artichokes are used, add the scrapings from leaves. Warm consommé, add gelatin which has been softened in cold water (see package directions). Season with lemon juice, Tabasco, salt and pepper. Add artichoke pieces, pour into mold and refrigerate. Serve on lettuce with mayonnaise. Serves 8.

Mrs. Ray C. McConnell

ASPARAGUS AND GRAPE SALAD MOLD

1 tablespoon unflavored gelatin
¼ cup asparagus juice
2 cups chicken consommé
2 small cans green asparagus tips
2 cups green grapes (halved)
1 cup celery, chopped fine

Soften gelatin in asparagus juice. Dissolve over hot water, add to consommé and mix well. Drain asparagus and place in oiled pan, sprinkling each layer with grapes and celery. Cover with gelatin mixture. Chill and serve on lettuce with homemade mayonnaise. Good with ham or Canadian bacon.

Mrs. Edward Baumhauer

CONGEALED ASPARAGUS SALAD

½ tablespoon gelatin
¼ cup cold water
1 cup boiling water
1 package lime gelatin
1 tablespoon grated onion
1 tablespoon vinegar
1 teaspoon salt
¼ cup green asparagus, mashed
¼ cup grated cheese (Cheddar)
1 cup mayonnaise

Soften gelatin in cold water. Pour boiling water over lime gelatin and add softened gelatin and other ingredients. Add mayonnaise last. Refrigerate to congeal. Makes nine small individual molds.

Mrs. George Shedd

ASPARAGUS SALAD

½ cup sugar
⅓ cup vinegar
1 cup water
¼ cup asparagus juice
1 teaspoon lemon juice
½ teaspoon salt

Boil ingredients five minutes. Add:

2 envelopes gelatin dissolved in
½ cup cold water
½ cup chopped pecans or almonds
1 cup chopped celery
1 can green asparagus, cut up
1 jar pimentos, drained

Congeal and serve.

Mrs. Russell Terry

AVOCADO RING

½ package gelatin	1 teaspoon salt
½ cup cold water	1 cup avocado, mashed
1 package lemon gelatin	1 cup whipped cream
1 cup boiling water	black cherries
1 cup mayonnaise	French dressing
3 tablespoons lemon juice	

Dissolve gelatin in cold water. Dissolve lemon gelatin in boiling water, add gelatin. Chill until partially set. When set, whip. To mayonnaise, add lemon juice, salt, and fold into whipped gelatin. Fold in avocado and whipped cream. Chill to congeal; serve with black cherries marinated in French dressing.

Mrs. H. R. Luscher, Jr.

AVOCADO SALAD

2 envelopes gelatin	1 carton sour cream
1 cup water	½ cup mayonnaise
2-3 avocados	2 teaspoons salt
3 tablespoons lemon juice	1 cup diced celery

Dissolve gelatin in water. Mash avocados with lemon juice. Combine and add remaining ingredients in order. Pour into greased mold and chill until firm. Serve with tomato and hard cooked egg wedges.

Mrs. Ernest L. Brown

AVOCADO ASPIC

1 cup mayonnaise	1 tablespoon caper juice
2 cups canned chicken broth	3 dashes Tabasco
2⅔ cups milk	1 teaspoon salt
4 envelopes unflavored gelatin	1 cucumber, finely chopped
1½ avocado, cubed	1 cup finely sliced scallions
½ cup lemon juice	½ green pepper, minced
3 tablespoons prepared mustard	1 cup diced celery

Mix mayonnaise, broth and 2 cups milk with gelatin. Heat together until gelatin dissolves, cool. In blender, buzz avocados, lemon juice. Mix in mustard, caper juice, Tabasco, ⅔ cup milk and salt. Mixture should be smooth and creamy. Combine mayonnaise, gelatin mixture with avocado mixture. Fold in vegetables, chill in mold.

Mrs. John Brady

CAULIFLOWER SALAD

½ cup oil	stuffed olives
½ cup vinegar	1 cauliflower
1 medium onion sliced	1 head lettuce

Mix oil and vinegar. Add sliced olives and cauliflower flowerettes. (Cut stems from flowerettes, which should be small.) Stir well and let stand in refrigerator for six to eight hours before serving. Tear the lettuce and put in large bowl, then add marinated vegetables and toss. Twelve generous servings.

Mrs. Samuel R. Stephenson, Jr.

GREEN BEAN SALAD I

2 cans Blue Lake green beans	chopped celery (½ stalk)
chopped olives	chopped green onions (1 bunch)
chopped pecans	

Dressing:

1½ cup salad oil	¼ teaspoon pepper
½ cup vinegar	¼ teaspoon paprika
2 teaspoons salt	½ teaspoon dry mustard

Mix all together and let chill in ice box for several hours. Serves 8.

Mrs. Harry Henson

GREEN BEAN SALAD II

1 small purple onion	⅝ cup sugar
½ green pepper	½ cup vinegar
1 can kidney beans	½ cup salad oil
1 can wax beans	1 teaspoon salt
1 can green beans	¼ teaspoon pepper

Slice onion and green pepper. Wash kidney beans and strain with other beans. Dissolve sugar in vinegar, add oil, salt and pepper. Stir and add other ingredients. Let stand in refrigerator, stirring occasionally. Serves 6-8.

Mrs. Samuel R. Stephenson, Jr.

BROCCOLI SALAD

1 package frozen broccoli	1½ teaspoon salt
3 hard boiled eggs	2 teaspoons lemon juice
¾ cup mayonnaise	2 teaspoons Worcestershire
2 envelopes plain gelatin	few drops Tabasco
1 can beef consommé	

Cook broccoli and mash. Soften gelatin in some of the consommé over hot water, mash eggs. Mix all together and put in ring mold. Serves 8.

Mrs. Ben Radcliff

FROZEN BROCCOLI OR SPINACH SALAD

2 packages frozen chopped broccoli (or spinach)	1¾ teaspoons salt
	4 teaspoons Worcestershire
3 hard cooked eggs, chopped	2 teaspoons lemon juice
¾ cup mayonnaise	dash of Tabasco
1½ envelopes gelatin	1 heaping teaspoon horseradish
¼ cup cold water	1 tablespoon vinegar
1 cup beef consommé	grated onion

Salt vegetable and cook without water. Combine vegetable, eggs, and mayonnaise. Soak gelatin in water and dissolve in hot consommé, combine with first mixture. Add seasonings, pour into ring mold and refrigerate to congeal. Serves 10.

Mrs. Tom Slade, III

CUCUMBER SALAD

1 tablespoon gelatin	3 medium cucumbers
2 tablespoons cold water	1 (8 ounce) cream cheese
¼ cup lemon juice	1 cup mayonnaise
½ cup boiling water	¼ cup minced parsley
2 tablespoons sugar	¼ cup minced onion
¾ teaspoon salt	

Soften gelatin in cold water and juice, dissolve in boiling water. Add sugar and salt. Halve the cucumbers and scrape out insides. Grind or mince very fine, should be about two cups. Soften cheese. Add cucumbers, mayonnaise, parsley and onion. Stir in gelatin. Pour into ring mold and chill. To serve, fill center with watercress and shrimp for a complete salad luncheon.

Mrs. Joseph Locke

PERFECTION SALAD

2 envelopes gelatin	1 cup cabbage, shredded fine
½ cup cold water	2 cups chopped celery
2 cups water	¼ cup chopped pimento
½ cup sugar	2 tablespoons chopped green
½ cup mild vinegar	pepper
2 tablespoons lemon juice	2 tablespoons chopped parsley
1 heaping teaspoon salt	3 tablesoons chopped olives

Soak gelatin in cold water. Heat two cups water and add sugar, vinegar, lemon juice and salt. Add gelatin to heated mixture and stir until gelatin is dissolved. Add remaining ingredients, mix well and pour into greased mold. A ring mold is best, filling center at serving time with following dressing: Mix a carton of cottage cheese, a half cup mayonnaise, salt, paprika and a few capers with juice.

Mrs. Ernest L. Brown

VEGETABLE ASPIC

2 envelopes gelatin	¼ teaspoon salt
1 cup cold water	1 can artichoke hearts
2 cups boiling water	stuffed olives
⅓ cup sugar	1 can French cut string beans
½ cup mixed lemon juice and	½ cup celery chopped
vinegar	1 small can green peas

Sprinkle gelatin on cold water to soften. Add sugar, salt and boiling water and stir until gelatin is dissolved. Pour small amount in bottom of greased mold and place artichokes and olives in desired design. Put mold in refrigerator or freezer to set. Meanwhile, let remainder of aspic thicken. When aspic is syrupy, add string beans (well drained), celery and green peas. Pour this mixture on top of artichokes in ring mold. Refrigerate to set. Serve with mayonnaise to which horseradish and sour cream have been added. Any combination of vegetables may be used following the same method of preparation.

Mrs. Richard Overby

TOMATO ASPIC RING

4 cups tomato juice	2 small bay leaves
1/3 cup chopped onion	4 whole cloves
1/4 cup chopped celery leaves	2 envelopes unflavored gelatin
2 tablespoons brown sugar	3 tablespoons lemon juice
1 teaspoon salt	1/2 to 1 cup finely chopped celery

Combine two cups tomato juice, onion, celery leaves, sugar, salt, bay leaves and cloves. Simmer uncovered five minutes; strain. Meanwhile soften gelatin in 1/2 cup of remaining tomato juice, dissolve in the hot tomato juice. Add remaining tomato juice and the lemon juice. Chill until partially set. Stir in celery. Pour into a five-cup ring mold. Chill until firm. Unmold on lettuce, fill center with shrimp or crabmeat. Serve with mayonnaise. Serves 6-8.

Mrs. John W. Donald

TOMATO ASPIC

4 envelopes unflavored gelatin	3 tablespoons vinegar
7 cups tomato juice	1 tablespoon salt
celery leaves	1 tablespoon sugar
1 bay leaf	1 large avocado, sprinkled with
3 tablespoons onion, grated	lemon juice

Sprinkle gelatin over 3/4 cup cold water. Let stand five minutes. Meanwhile, heat tomato juice, adding a few celery leaves, bay leaf and onion, vinegar, salt and sugar. Simmer ten minutes. Strain, add softened gelatin to hot juice, stir until dissolved. Chill until thick and syrupy. Arrange avocado slices in bottom of ten inch ring mold. Pour in a little of tomato and chill until firm. Add any remaining avocado slices, rest of tomato mixture and chill until firm. (overnight) Serves 14-16.

Mrs. M. B. McMurphy

TOMATO ASPIC WITH CREAM CHEESE FILLING

1 large can tomatoes	few sprigs parsley
1/3 green pepper, chopped	1/3 cup sugar
1/3 medium onion, chopped	3-4 bay leaves
1 tablespoon whole cloves	salt to taste
dash of red pepper	2 1/2 envelopes gelatin
3 celery stalks, chopped	1 1/2 lemons

63

Cook these ingredients together, slowly, until thoroughly done, about one hour. Drain into gelatin after pressing through a colander. Add lemon juice. Use about ⅓ of this mixture as bottom layer in mold. Congeal thoroughly.

CREAM CHEESE FILLING:

1 package (small) cream cheese	3-4 tablespoons mayonnaise
1 teaspoon chopped onion,	½ envelope gelatin
chives or cucumber	½ cup water

Mash cream cheese, seasoning and mayonnaise. Add boiling water to gelatin. Mix together cream cheese and gelatin for middle layer in mold. Add to mold and again allow to congeal thoroughly. Add remaining tomato, gelatin mixture. Congeal. Serves 12.

Mrs. Robert D. Hays

FROZEN EYEOPENER

1 (No. 2) can tomato juice	½ teaspoon allspice
1 teaspoon minced onion	juice of 1 lemon
1 teaspoon minced parsley	½ heaping teaspoon salt
1 teaspoon horseradish	Tabasco to taste
3 teaspoons wine vinegar	2 egg whites
½ teaspoon celery seed	shredded lettuce

Blend all ingredients except egg whites and lettuce in electric blender. Pour into ice cube tray and put in freezing compartment. When partially frozen, remove and in same container, stir in beaten egg whites. Replace in freezing compartment, stirring occasionally, until serving time. Serve on shredded lettuce. Serves 8-10.

Mrs. Jere Austill, Jr.

FROZEN TOMATO SALAD I

1 quart tomato juice	1 pint mayonnaise
1 pint crushed pineapple,	2 tablespoons grated onion
well drained	few dashes Tabasco
1 cup cream cheese	salt and pepper to taste

Mix thoroughly and freeze. Serve with mayonnaise, lightly flavored with curry powder. Serves 10.

Mrs. Clarence V. Partridge

FROZEN TOMATO SALAD II

2 1 lb. cans tomatoes, well drained	1 teaspoon Worcestershire
1⅓ cups mayonnaise	2 drops Tobasco
juice of 1 very juicy lemon or 1½ not so juicy	1 teaspoon salt
	a shake of cracked pepper
3 teaspoons finely chopped green onion	1 envelope gelatin dissolved in ⅓ cup water

Combine all ingredients in blender and whip on high until well blended. Place liquid in container in freezer and beat a couple of times as it freezes. When frozen, scoop out with ice cream scoop, refreeze individual servings. Yield six or eight servings. (This is highly seasoned, so homemade mayonnaise is sufficient for topping. If you really like it rich, a sliced hard boiled egg and horseradish dressing is a grand topping or you may eliminate onion and Tabasco in recipe and substitute horseradish dressing. All ways are excellent!)

Mrs. Selwyn Turner, Jr.

COLE SLAW

½ head white cabbage	1 stalk celery, grated
1 small onion, grated	1 teaspoon salt
1 dill pickle, grated	1 tablespoon horseradish
¼ pound Roquefort cheese, grated	½ cup mayonnaise

Wash cabbage, drain and chill. When ready to serve, grate cabbage, onion and pickle, Roquefort and celery. Add seasonings with mayonnaise. Serves 6.

Mrs. Harry A. Partridge

CHINESE SALAD

½ can (5 ounce can) Chinese noodles	1 teaspoon Worcestershire sauce
1½ tablespoons melted butter	1 quart salad greens
½ teaspoon garlic salt	1 tablespoon sliced ripe olives
½ teaspoon curry powder	vinegar & oil dressing

Heat noodles with butter and seasonings in 200° oven for fifteen minutes. Toss hot with greens, olives and dressing. Serve at once. Serves 8.

Mrs. Tom Perry

SALAD JAMBOREE

GARDEN CRISP SALAD

1 envelope unflavored gelatin	1 small onion, grated
¼ cup cold water	1 cup crisp, shredded cabbage
1 cup boiling water	2 tablespoons chopped green
1 teaspoon salt	pepper
½ cup sugar	½ cup julienne cut carrots
¼ cup lemon juice	1 cup chopped celery
¼ cup vinegar	¼ cup sliced stuffed olives

Soften gelatin in cold water, dissolve in boiling water. Add salt, sugar, lemon juice and vinegar, stir to dissolve sugar. Chill until partially set. Add remaining ingredients. Chill in oiled salad mold. Serves 6.

Mrs. M. B. McMurphy

CAESAR SALAD

1 garlic pod	½ head lettuce
½ cup salad oil	½ bunch curly endive
1 egg, beaten	1 cup croutons (made by
1 tablespoon Worcestershire	spreading mixture of
sauce	Worcestershire and butter
¼ cup lemon juice	on stale bread slices,
½ teaspoon salt	cutting into cubes and
½ teaspoon coarsely ground	toasting in slow oven)
pepper	1 2 ounce can flat anchovy fillets
½ cup Parmesan cheese	2 or 3 tomatoes diced

Mash garlic in press and add to salad oil. Mix egg, Worcestershire, lemon juice, salt, pepper and cheese in jar and shake well. Just before serving break lettuce and endive into bowl, strain oil over this, add tomatoes, anchovies and croutons to lettuce. Pour above mixture over all and toss well. Serves 4-6.

Mrs. Kenneth Hannon

FIVE CUP SALAD

1 cup mandarin orange sections, drained	1 cup grated coconut
1 cup pineapple chunks, drained	1 cup miniature marshmallows
	1 cup sour cream

Mix in bowl and chill well. Serve on lettuce.

Mrs. Carl Hardin

66

SALAD JAMBOREE

CONGEALED FRUIT SALAD

1 small pack lime or lemon gelatin	1 small can crushed pineapple
¾ cup boiling water	⅓ cup mayonnaise
1 small pack cream cheese	2 diced bananas
14 small marshmallows	1 teaspoon lemon juice
½ cup evaporated milk	¾ cup chopped pecans

Mix gelatin, boiling water, cream cheese and marshmallows over low heat until dissolved. Add milk, pineapple, mayonnaise, bananas, lemon juice and pecans. Pour into medium sized ring mold and refrigerate until set.

Mrs. Albert Reynolds, Jr.

FROZEN FRUIT SALAD

1 large can fruit salad	½ cup cherries, chopped
1 envelope gelatin	½ cup pecans or walnuts, quartered
½ cup fruit juice	
3 tablespoons sugar	1 can peaches, cut fine
1 cup mayonnaise	1 cup whipped cream
1 package frozen strawberries	

Drain fruit. Dissolve gelatin in heated fruit juice to which sugar has been added. Add a drop of lemon juice and cool. Mix mayonnaise, fruits and nuts and fold into the partially congealed gelatin. Fold in whipped cream, pour mixture into ice trays and freeze, stirring several times during freezing process. Serves 12.

Mrs. Mac B. Greer

FRUIT SALAD AND DRESSING

2 grapefruit, peeled and sectioned	20 marshmallows, chopped
2 oranges, peeled and sectioned	½ pound blanched almonds
1 can pineapple tidbits, drained	

Dressing:

4 egg yolks	2 tablespoons water
1 teaspoon mustard	juice of one lemon
4 teaspoons sugar	1 pint whipping cream
2 tablespoons vinegar	

67

Mix all ingredients except cream and cook over low heat until thick. Cool and add a pint of whipped cream. Serves 12.

Mrs. Frank Courtney

24 HOUR SALAD

2 eggs, beaten
4 tablespoons vinegar
4 tablespoons sugar
2 cups Queen Anne cherries, halved

4 tablespoons butter
2 cups pineapple, cut in pieces
2 oranges, cut in pieces
2 cups marshmallows, cut
1 pint whipping cream

Cook eggs in double boiler with vinegar and sugar, beating constantly until smooth and thick. Remove from heat, add butter and cool. Whip cream. Fold cream and mixed fruit into cooled egg mixture. Put in mold and refrigerate for 24 hours. Serve on lettuce. 8 to 12 generous servings.

Mrs. S. A. Barrett

CRANBERRY MOLD RELISH

juice of 6 oranges
orange pulp and rind
6 cups cranberries

6 cups sugar
3 packages cherry gelatin

Squeeze juice from oranges. Grind together oranges, minus seeds, and cranberries. Add sugar and mix well. Dissolve gelatin in three cups orange juice. Mix all together, pour into mold and refrigerate. This relish serves 18.

Mrs. Jack Friend, Sr.

CRANBERRY DELIGHT

1 package raspberry gelatin
1 tablespoon sugar
¼ pound cranberries, ground
½ cup chopped celery

½ apple, chopped
1 small can crushed pineapple
¼ cup chopped pecans

Prepare gelatin, allow to set, add remaining ingredients. More sugar may be added for a sweeter salad. (When short of time, add an envelope of plain gelatin for quicker results.) Serves 10.

Mrs. Paul Thompson

CRANBERRY SALAD I

1½ envelopes gelatin
¼ cup cold water
10 ounce can crushed pineapple,
    juice reserved
1 can cranberry jelly

1 cup fresh grapes, peeled and
    seeded
1 cup chopped pecans
juice of 1 lemon
pinch of salt

Dissolve gelatin in cold water. Heat juice of pineapple and pour over gelatin. Dissolve cranberry jelly in double boiler. Mix in grapes, nuts, etc. Pour into greased molds. Serve with cream cheese dressing. Serves 8-10.

Mrs. Randall Hollinger

CRANBERRY SALAD II

1 cup ground, raw cranberries
    (measure after putting
    through blender)
1 cup sugar
1 package lemon gelatin

½ cup boiling water
¼ cup orange juice
1 teaspoon grated orange rind
1 9 ounce can crushed pineapple
½ cup chopped celery

Mix ground cranberries and sugar together and let stand overnight. Add gelatin to boiling water and dissolve. Add other ingredients and pour into either one large or individual molds. Serve with turkey or other fowl or game.

Mrs. Robert T. Clark

SAUTERNE SALAD

1 package lemon gelatin
1 cup fruit juice, boiling
½ cup sauterne
¼ cup lemon juice

sugar to taste
1 cup seedless grapes
1 cup drained, diced pineapple

Dissolve gelatin in boiling fruit juice, add sauterne, lemon juice and sugar. Chill until syrupy. Add grapes and pineapple. Refrigerate until firm.

Mrs. W. B. Erickson, Jr.

69

FROZEN GINGER ALE SALAD

1 tablespoon gelatin	¼ cup crushed strawberries
¼ cup orange juice	or raspberries
2 tablespoons lemon juice	½ cup diced pears
¼ cup sugar	¾ cup mayonnaise
1 cup ginger ale	1 cup whipping cream

Soak gelatin in orange juice for five minutes, add lemon juice and sugar. Place over double boiler and stir until gelatin and sugar are dissolved. Add fruit and ginger ale and cool until slightly thickened. Fold in mayonnaise and stiffly beaten cream. Freeze.

Mrs. Leon McVay, Jr.

LIME FRUIT SALAD

2 packages lime gelatin	2 small cans crushed pineapple
2 cups boiling water	2 (No. 2) cans white cherries
2 large packages cream cheese	1 cup chopped pecans or
⅔ cup mayonnaise	½ cup chopped almonds

Dissolve gelatin in boiling water. Add softened and whipped cream cheese. Add remaining ingredients. (Fruits should be drained before adding.) Pour into ring mold or twelve individual molds, refrigerate.

Mrs. Marion S. Adams, Jr.

LIME SALAD

1 package lime gelatin	1 teaspoon grated onion
1 cup hot water (boiling)	½ cup mayonnaise
½ cup crushed pineapple	1 cucumber, chopped fine
(undrained)	3 tablespoons white vinegar
½ teaspoon salt	

Dissolve gelatin in boiling water. Add other ingredients, refrigerate to congeal. Serve with mayonnaise and sour cream dressing.

Mrs. A. A. Hory

SALAD JAMBOREE

LIME PINEAPPLE MOLDED SALAD

1 package lime gelatin	1 small can crushed pineapple,
1 cup hot water	drained
1 small package cream cheese	½ cup orange juice

Add hot water to package of gelatin. Add cream cheese and mix well. Add pineapple and orange juice. Pour into 8 small individual molds and top each with a red cherry, if desired.

Mrs. Manson Murray

BING CHERRY SALAD

1 package lemon gelatin	1 can pitted bing cherries
1 package cherry gelatin	lemon juice to taste
1 grapefruit, sectioned	

Heat juice from grapefruit and cherries plus enough water to make one and a half pints. Dissolve gelatin in hot liquid, add fruit and lemon juice, pour in mold and refrigerate to congeal.

Mrs. Manning McPhillips

WEST INDIES SALAD

1 medium onion, chopped fine	3 ounces cider vinegar
1 pound fresh lump crabmeat	4 ounces ice water
4 ounces Wesson Oil	salt and pepper

Spread half of onion over bottom of large bowl. Cover with separated crab lumps and then remaining onion. Salt and pepper. Pour oil, vinegar, ice water over all. Cover and marinate for two to twelve hours. Toss lightly before serving.

William Bayley
Bayley's Steak House

CHERRY AND GRAPEFRUIT SALAD

1 package lemon gelatin	1 cup cherry juice
1 cup hot water	1 tablespoon fresh lemon juice
1 large can pitted black cherries	2 small grapefruit (sectioned)

Dissolve gelatin in hot water. Drain cherries and add cherry juice and

71

lemon juice to gelatin. Stir in cherries and grapefruit. Turn into mold and chill until firm.

Mrs. H. C. Slaton, Jr.

GRAPEFRUIT SALAD

1 whole grapefruit   1 scant cup sugar
1 package lemon gelatin

Heat grapefruit juice. (As about a pint is needed, you may need extra juice for this.) Dissolve gelatin in heated juice, add grapefruit pulp. Add sugar to this mixture. Mould in grapefruit shells. Refrigerate. When this has set and firmed, cut the halves into halves again, providing four half moons of molded salad.

Dressing:
Blend
1 package (3 ounce) cream cheese   juice of one large lime
2 tablespoons honey

Fold in one cup whipped cream. Chill.

Mrs. Taylor Morrissette

GRAPEFRUIT RING

3 tablespoons gelatin   ¼ teaspoon salt
½ cup cold water   avocado slices
1 cup sugar   fresh grapefruit sections
½ cup water   cream cheese
2 cups plus 6 tablespoons fresh   crushed pecans
   squeezed grapefruit juice   pomegranate seeds
3 tablespoons lemon juice   French dressing (mild sweet)
½ cup sherry

Soak gelatin in cold water. Stir combined sugar and water over low heat and pour over gelatin, cool. Add grapefruit and lemon juices, sherry and salt. Pour into well greased nine inch mold and refrigerate until congealed. Turn on tray and surround with avocado slices and fresh grapefruit sections. Fill center with cream cheese balls rolled in pecans. Sprinkle with seeds and serve with dressing.

Mrs. Carl Hardin

72

MINT FLAVORED PEAR SALAD

10 ounce glass of mint jelly	green food coloring
½ cup pear juice	8 canned pear halves

Heat together mint jelly and pear juice. Add several drops of green food coloring. Place pear halves in the melted jelly, let stand, basting occasionally, until light green in color. Drain the pears. For each serving place two pear halves, cut side up, on a salad plate using a spoonful of your favorite salad dressing. Arrange on Bibb lettuce and garnish with tiny leaves. Wonderful with lamb.

Mrs. Gordon Stimpson

CREAMY PEACH SALAD

1 pound can cling peach slices	1 cup hot water
1 (3 ounce) package cream cheese	1½ tablespoons lemon juice
1 (3 ounce) package peach flavored gelatin	3 tablespoons chopped crystallized ginger

Drain peaches, reserving syrup. Allow cream cheese to stand at room temperature until soft. Dissolve gelatin in hot water, add cream cheese in chunks. Beat with rotary beater until smooth. Combine peach syrup and lemon juice and add water to make one cup, stir into gelatin. Chill in refrigerator until partially set. Fold in peaches and ginger. May be put into one 4 cup mold or individual molds. Chill unil firm, unmold and serve on lettuce. Top with mayonnaise. Serves 8.

Mrs. James Craig

FRESH PINEAPPLE SALAD PLATE

2 fresh pineapples	½ cup miniature marshmallows
1 small can sliced peaches, cut up	1 cup green grapes, chopped
1 small jar red maraschino cherries	1 package frozen strawberries, drained
½ cup chopped pecans or walnuts	½ cup mayonnaise
1 apple, diced	whipping cream

Split pineapples in half, from top to bottom. Do not cut tops off pineapples. Cut out pineapple meat, as close as possible to rind, cut into bite size pieces. Add peaches, cut or whole cherries, nuts, apple, marshmallows, grapes and strawberries. Mix the mayonnaise with juice from strawberries. Some of

the peach juice may be added. Toss fruits lightly with dressing. Fill pineapple halves and top with whipped cream. Delicious served with toasted
pecan bread.

Mrs. Mac Greer

SPICED PEACH SALAD

1 package lemon gelatin	1 can crushed pineapple, drained
1 package orange gelatin	1 cup nut meats (your preference)
juices from canned fruit	1 large jar spiced peaches,
½ cup sugar	chopped or sliced
1 can white cherries, drained	

Make gelatin according to package directions, using juices from canned
fruit and adding sugar. Pour into well greased mold and when beginning
to set stir in fruits and nuts. Serve with whipped cream and mayonnaise
mixed together, using more cream than mayonnaise.

Mrs. Carl Hardin

CONGEALED PINEAPPLE SALAD

1 envelope gelatin	1 cup undrained crushed
¼ cup cold water	pineapple
1 tablespoon sugar	2 three ounce packages cream
¼ teaspoon salt	cheese, softened
½ cup boiling water	½ cup whipping cream
2 tablespoons lemon juice	

Place gelatin in cold water. In top of double boiler put sugar, salt, lemon
juice and pineapple, add the boiling water and cook until sugar is just
dissolved, only a few minutes. Remove, add gelatin and set aside to cool.
Slowly stir this cooled mixture into cream cheese, blending well. Fold in
whipped cream. Since this mixture has no color it may be made more
attractive by the addition of a few drops of green food coloring, added
carefully and slowly. The addition of almonds, whole or chopped makes
a more festive salad. Pour into a slightly greased mold or dish. Place in
refrigerator to set. Best served with homemade mayonnaise. Serves 4.

Mrs. John Scott

SUMMER TREAT CHICKEN MOLD

8 hard cooked eggs (grind whites and yolks separately)
Boil medium sized hen, remove meat and grind (season with salt, celery salt, 2 tablespoons grated onion)
Grease loaf mold and fill as follows:
1st. layer—all chicken meat packed loosely
2nd. layer—all ground yolks
3rd. layer—all ground whites
Dissolve 1 package plain gelatin in ½ cup cold water. Dissolve in 1 cup hot, strong chicken broth. Pour over loaf. Allow several hours to set. Serve with lettuce and tomato wedges. 12 generous servings.

Mrs. R. O. Garrett

CHICKEN SALAD

1 large chicken	several small sour pickles
8 hard boiled eggs	½ cup chopped nuts
1 cup celery, chopped	pimento
1 apple, chopped	mayonnaise

Boil chicken in water to cover until meat begins to fall off. Cut with scissors into small pieces. Add chopped eggs, celery, apple, pickle, nuts and small bit of pimento. Mix well with mayonnaise. Add salt and pepper to taste. Serve on lettuce leaf with spoonful of mayonnaise on top of each serving. Serves 10-12.

Ann Goode

MY FAVORITES

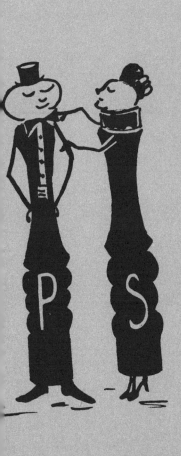

Salad Dressings

SALAD DRESSINGS

LIME SALAD DRESSING

¾ cup salad oil
2 teaspoons cider vinegar
3 tablespoons lime juice
¼ cup orange juice

2 tablespoons sugar
½ teaspoon salt
3 tablespoons chopped fresh mint

Combine all ingredients and put in a jar. Shake vigorously. Refrigerate. Delicious with fruit salad.

Mrs. F. L. DuValle

DRESSING FOR FRUIT SALAD

½ cup mayonnaise
1 tablespoon honey
1 tablespoon lemon juice

1 teaspoon grated lemon rind
2 tablespoons soft cream cheese

Combine all ingredients and mix until well blended.

Mrs. H. C. Slaton, Jr.

COOKED FRUIT SALAD DRESSING

¾ cup sugar
vinegar
2 eggs
2 tablespoons mustard

¼ teaspoon salt
1 tablespoon butter
2 tablespoons mayonnaise

Fill cup with ¾ cup sugar and add vinegar until cup is full. Beat eggs until light and fluffy, add mustard and salt, then sugar and vinegar. Mix well.

Cook, stirring constantly, until mixture is thick when dropped from a spoon. Add butter. When almost cold, whip with mayonnaise. Delicious over fruit salad.

Mrs. J. Manson Murray

POPPY SEED DRESSING

½ cup sugar	1 teaspoon poppy seed
½ teaspoon salt	4 tablespoons vinegar
1 tablespoon dry mustard	2 teaspoons grated onion
1 tablespoon paprika	1 cup salad oil

Blend with mixer all ingredients except oil. Add salad oil in thirds, beating after each addition. This dressing will keep for several weeks in refrigerator.

Mrs. Marshall J. DeMouy

HONEY—FRUIT SALAD DRESSING

⅔ cup sugar	⅓ cup honey
1 teaspoon dry mustard	5 tablespoons vinegar
1 teaspoon paprika	1 tablespoon lemon juice
¼ teaspoon salt	1 tablespoon grated onion
1 teaspoon celery seed	1 cup salad oil

Mix dry ingredients, add honey, vinegar, lemon juice and onion. Beat with rotary beater or electric mixer. Add oil gradually while beating. Chill thoroughly. Delicious on fresh fruits.

Mrs. J. C. Sutherland

MAYONNAISE I

2 eggs	2 teaspoons salt
1 quart (or 5 cups) salad oil	1 teaspoon pepper
1 tablespoon Worcestershire	juice of 1 lemon
2 teaspoons mustard	

Beat eggs thoroughly in mixer. Add oil very, very slowly, beating well after each addition. When mixture begins to thicken add remaining ingredients slowly, continuing to beat. (Grated onion may be added, if desired.) If mayonnaise separates after a period of refrigeration, beat one egg and a small amount of oil to thicken and add gradually to cold mayonnaise.

Mrs. Jere Austill, Jr.

MAYONNAISE II

2 egg yolks	1 tablespoon wine vinegar
1 teaspoon salt	1 pint Wesson Oil
1 heaping teaspoon sugar	dash of red pepper
juice of one lemon	1 tablespoon hot water

Place egg yolks in small electric mixer bowl. Turn on to speed seven. Add salt and sugar, beat until well blended. Continue beating as you add lemon juice and vinegar. Slowly add Wesson Oil. When thickened, add pepper and hot water.

Mrs. Austill Pharr, Jr.

BLEU CHEESE DRESSING

2 4 ounce packages bleu cheese	1 teaspoon salt
½ cup vinegar	½ teaspoon dry mustard
1 teaspoon sugar	1½ cups salad oil

Mix ⅓ crumbled cheese with vinegar, sugar, salt and mustard in a bowl, using fork to mash cheese into mixture. Slowly add oil, beating constantly with rotary mixer, until well blended. Stir in remaining cheese and refrigerate.

Mrs. T. M. Taul, Jr.

CREAM GARLIC SALAD DRESSING

2 cups mayonnaise	½ teaspoon garlic salt
1 garlic clove, crushed	¼ cup milk
¼ teaspoon horseradish	

Combine all ingredients and shake well. Best if made at least one hour before serving. Serve on green salad.

Mrs. Kenneth Granger

ROQUEFORT-CREAM DRESSING

⅓ cup green onions, chopped fine	2 tablespoons anchovy paste
2 cups mayonnaise	½ cup vinegar
2 garlic cloves, grated	2 tablespoons lemon juice
½ cup chopped parsley	1-2 packages Roquefort
1 cup thick sour cream	

Add onions to mayonnaise. Add garlic and parsley. Mix anchovy paste with sour cream and add to mayonnaise. Thin this mixture with vinegar and lemon juice. Crumble cheese and beat into dressing. Season to taste with salt and pepper.

Mrs. Marion B. McMurphy

TOMATO DRESSING

3 large tomatoes, grated
3 small bottles of olive oil
1 olive oil bottle of vinegar
1 tablespoon Worcestershire

1 teaspoon mustard (dry)
½ teaspoon salt
1 pod garlic

Grate tomatoes, add olive oil, vinegar, Worcestershire, mustard and salt. Squeeze pod of garlic, for juice, into mixture. Shake well in jar. Refrigerate. Serve dressing at room temperature over greens. Makes almost 1 quart.

Mrs. T. Massey Bedsole

FAUCON DRESSING

5 pods garlic
3 tablespoons vinegar
3 hard boiled eggs
1 teaspoon salt
2 full tablespoons Durkee's dressing

paprika to taste
1 tablespoon Worcestershire
4 drops hot sauce
½ pint olive oil
½ pound Roquefort cheese
1 cup vinegar

Cut garlic fine and soak in three tablespoonsful vinegar for about four hours. Crush garlic after it has soaked for a while. Mash hard boiled egg yolks with salt and paprika. Stir in Durkee's dressing, Worcestershire and hot sauce. Stir in olive oil slowly and mix well. Now add garlic mixture and blend well. Add Roquefort, broken into small pieces and mix thoroughly. Add vinegar slowly, continuing to stir well.

Mrs. Franklin King

COOKED SALAD DRESSING

4 tablespoons butter
2 tablespoons flour
1 cup milk
3 eggs
1 tablespoon dry mustard

1 teaspoon salt
⅛ teaspoon Cayenne pepper
¼ teaspoon paprika
1½ tablespoons sugar
½ cup cider vinegar

Melt butter, add flour, then add half the milk. Place in double boiler. Beat eggs, add all seasonings and vinegar. Stir this into mixture in double boiler. Add remaining milk and cook, stirring constantly until custard consistency. Pour into a jar and keep covered in refrigerator. This dressing is very good with slaw and potato salad and will keep for weeks.

Mrs. C. D. Wilson

SINA SKINNER'S SALAD DRESSING

1 pint home-made mayonnaise	1 minced green onion
5 teaspoons tarragon vinegar	1 teaspoon minced chives
1 tube anchovy paste	1 teaspoon minced garlic
2 teaspoons minced parsley	

Mix well, chill and serve with green salad.

Sina Skinner

THOUSAND ISLAND DRESSING

1 cup mayonnaise	1 tablespoon parsley flakes,
1 cup tomato catsup	dried or fresh
1 garlic pod, minced	8 small green olives, chopped fine
1 small onion, grated	1 hard boiled egg, grated
juice of one lemon	salt to taste
1 teaspoon mustard	pepper to taste
½ teaspoon Worcestershire	

Mix as listed, store in jar in refrigerator.

Mrs. Ernest L. Brown

OUR HOUSE FRENCH DRESSING

2 garlic cloves, peeled and split	½ cup lemon juice
1 tablespoon granulated sugar	6 tablespoons tarragon vinegar
¼ cup seasoned salt	2 cups good salad oil

Combine all ingredients in a jar with a tight top, shake well and store in refrigerator. The garlic remains in the mixture. To the desired amount of dressing, poured into a small bowl you may add crumbled blue or Roquefort cheese, fine herbs, such as minced parsley, chives, chervil, shredded green onion and the like: chutney, finely chopped, a good chili sauce— any of these make an interesting change.

Frank Kohler
"Skillet Club for Men"

81

SALAD DRESSINGS

HORSERADISH DRESSING

1 cup mayonnaise	4 teaspoons undrained horseradish
½ cup sour cream	2 pods garlic, pressed
¼ teaspoon dry mustard	2 teaspoons chives

Put in blender. Then add two teaspoons chives and refrigerate. Serve on frozen tomato salad or fried shrimp.

Mrs. Selwyn Turner, Jr.

FRENCH DRESSING WITHOUT GARLIC

1 teaspoon sugar	3 tablespoons lemon juice
1 teaspoon celery salt	¾ cup olive oil
⅛ teaspoon dry mustard	½ teaspoon onion scraped
¼ teaspoon paprika	2 teaspoons Worcestershire sauce
1 tablespoon vinegar	

Mix all well and refrigerate.

Mrs. Jack Gallalee

CHEESE CROUTONS FOR SALAD

Toss 1½ cups bite size shredded wheat biscuits in three tablespoons melted butter or margarine over low heat for five minutes. Sprinkle with one half cup grated parmesan cheese and spread to cool.

Mrs. Robert Meador

FRENCH DRESSING WITH GARLIC

1¼ cup olive oil	¾ teaspoon sugar
6 tablespoons vinegar	1½ tablespoon catsup
2 teaspoons salt	1½ teaspoon chili sauce
⅛ teaspoon pepper	1 tablespoon lemon juice
¼ teaspoon paprika	1½ teaspoon Worcestershire
celery salt	2 garlic buds

Combine all ingredients. Beat well until smooth, adding oil last and very slowly. Let peeled garlic buds remain in dressing several hours then remove. Makes 2 cups.

Mrs. Manning McPhillips, Jr.

MY FAVORITES

MY FAVORITES

Seafood Jubilee

SEAFOODS

GENERAL RULES FOR PREPARING SEAFOOD

1. All seafoods served in salads or cocktails must be served ice cold.
2. Oysters, clams and shrimp should not be cooked too long as over cooking toughens them and destroys the delicious flavor.
3. Fish should always be cooked until well done, which can be detected when flesh easily separates from the bone.
4. In frying fish, care should be taken to have fat the proper temperature. If too hot, the fish will burn before cooking and if not hot enough, the fish will absorb grease and will not crisp.
5. Fish should be served piping hot, immediately after cooking. This is especially true of fried fish. It is doubly delicious when served right from the frying pan.
6. Fish having a thick skin will be found more palatable if skinned before cooking, except when it is baked. To skin a fish, make a slit crossways near the tail down to meat. Grab skin with pliers and pull toward head.
7. The shell of crab and lobster is removed more easily after boiling than in raw state.
8. Whenever possible, fish should be prepared at least a half hour before cooking and seasoned with salt and lemon juice. This takes away much of the strong "fishy" flavor, considered objectionable by many.
9. Large, fleshy fish are better broiled than baked. Small fish lend themselves better to frying.
10. Spicy, piquant sauces are delicious with all fish and do much to bring out the natural flavor. However, delicately flavored fish, such as pompano and flounder are good with little flavor other than lemon juice.
11. Salt fish may be prepared in many appetizing ways, in salads, cro-

quettes, casseroles, jambalayas, etc. It may also be shredded, seasoned anew and served with macaroni.

12. Delicious sandwiches may be made by combining fried fish with mustard, mayonnaise or catsup and using either tomato, lettuce, celery or bacon in combination.

13. To clean a crab, lift the shell off; remove all legs and feelers; remove the mushy tan substance on each side known as the "dead man's fingers", clean out the cavity in the middle, break in half, wash well, and the crab is ready!

14. To freeze crabs leave them uncooked and clean them alive. This prevents the meat from becoming stringy. Follow the above directions for cleaning. After they are broken and washed, put 10 to 12 raw crab halves into a plastic container. Fill with water, cover tightly, and store in freezer.

FRIED CRABS

12-14 whole boiled crabs	2 eggs
cracker meal seasoned with	bacon drippings or shortening
salt and pepper	

Remove back, feelers, et cetera, from crabs. Wash thoroughly and break in half. Dip each half in beaten egg and then in cracker meal. Fry (in bacon drippings for better flavor) until cracker meal is golden brown. Eat as you would boiled crabs. This is not a very neat dish and is recommended for informal meals. The flavor is delicious and very different from boiled crabs.

Mrs. John Brady

CRAB OMELETTE

2 green onions, diced	½-¾ pound crabmeat
1 celery stalk, chopped	few drops Tabasco
½ small bell pepper, chopped fine	salt and pepper to taste
3 eggs, separated	

Sauté onion, celery and bell pepper until soft—not brown in bacon grease. In a bowl, mix egg yolks and crabmeat. Scoop onion, celery and bell pepper from skillet and add to egg yolks and crabmeat. Add Tabasco, salt and pepper. Beat egg whites until stiff. Fold into other mixture. Spoon into skillet with hot grease. Turn as soon as lightly browned.

Mrs. John Brady

86

INDIVIDUAL CRABMEAT OMELETTES

4 eggs
1 teaspoon onion, chopped fine
1 teaspoon chives, chopped
1 teaspoon shallots, chopped

1 teaspoon chervil
1 teaspoon parsley, chopped fine
½ to ¾ pound crabmeat

Stir herbs into well beaten eggs. Add crabmeat and fry in butter, cooking one large spoonful at a time.

Mrs. Selwyn Turner, Jr.

SOFT SHELL CRABS

Soft shell crabs are young blue crabs that have shed their old shells and have only a soft covering. They are cleaned and cooked whole, either sautéed or deep fried.

FRIED:

Soak cleaned crabs in egg, beaten with a little milk. Then dip in salted corn meal. Fry in deep fat (360°) five to ten minutes until well browned. Drain on paper and serve hot.

SAUTÉED:

Soak cleaned crabs in egg beaten with a little milk and dip in seasoned flour. Melt butter until bubbly hot and sauté crabs about ten minutes until brown. Serve with lemon wedges.

Mrs. Kenneth Hannon

CRABMEAT AMANDINE SUPREME

¼ cup butter
½ bell pepper
4 tablespoons flour
1 cup evaporated milk
⅓ cup water
½ teaspoon chervil

1 cup chopped celery
1 pound crabmeat
2 hard-boiled eggs, chopped
½ cup toasted almonds
½ cup corn flake crumbs
½ cup grated cheese

Melt butter. Add bell pepper and cook until tender. Remove from burner. Add flour combined with milk and water. Cook over low heat until thick. Stir in chervil, celery and crabmeat. Add eggs, almonds and pour into casserole. Top with combined crumbs and cheese. Bake in 350° oven for thirty minutes. Serves 6.

Mrs. Selwyn H. Turner, Jr.

CRAB CAKES

1 medium onion, chopped	1 pound white lump crabmeat
½ medium bell pepper, chopped	salt and pepper to taste
2 tablespoons cooking oil	1 egg, beaten
2 medium size potatoes	corn flake crumbs

Sauté onion and bell pepper in oil, until soft, not brown. Boil potatoes with salt until done. Mash thoroughly. (You need only enough potato to hold mixture together.) Scoop onion and bell pepper from oil and mix with crabmeat and potatoes. Season with salt and pepper. Form into cakes about the size of a hamburger patty. Dip in egg and roll in crumbs. Fry in oil until golden brown.

Mrs. J. C. Carrington

CRAB MORNAY

4 tablespoons margarine	½ pound Swiss cheese, cut up
4 tablespoons flour	1 pound crabmeat
2 garlic cloves, minced	dash of Tabasco
2 cups milk	Parmesan cheese
salt to taste	

Melt margarine. Add flour and garlic. Mix well. Slowly add milk. Cook and stir until thick. Add salt. Add Swiss cheese, crabmeat and Tabasco. Mix well. Pour into ramekins and sprinkle with Parmesan cheese. Bake in 350° oven for thirty minutes. Serves 8.

Mrs. John Warren

CRABMEAT CASSEROLE

4 tablespoons butter	dash of pepper
3 hard-boiled eggs	2 eggs yolks
4 tablespoons flour	1 small onion, chopped
4 tablespoons vinegar	1 cup heavy cream
2 teaspoons prepared mustard	1 pound crabmeat
2 tablespoons Worcestershire	2 egg whites
½ teaspoon salt	½ cup buttered bread crumbs

Melt butter in double boiler. Separate hard-boiled eggs. Mash yolks in butter. Add flour, vinegar, seasonings and stir well. Chop egg whites and combine with beaten yolks and onion. Pour in cream and cook over hot water until very thick. Add crabmeat. Remove from heat and fold in well

88

beaten egg whites. Fill greased casserole. Cover with crumbs and bake twenty minutes in 350° oven.

Mrs. W. B. Erickson, Jr.

CRAB MOUSSE

2 envelopes gelatin
¼ cup cold water
2 small packages cream cheese
1 can mushroom soup
1 cup mayonnaise
¼ teaspoon salt
1 teaspoon Worcestershire

1 (8 ounce) can crabmeat or
  ½ pound fresh crabmeat
1 cup minced celery
1 tablespoon minced chives
1 small onion, grated
cranberry jelly slices

Dissolve gelatin in cold water. In double boiler top, over low heat, stir cheese, soup, mayonnaise, salt and Worcestershire. Remove from heat. Add gelatin and stir until melted. Let cool and add crabmeat, celery, chives and onion. Fill eight well greased individual molds with mixture. Chill and serve on cold, thickly sliced cranberry jelly.

Mrs. Ernest Brown

CRAB STUFFED POTATOES

4 baking potatoes
½ cup milk
½ cup margarine
1 teaspoon salt

½ onion, grated
½ pound crabmeat
sharp cheese, grated

Bake potatoes for about one hour in 450° oven. Remove from oven and take pulp from shell. To pulp, add milk, margarine, salt and onion. Whip. Add crabmeat and stuff potato shells with this mixture. Sprinkle with grated cheese. This can be done well in advance. Heat thoroughly in moderate oven before serving. (15-20 minutes)

Mrs. John Warren

DEVILED CRAB WITH MAYONNAISE

1 can white or claw crabmeat
1 teaspoon mustard
½ cup cracker crumbs
2 hard-boiled eggs, chopped fine

½ teaspoon horseradish
a little onion juice
a little lemon juice
red pepper and salt to taste

Mix all ingredients. Add enough salad dressing to make mixture stick together. (Usually one-half to three-fourths cup.) Dot with cracker crumbs and butter and bake in 350° oven for thirty minutes or until thoroughly heated.

Mrs. Russell Terry

DEVILED CRAB

4 tablespoons butter	⅛ teaspoon black pepper
2 tablespoons flour	pinch of red pepper
1 cup chopped celery	1 tablespoon lemon juice
½ green pepper, chopped	1 tablespoon Worcestershire
1 small onion, chopped	1 tablespoon prepared mustard
1 cup milk	½ teaspoon salt
1 pound crabmeat	toasted bread crumbs
1 egg	butter

Melt butter in saucepan. Add flour, celery, green pepper, onion and milk. Stir this mixture until well blended and slightly thickened. Pour this sauce over crabmeat in bowl. Add beaten egg and seasonings. Add enough bread crumbs to thicken. (About two tablespoonfuls.) Grease individual baking shells or casserole and fill with crab mixture. Sprinkle with bread crumbs and top with small slices of butter. Bake fifteen to twenty minutes in 400° oven.

Mrs. A. A. Hory

BAKED CRABS

1 large onion, minced	1 tablespoon prepared mustard
½ cup minced celery	1 tablespoon mayonnaise
1 small green pepper, minced	2 eggs, well beaten
½ stick butter or margarine	¼ teaspoon garlic salt
1 pound crabmeat	salt and pepper to taste
1 cup bread crumbs	10 medium crab shells

Sauté minced seasoning in butter until it becomes glazy, but not brown. Mix crabmeat and bread crumbs and add cooked seasoning. Add mustard, mayonnaise, eggs, garlic salt and pepper. Mix until well blended. Pack into well greased shells. Top lightly with bread crumbs. Bake in 400° oven until lightly browned. Serves 10.

J. O. Wintzell, Wintzell's Oyster House

CRABMEAT SEA SHELLS

3 tablespoons butter
3 green onions, chopped
1½ celery stalks, finely chopped
1 teaspoon dry mustard
1 teaspoon Worcestershire
½ teaspoon salt
dash of pepper

1 cup mayonnaise
½ cup undiluted evaporated milk
2 tablespoons sherry
1 pound lump crabmeat
3 tablespoons butter
1 garlic clove
1 cup bread crumbs

Melt three tablespoonfuls butter in pan. Sauté onions and celery until tender. Stir in seasonings, mayonnaise, milk and sherry. Add crabmeat and pour into six individual seafood shells or ramekins. Heat remaining butter with cut garlic clove and toss crumbs in butter. Sprinkle over seafood. Bake in 350° oven for about thirty minutes.

Mrs. Robert Mudd

CRABMEAT AND SPINACH CASSEROLE

4 tablespoons butter or
   margarine
¼ cup chopped onion
2 cans (11 ounce) condensed
   cream of mushroom soup
1 cup sour cream
1 can (6 ounce) sliced
   mushrooms, plus liquid
½ cup grated Parmesan cheese
dash of Angostura bitters

½ teaspoon dry mustard
½ teaspoon monosodium
   glutamate
1 pound can crabmeat
2 tablespoons sherry
1 tablespoon chopped chives
   or parsley
2 packages frozen chopped
   spinach

Melt butter in saucepan. Sauté onions until tender. Add soup, sour cream, mushrooms, grated cheese and seasonings. Cook until smooth and thoroughly heated. Stir in crabmeat, sherry and chives. Place in serving dish, alternating layers of crabmeat mixture and cooked spinach. Serves 8.

Mrs. Marion H. Dodson

CRABMEAT NORFOLK

dash of nutmeg
1 pint crab meat (lump preferred)
1 cup home-made mayonnaise

salt and pepper to taste
¼ cup sherry or vermouth

91

SEAFOOD JUBILEE

Combine ingredients. Fill crab shells. Sprinkle tops lightly with paprika and heat in 375° oven for 20 minutes. Serves 8. (Also good in chafing dish served with patty shells. If bought mayonnaise is used, add juice of ½ lemon to mixture.)

Mrs. C. M. A. Rogers

CRAB CASSEROLE

4 tablespoons butter	½ pound fresh mushrooms
4 tablespoons flour	butter
2 cups thin cream	1 pound lump crabmeat
2 egg yolks	3 tablespoons chopped parsley
½ teaspoon salt	¼ cup Rhine wine
1 teaspoon Worcestershire	buttered bread crumbs

Make cream sauce with butter, flour and cream. Remove from heat and add well beaten egg yolks, salt, Worcestershire. Broil mushrooms in butter and combine with crabmeat, parsley and wine. Bake in 350° oven for fifteen minutes. Cover with buttered bread crumbs and bake fifteen to twenty minutes longer.

Mrs. Dewitt King
Mobile Country Club

CRABMEAT IN AVOCADO

¼ cup butter	2 cups crabmeat
¼ cup flour	2 hard-boiled eggs, chopped
¾ teaspoon salt	½ cup sliced mushrooms
dash of pepper	3 tablespoons sherry
⅛ teaspoon nutmeg	4 avocados
2 cups milk	⅓ cup cracker crumbs
½ teaspoon scraped onion	2 tablespoons melted butter

Melt one-fourth cup butter in double boiler top over direct heat. Combine flour, salt, pepper and nutmeg and stir into butter. Cook until bubbly. Set over boiling water. Gradually add milk. Add onion and continue stirring until smooth. Add crabmeat, eggs and mushrooms. Mix well. Stir in sherry and keep warm over hot water. Cut avocados in half and place in a baking dish or pan, and fill each three-fourths full with crabmeat mixture. Sprinkle with bread crumbs and drizzle butter over crumbs. Bake in 350° oven about twenty minutes or until crumbs are golden.

Mrs. Jack Flautt

92

CRABMEAT SAUTÉ AMANDINE

½ pound butter, clarified
2 ounces slivered or
blanched almonds
2 pounds lump crabmeat

lemon juice
8 puff-paste toast points
4 lemon twists
fresh parsley

In clarified butter, sauté almonds to hazel color and remove from butter, reserving on side dish. In same butter, sauté crabmeat until thoroughly heated. Squeeze lemon juice over crabmeat to taste and pour into casserole. Sprinkle almonds over crabmeat and garnish each entrée with two puff-paste toast points and place one lemon twist in center of each. Add sprig of fresh parsley. Serves 4.

Sheraton—Battle House

CRABMEAT RECTOR

1 bunch scallions, diced
3 garlic cloves, diced
½ green pepper, diced
¼ pound butter
2 peeled tomatoes, sliced
4 ounce can chopped mushrooms

½ cup white wine (Sauterne)
1 pound lump crabmeat
salt to taste
crushed red pepper
grated Parmesan cheese

Sauté scallions, garlic and green pepper in butter until golden. Add sliced tomatoes and cook until tomatoes are soft. Add mushrooms and cook five or ten minutes longer. Add wine, then crabmeat, salt and pepper (generously) to taste. Sprinkle cheese (generously) over all. Cook ten minutes longer, turning crabmeat gently to prevent breaking. Serve hot, as first course or main dish.

Dr. Jack Hyman

CRABMEAT IN PATTY SHELLS

½ pound mushrooms
3 tablespoons butter
3 tablespoons flour
1 cup chicken stock or bouillon
½ cup cream
1 pound lump crabmeat

½ cup Parmesan cheese
½ teaspoon salt
¼ teaspoon pepper
¼ teaspoon paprika
2 tablespoons sherry
6 patty shells

Sauté mushrooms. Melt butter and stir in flour until well blended. Stir in chicken stock and cream. When sauce is boiling, add crab meat and mush-

93

rooms. When it comes to a second boil, add cheese, and seasonings. Remove from fire, add sherry and serve in patty shells. Serves 6.

Mrs. Franklin King

CRABMEAT IN CHEESE SAUCE

4 small green onions	1 tablespoon Worcestershire
1½ tablespoons butter	1 scant tablespoon mushroom
6 tablespoons butter	powder
6 tablespoons flour	½ teaspoon Cayenne
3 cups milk	5 or 6 shakes seasoned pepper
1 cup grated cheese	½ teaspoon paprika
½ cup Parmesan cheese	salt to taste
1 tablespoon dried parsley	¾-1 cup white wine (Sauterne)
1 teaspoon dry mustard	2 pounds lump crabmeat
1 teaspoon celery flakes	

Sauté onions, tops and all, in 1½ tablespoons butter over low heat until soft but not brown. Make white sauce with butter, flour and milk. Add cheeses to sauce. Stir until cheese is dissolved. Add parsley, mustard, celery flakes, Worcestershire, mushroom powder, cayenne, seasoned pepper, paprika and salt. When this is well mixed, add sautéed onions and wine, then gently stir in crabmeat. This can be served in patty shells or on artichoke bottoms.

Mrs. Ernest Brown

SOUR CREAM CRAB WITH MUSHROOMS

1 pound mushrooms	10 tablespoons flour
(or 1 large can)	2½ pints sour cream
2½ sticks butter	salt and pepper to taste
½ onion, chopped	4 pounds crabmeat
5 tablespoons chopped chives	sherry to taste
5 tablespoons chopped parsley	truffles (optional)

Wash and slice mushrooms. Cook stems in water and set stock aside. Heat butter. Add mushrooms, onions, chives and parsley. Cook three or four minutes. Stir in flour gradually. Add sour cream mixed with mushroom stock. Season with salt and pepper. Add crabmeat and cook five minutes. Add sherry and serve in chafing dish with toast rounds.

Mrs. Cowan Butler

CRABMEAT CANAPÉ SWISS CHALET

¾ pound cream cheese
½ cup whipping cream
pinch of salt
½ cup home-made mayonnaise
1 tablespoon finely chopped
  chives
1 garlic clove, finely minced

½ pound select white crabmeat,
  marinated for one hour in:
lemon juice
few drops Tabasco
few drops Worcestershire
dry, dry, dry toast

In electric mixer combine cream cheese with whipped cream until mixture is smooth. Add salt, mayonnaise, chives and garlic. Blend well. Fold into crabmeat (which has been marinated in lemon juice for one hour). Add Tabasco and Worcestershire and serve cold on dry toast rounds as a first course. Serves 6-8.

Mrs. Gillette Burton

CRABMEAT CROUSTADES

8 tablespoons shortening
12 tablespoons (¾ cup) flour
3 cups hot milk
1 pound crabmeat
4 hard-boiled eggs
4 tablespoons lemon juice
2 tablespoons grated onion
1½ teaspoons salt

1 cup slivered, salted almonds
1 large can mushrooms or 1 pound
  fresh mushrooms, sliced
1 loaf unsliced sandwich bread
fresh shortening
paprika
fresh parsley sprigs

Melt shortening. Remove from heat. Blend in flour. Gradually add hot milk over low heat. Cook until sauce comes to a boil, stirring constantly. Add eggs, lemon juice, onion, salt, crabmeat, almonds and mushrooms. (To prepare fresh mushrooms: slice, sauté in 2 tablespoons butter, add 4 tablespoons dry sherry or Chablis. Cover and marinate ten minutes.) Stir lightly and as little as possible to mix well. Remove crusts from bread which has been cut in two-inch slices. With scissors carefully cut out center, leaving about one-half inch on sides and bottom. Melt fresh shortening in deep, narrow saucepan. Heat until a small piece of bread browns quickly. Using long handled fork and slotted spoon, lower bread cups into hot shortening, turning to brown evenly. Keep croustades warm by placing in low oven, door open, on paper toweling over cookie sheet. To serve, pile crabmeat mixture into cups generously and garnish with paprika and a sprig of parsley.

Yvonne Jackson

FRIED FISH

The old fishermen of the area say, "If they are small enough to put in the pan, fry 'em!"

After cleaning the fish and washing it thoroughly, wipe dry and roll in corn meal that has been seasoned with salt and pepper. In a thick pan (an old iron skillet is best) put enough lard or oil to half cover fish. When lard is very hot put in fish. Brown well, then turn once. When that side is browned, lift carefully from pan and drain on brown paper before serving.

Mrs. John Brady

BROILED POMPANO WITH CAPER SAUCE

1 broiled pompano	⅛ teaspoon pepper
½ cup butter	½ cup capers
4 tablespoons flour	1 hard-boiled egg, chopped
2 cups boiling water	paprika
½ teaspoon salt	

To broiled pompano add caper sauce made as follows: Melt half the butter; add flour; stir while gradually adding boiling water; boil five minutes and add seasonings, remainder of butter and drained capers. Pour over fish and sprinkle with finely chopped egg and paprika.

Mrs. Arthur S. Gonzales

FISH IN SOUR CREAM

3½ pounds flounder	¾ teaspoon dried dill
5 tablespoons melted butter	¼ teaspoon salt
½ teaspoon thyme	¼ teaspoon pepper
1 bay leaf, chopped	1 cup sour cream
1 tablespoon minced onion	¼ cup light cream

Put fish in greased baking dish. Combine remaining ingredients to make sauce and pour over fish. Bake in 375° oven for thirty-five minutes or until flakey. Baste often. Serves 6.

Mrs. Willis R. Brown

BROILED FLOUNDER

Clean and wash fish. Dry on clean towel. Rub the entire fish with salt, pepper, and lemon juice. Make deep gashes in fish and fill with chopped parsley and onion. Dot fish with butter. Bake in 350° oven until fish is two-thirds done, (about twenty-five minutes). Then broil to desired brownness, (about fifteen minutes). Serve on platter garnished with parsley and lemon wedges. A whole four pound flounder should serve six generously.

Mrs. Arthur S. Gonzales

FLOUNDER FLORENTINE

1 package frozen chopped spinach, cooked and well drained	2 tablespoons salad oil flounder fillets, cut in serving pieces (fresh fish only— not frozen)
2 tablespoons chopped onion	
1 teaspoon salt	½ cup medium white sauce
¼ teaspoon pepper	2 tablespoons dry vermouth
½ teaspoon seasoned salt	½ cup grated American cheese

Place spinach in greased shallow casserole. Add onion, seasonings and oil. Put fish fillets in layer over spinach. Make white sauce, adding vermouth to finished product and pour over spinach. Sprinkle well with cheese and bake in 350° oven forty-five minutes. Serves 2-3.

Mrs. Sam Betty

FISH FILLETS

8 fillets of snapper or trout	½ stick butter
1½ cups milk	1 teaspoon paprika
flour seasoned with salt	1 tablespoon lemon juice

Soak fillets in milk for thirty minutes. Dust with salted flour. Melt butter in skillet and heat until bubbly. Sauté fillets ten to twenty minutes depending on thickness. Turn once. Remove fillets from pan and sprinkle with paprika. Add lemon juice to butter remaining in skillet and pour over fish before serving.

Mrs. Willis R. Brown

FISH 'N ONIONS

10 firm fillets of snapper or speckled trout	1 cup flour
	¼ teaspoon salt
1 cup milk	2 Bermuda onions, sliced
3 eggs, beaten	(soak slices in milk ½ hour)

Cut fish fillets into pieces about one inch by two inches. Combine milk, eggs, flour and salt. Stir well. Dip fish in batter and fry in deep fat (400°).

Drain and keep warm in low oven. Dip onions in batter and fry in same fat. Serves 6.

Mrs. Willis R. Brown

BAKED STUFFED FISH

2 pound sheephead, snapper or redfish	¼ cup chopped onion
butter	2 tablespoons chopped parsley
salt and pepper	¼ cup chopped celery
paprika	1 tablespoon chili sauce
2 slices white bread	salt and pepper
¼ cup white wine	½ stick butter
3 tablespoons butter	juice of one lemon
	¼ cup white wine

Slit a pocket for stuffing in the back of fish, using a sharp knife. Rub fish with butter, salt and pepper, and sprinkle with paprika. In a very slow oven dry out the bread slices. Crumble and soak in ¼ cup wine for ten minutes. Sauté onion, parsley and celery in 3 tablespoons butter, then add to crumbs. Add chili sauce. Season with salt and pepper. Add a little milk if needed to moisten. In pan melt ½ stick butter and add lemon juice and ¼ cup wine. Place stuffed fish in pan and bake in 325° oven for fifty to sixty minutes, basting frequently.

Mrs. Marion S. Adams, Jr.

SAUTÉED RED SNAPPER BOMBAY

1¾-2 pounds red snapper (cut into three 2½-ounce strips per person)	½ cup butter
	1 teaspoon curry powder
	1 cup hot milk
seasoned flour	1 cup coconut milk
½ pound clarified butter	1 cup chicken stock
¼ cup chopped onion	¼ apple, chopped
½ pound rice, cooked	2 tablespoons grated fresh coconut meat
2 bay leaves	
2 ounces butter	1 tablespoon chopped pimento
1 teaspoon curry powder	chopped parsley
¾ cup boiling chicken stock	chutney torte
½ cup flour	

Dip tiny snapper steaks into seasoned flour and sauté in clarified butter. In oven pot, sauté onion, rice and bay leaves in two ounces of butter.

SEAFOOD JUBILEE

Add one teaspoon curry powder and boiling chicken stock. Cover with greased paper, leaving a small hole in paper for steam vent. Bake in 350° oven for eighteen minutes and remove. For curry sauce, make roux of flour and one-half cup butter. Cook five minutes. Add curry powder and break roux with milks. In chicken stock, poach apple and grated coconut meat. Add all to sauce. Add pimento. Make ring mold of rice on plate. Place snapper steaks inside. Top two-thirds with curry sauce, leaving one-third exposed to view for color contrast and also to show guests what is being served. Sprinkle chopped parsley over all and place chutney torte on side.

Sheraton—Battle House

BAKED SNAPPER

3 pound snapper or other
  large fish
salt
pepper
flour
1 stick butter
1 onion, finely chopped
2 cups chopped celery
¼ cup chopped green pepper

3 cups canned tomatoes
1 tablespoon Worcestershire
1 tablespoon catsup
1 teaspoon chili powder
½ lemon
1 garlic clove, minced
1 teaspoon salt
Cayenne

Dredge fish inside and out with salt, pepper and flour. Melt butter; add onion, celery, green pepper and simmer until tender. Add tomatoes, Worcestershire, catsup, chili powder, lemon, garlic, salt and Cayenne. Cook for about forty-five minutes, then pour over fish and bake an hour or longer, basting frequently.

Mrs. J. P. Courtney, Jr.

SNAPPER PUDDING

1 four-pound red snapper
1 bay leaf
1 onion, sliced
3 cloves
½ cup butter
½ cup all purpose flour

2 teaspoons salt
4 cups milk
1 (8 ounce) can mushrooms,
  thinly sliced
½ cup Parmesan cheese
2 tablespoons butter

Cook fish for ten minutes in water with bay leaf, onion and cloves. Let cool in liquor. Shred. Make white sauce of butter, flour and milk. Cook until thick and smooth. Add mushrooms and shredded fish. Put in buttered baking dish. Cover with cheese, dot with butter and bake in 350° oven fifteen minutes. Serves 20-24.

Mrs. Charles R. Hicks

STUFFED FLOUNDER

1 large flounder	2 hard-boiled eggs, chopped
½ cup chopped green onions	½ pound crabmeat
½ stick butter	½ teaspoon pepper
2 tablespoons chopped parsley	1 teaspoon salt
⅓ cup bread crumbs	dash Tabasco

Prepare flounder for cooking. Slit a pocket for stuffing in the back of the flounder, using a shark knife. Brown onion in butter; add parsley, crumbs, eggs, crabmeat and seasoning. Mix well and stuff in the pocket. Brush flounder with melted butter. Sprinkle with paprika. Bake 30 minutes in 375° oven. 5-pound flounder provides six medium servings.

Mrs. Willis R. Brown

MACKEREL HOLLANDAISE

3 two-pound mackerel	1 cup dry white wine
2 tablespoons butter	½ cup hollandaise sauce
1 tablespoon chopped onion	

Fillet fish. Melt butter in skillet, add onion and cook two or three minutes. Add fish fillets. Cover with wine and bring to a boil. Bake in 250° oven for twelve minutes. Remove fillets and keep warm. Return skillet to burner and reduce liquid by boiling three minutes. Add hollandaise. Pour over fillet and serve.

Mrs. Willis R. Brown

GRILLED FISH

6 medium speckled trout	cooking oil
or Spanish mackerel	bacon slices
salt and pepper	

Fillet fish lengthwise. Salt and pepper well. Wipe both sides of each piece well with cooking oil. Wrap a slice of bacon several times around each piece. Place fish in a wire hamburger rack and grill over charcoal fire until bacon is done. When bacon is done, fish will be also.

Mrs. James C. Bledsoe

VARIATION OF GRILLED FISH

Fillet, season and wipe fish with oil as in above recipe. Instead of wrapping with bacon, baste with sauce made of:

1 stick butter   juice of 2 lemons
3 teaspoons Worcestershire

and serve with tartar sauce.

Mrs. Selwyn H. Turner, Jr.

KING MACKEREL MARGUERY

1 6-pound King Mackerel	juice of 2 lemons
(ling, trout or snapper)	3 dozen de-veined shrimp
6 tablespoons olive oil	(fresh or canned)
salt and pepper to taste	2 four-ounce cans sliced
1 cup water	mushrooms, drained
4 egg yolks	1 can truffles (optional)
1 pound butter, melted	

Skin, bone and fillet fish. Roll in olive oil and place in greased baking pan. Add salt, pepper and water. Bake in 450° oven for about twenty-five minutes, or until done. Place on individual plates and keep hot. Put egg yolks in double boiler top. Drip in melted butter, while beating constantly, until thick. Add lemon juice, shrimp, mushrooms and truffles. Mix in small portion of drippings from the fish. Pour over fish and serve immediately. Serves 6.

Mrs. Clarence V. Partridge

KING SPECIAL

4 large King mackerel fillets	seasoned pepper
(about 8 inches long,	2 sticks butter
½ to ¾ inches thick)	juice of 6 lemons
seasoned salt	4 tablespoons Worcestershire

Sprinkle fillets liberally with seasoned salt and seasoned pepper. Dot with pats of butter. Place fillets in baking pan, greased with butter, and place

101

in preheated 350° oven. Melt butter in saucepan, add lemon juice and Worcestershire. Simmer. When fish has baked ten minutes, spoon sauce over fillets. Do not turn fish, but raise around edges to keep from sticking and to allow sauce to reach bottom of fish. Bake until fish begins to flake when fork tested. Serve garnished with lemon slices and topped with remaining sauce. Excellent with grits.

Mrs. Jere Austill, Jr.

TROUT AMANDINE

Sauce:

½ cup butter	2 tablespoons chopped parsley
juice of ½ lemon	¼ cup browned, blanched,
2 tablespoons Worcestershire	chopped almonds

Melt butter. Add lemon juice, Worcestershire and cook, stirring, for two minutes. Add parsley and almonds.

Fish:

| trout fillets | ½ cup milk |
| 2 egg yolks | flour |

Beat egg yolks and add milk slowly, mixing well. Dip fillets in this mixture and roll in flour. Heat fat and cook fish three to five minutes or until brown. Pour sauce over fish and serve.

Mrs. John B. Flynn

SALMON MOLD

¼ cup butter	6 eggs, lightly beaten
1 medium onion, chopped	1 teaspoon salt
¼ cup flour	dash Cayenne
1 cup milk	1 tablespoon Worcestershire
2 (one pound) cans salmon,	¼ cup lemon juice
drained and flaked	1 cup bread crumbs

Sauté onion in butter. Add flour and stir until bubbly. Gradually add milk, and cook over low heat until thickened. Add salmon, eggs, salt, Cayenne, Worcestershire, lemon juice and crumbs. Turn into two quart casserole or mold. Place bowl in pan containing one inch of hot water. Bake in 350° oven for one hour and a half. Serve with mushroom sauce or cheese sauce. Serves 8-10.

Mrs. Marion S. Adams, Jr.

OYSTERS ON THE GRILL

Leave oysters in shell and place on charcoal grill when fire reaches white ash stage. Cover with a *wet* burlap bag and when oysters pop open, serve immediately.

They may be served with a lemon-butter sauce or eaten plain. Delicious as an hors-d'oeuvre when having a fish fry or a barbeque.

Mrs. Jere Austill, Jr.

FRIED OYSTERS

Fried oysters are easy to prepare and superb if a few basic rules are followed. Drain them well on a paper towel. Some people roll them in cracker meal and some in corn meal. It is really a matter of taste, but add salt and pepper to whichever is used. However, the important things are the grease and skillet. An old iron skillet is best. Have plenty of *hot* grease and do not crowd the oysters in the pan. If the grease is not hot enough, or if they are crowded, they will be soggy. Given plenty of space and hot grease, they will be crisp and delicious.

Mrs. John Brady

BROILED OYSTERS

1 pint oysters	1 teaspoon black pepper
1 stick butter	salt to taste
1 teaspoon dried chopped chervil	lemon juice
1 cup fresh parsley, chopped	Tobasco to taste

Melt butter. Add parsley, chervil, pepper and salt. Add lemon juice and Tabasco to taste. Place oysters in flat pan and cover with butter mixture. Broil until edges of oysters curl. Serve on hot buttered toast.

Anne Goode

OYSTERS ARISTIDE

Drain oysters well. (Use one-half pint per person.) Place in shallow baking dish. Sprinkle liberally with lemon juice. Season with salt, pepper, Tabasco, Worcestershire, mace, finely chopped green onion or chives, and garlic, if desired. Also add finely chopped celery and parsley. Dot with butter. Cover with strips of bacon. Bake in 400° oven about fifteen minutes (shorter time if oysters are small), or until bacon is crisp.

Mrs. Jackson Corley

SCALLOPED OYSTERS

½ cup butter
¾ cup flour
3 teaspoons paprika
1 teaspoon salt
½ teaspoon black pepper
4 tablespoons chopped green
  pepper

4 tablespoons chopped onion
½ teaspoon garlic, finely
  chopped
2 tablespoons lemon juice
1 tablespoon Worcestershire
1 quart oysters
cracker crumbs

Cook together butter and flour until mixture is a dark brown roux. To this roux add paprika, salt and black pepper. Cook for several minutes before adding green pepper, onion and garlic. Cook slowly for about five minutes. Remove from fire and add lemon juice, Worcestershire and oysters which have been heated in their own liquor. Pour into baking dish and sprinkle cracker crumbs over top. Bake in 400° oven for thirty minutes. Serves 6.

Mrs. Robert T. Clark

OYSTERS LONGCHAMP

2 tablespoons butter
1 medium can sliced mushrooms
2 small onions
2 tablespoons flour

2 tablespoons fresh parsley
1 pint oysters, drained
⅓ cup sherry
salt and pepper to taste

Cook butter, mushrooms and onions together in a skillet until onions are transparent and then thicken with flour. Add other ingredients and cook for about one minute. Pour into shallow casserole, cover with cracker crumbs and bake in 375° oven about 45 minutes. Delicious with rice, potatoes or grits. Serves four.

Mrs. Tom Horst, Jr.

OYSTER ROCKEFELLER SAUCE

⅓ bunch spinach
⅔ bunch green onions
  (3 or 4 stalks)
celery leaves (4 or 5 tops
  of stalks)
⅓ bunch parsley
⅓ cup butter or margarine

⅓ cup fine bread crumbs
1 tablespoon Worcestershire
1 teaspoon anchovy paste
dash of Tabasco
¾ ounce absinthe
Parmesan cheese
⅓ teaspoon salt

104

Place all greens in blender. Add butter and bread crumbs to thicken mixture. Add remaining ingredients, except cheese. Makes about one pint. Place oysters, already drained, in individual oyster shells or several oysters can be placed in baking shells. Place shells on a pan of hot ice cream salt. Spread sauce over oysters. Sprinkle with cheese. Bake in 450° oven for thirty minutes, then place under broiler until brown, (about five minutes). Serves 4.

Mrs. O. M. Otts, Jr.

OYSTER PIE

1 quart oysters	½ cup flour
salt	1 stalk celery, chopped fine
pepper	3 cups oyster liquor and milk
2 garlic pods, chopped fine	combined
1 tablespoon Worcestershire	½ stick butter
½ teaspoon ground celery seed	½ pound mushrooms
dash of Cayenne	2 hard-boiled eggs
½ teaspoon chervil	2 tablespoons parsley
½ stick butter	pastry

Place oysters, salt, pepper, garlic, Worcestershire, celery, Cayenne and chervil in pan, and cook until oysters curl. Drain well, reserving liquid. Melt one-half stick butter. Add flour and stir, making a brown sauce. Add celery and combined milk and oyster liquor. Stir until bubbly. Melt one-half stick butter and broil mushrooms until done. Combine oysters, brown sauce, mushrooms with butter, and sliced hard-boiled eggs. Add parsley. Pour into greased casserole and cover with pastry. Bake in 425° oven until crust is brown—about thirty minutes. Serves 4-6.

Mrs. Dewitt King
Mobile Country Club

BAKED OYSTERS

1 stick butter	Tabasco to taste
1 large onion, chopped	Worcestershire to taste
1 large bell pepper, chopped	chili powder (lots) to taste
5-6 celery stalks, chopped	1 quart oysters
5-6 large parsley sprigs, chopped	8-10 slices toasted bread, grated
salt and pepper to taste	

Sauté onion, bell pepper, celery and parsley in butter until very tender. Add Tabasco, Worcestershire, salt, pepper and chili powder. Add oysters

105

and cook thirty minutes. Add bread crumbs until mixture is firm, but not dry, and will not run. Fill eight baking shells. Sprinkle with break crumbs and dot with butter. Place in oven thirty minutes before serving. Serve very hot. This can be prepared a day ahead, refrigerated and heated thoroughly before serving.

Mrs. Robert T. King

OYSTER AND SPINACH CASSEROLE

1 pint fresh oysters
1 pack frozen chopped spinach
2 tablespoons flour
2 tablespoons butter or
   margarine
⅓ cup milk

salt and pepper to taste
¼ teaspoon savory
¼ teaspoon thyme
¼ cup grated cheese
¼ cup bread crumbs, toasted

Thaw spinach in colander. Squeeze out liquid with spoon. Drain oysters. In buttered baking dish, arrange alternate layers of oysters and spinach, sifting flour between layers. Mix melted butter, warm milk, salt, pepper, savory and thyme and pour over casserole. Combine grated cheese and bread crumbs and sprinkle over top. Bake in moderate oven (350°) about 45 minutes. Serves 2 to four.

Mrs. Joe M. Courtney

WILD RICE AND OYSTER CASSEROLE

2 cups wild rice (cooked in beef
   consommé and water)
¼ pound butter
2 quarts oysters
salt and pepper
hot pepper sauce
1 can cream of mushroom soup

1 cup light cream
1½ teaspoon onion powder
¾ teaspoon thyme
1½ tablespoon curry powder
   (dissolved in hot water)
½ cup finely minced parsley

Cook and drain rice. Add butter. Place half in bottom of baking dish. Cover rice with oysters, seasoned with salt, pepper and pepper sauce. Top with remaining rice. Heat soup. Add cream, onion powder, thyme and curry powder. Pour over rice—oyster mixture. Bake in 325° oven forty-five minutes. Garnish with parsley. Serves 10-12.

Mrs. H. W. Thurber, Jr.

SEAFOOD JUBILEE

JAMBALAYA

1 cup uncooked rice	1 small green pepper, minced
3 heaping tablespoons lard or	2 cups boiling water
cooking oil	½ cup oyster juice, heated
½ cup onions, minced	salt and pepper to taste
½ cup minced celery	1 pint oysters
2 garlic cloves, minced	

Put rice into heated fat in a heavy saucepan. Stir until lightly browned. Add minced ingredients and sauté for about a minute. Add boiling water, juice, salt and pepper. Mix thoroughly. Add oysters or other seafood. Stir once, then reduce heat to simmer. Cover and cook about fifteen minutes or until rice is tender. If desired, after rice is done, place about four pats of real butter on top. Cover and allow butter to melt. Serve as a main course.

J. O. Wintzell
Wintzell's Oyster House

HAM AND OYSTER CHAFING DISH SPECIALTY

4 cups milk	Cayenne to taste
1 cup cream	1 quart oysters
5 tablespoons butter	2 cups cold, diced ham
5 tablespoons flour	1 can mushrooms
salt and pepper to taste	

Make a rich cream sauce of first five ingredients. Add oysters, ham and mushrooms to sauce and pour into chafing dish, adding flour to desired consistency. Serve on favorite wafers, pastry shells or biscuits.

Mrs. Jere Austill, Jr.

CHAFING DISH OYSTERS

3 tablespoons butter	3 dozen oysters
4 tablespoons flour	2 cans sliced mushrooms
1 large onion, chopped	1 tablespoon Worcestershire
sprig of thyme	red pepper to taste
1 stalk of celery, chopped	salt and pepper to taste
1 bay leaf	

Melt butter in large skillet, add flour and brown. Add onion, thyme, celery and bay leaf and cook forty-five minutes. (Looks unattractive). Place oysters in another pan and simmer until curled. Add oysters to brown sauce, reserving oyster liquor. Add mushrooms and seasonings. Do not add

107

water at any time. Oyster liquor may be added to obtain desired consistency. May be prepared a day ahead, adding oyster liquor before serving.

Mrs. Charles O. Ditmars

MAMIE'S OYSTERS

2 sticks butter	4 tablespoons Beau Monde
1 cup flour	seasoning
2 quarts oysters	juice of 1 large onion
2 teaspoons summer savory	4 teaspoons Worcestershire
2 teaspoons marjoram	salt and pepper to taste
½ cup parsley, cut	½ cup onion, chopped fine

Melt butter in large iron pan. Add flour and cook together for about a half hour. Drain oysters, reserving liquid. Cook oysters in a separate pot until they curl. Add to butter and flour. Add seasonings and stir until the mixture is heated through. If mixture is too thick, add oyster liquid until mixture reaches consistency of heavy cream. Serve at a party with bite-size patty shells. This should serve about thirty people.

Mrs. Gillette Burton

OYSTERS SUPREME

2 quarts oysters	1 tablespoon sweet basil
1 cup butter	½ cup sherry
1 cup flour	1 tablespoon Scotch
2 garlic cloves, chopped fine	3 tablespoons catsup
1 tablespoon grated onion	3 tablespoons Worcestershire
1 tablespoon chopped parsley	3 tablespoons lemon juice
1 tablespoon paprika	¼ teaspoon Tabasco
1 tablespoon monosodium	1 tablespoon dill seed
glutamate	½ cup red wine
3 tablespoons A-1 sauce	salt and pepper to taste

Drain oysters well. Simmer in skillet until curled. Drain again and save some of the liquid. Brown butter and flour in heavy skillet or Dutch oven, as for gravy. Thin with some of the oyster liquid. Do not make too thin as seasonings will help to thin sauce. Add all seasonings and simmer until thick. Add oysters. Do not cook any more. This can be prepared ahead and refrigerated or frozen. Serve hot in patty shells.

Mrs. Glenn Cobb, Jr.

SEAFOOD JUBILEE

BARBECUED SHRIMP

Split large shrimp down the back and place over a low fire. Baste with lemon butter and Worcestershire sauce until shrimp begin to curl around edges. Use more lemon butter than Worcestershire—all to taste.

Mrs. T. M. Taul, Jr.

BROILED SHRIMP

½ stick butter	juice of one lemon
1 pound shrimp, peeled	salt and pepper
and de-veined	chopped parsley

Melt butter in skillet and add lemon juice. Place shrimp in single layer and sprinkle salt and pepper over shrimp. Cook until shrimp begin to get pink. Turn and sprinkle with more salt and pepper. Cook until shrimp are pink throughout. Cook very slowly over low heat to keep shrimp tender. Serve hot with a little chopped parsley over all.

Mrs. Tom Horst, Jr.

SHRIMP BOILED IN GULF WATER

For five pounds of shrimp with heads:
Bring five quarts of clean Gulf water to a rolling boil, season with 1 large lemon thinly sliced, and enough red pepper to turn water pink. Put in shrimp, bring to second boil, cook 5 to 10 minutes. Drain, cool and put on ice.

SHRIMP BOILED WITH ICE CREAM SALT

For five pounds of shrimp with heads:
Use 5 quarts of water. Keep adding ice cream salt until water is almost briney. Season with one large lemon sliced thin and enough red pepper to turn water pink. Bring to rolling boil, add shrimp, and boil 5 to 10 minutes. Drain, cool and ice down.

Mrs. Jere Austill, Jr.

FRIED SHRIMP

Peel and de-vein shrimp and put in a bowl. Squeeze lemon juice over all and sprinkle with Cayenne. Let sit for a half-hour. Dredge in flour to which salt and pepper have been added. Let sit another half-hour. Dip in

109

SEAFOOD JUBILEE

beaten egg and dredge in cracker meal. Fry in hot fat until golden brown, three to five minutes depending on size of shrimp. Drain on paper towel and serve with horseradish dressing, catsup or tartar sauce.

Mrs. Selwyn H. Turner, Jr.

FRENCH FRIED SHRIMP

2 pounds shrimp	¾ cup ice water
1 cup flour	2 tablespoons melted
½ teaspoon sugar	fat or salad oil
½ teaspoon salt	1 egg

Clean and de-vein shrimp. Slit down vein side almost through. Dry shrimp thoroughly. Mix all remaining ingredients. Dip shrimp in batter and fry in deep fat (375°) until golden brown. Drain on paper towel. Serves 6-8.

Mrs. Richard Cunningham

SHRIMP BOILED IN BEER

3 bottles beer	1 onion, chopped
3 bottles water	3 whole peppercorns
3 tablespoons salt	1 bay leaf
½ box celery seed	3 pounds shrimp

Boil all ingredients, except shrimp, a few minutes. Add shrimp (in shells) and cook fifteen minutes. Serve chilled with "sauce for boiled shrimp."

Mrs. John Howard Wilson

FRENCH BOILED SHRIMP

1 pound large shrimp	½ bay leaf
liquid (½ water, ½ vinegar)	1 celery stalk
enough to cover all	¼ teaspoon black pepper
ingredients	salt to taste
1 garlic clove	dash of Cayenne

Rinse shrimp. Boil water and vinegar (to which has been added all seasonings) for two minutes. Add shrimp and boil for approximately fifteen minutes. Allow to cool in liquid in which they were cooked. Drain and shell, removing the vein. Serve on lettuce in a cocktail cup with light mayonnaise or French dressing, or with hot sauce.

Mary Koehler

110

SEAFOOD JUBILEE

SHRIMP CURRY

6 tablespoons butter	2 tablespoons lemon juice
4 tablespoons curry powder	2 teaspoons grated lemon rind
4 tablespoons flour	salt and pepper to taste
2 garlic cloves, minced (optional)	5 cups hot water
1 large onion, chopped	5 chicken bouillon cubes
1 cup chopped apple	4 pounds fresh cleaned shrimp
3 tablespoons chopped green	½ cup white wine
pepper	2 (1½ ounce) boxes of raisins
3 or 4 bay leaves	

Melt butter in pan and blend in curry powder mixed with flour. Add garlic, onion, apple, green pepper, bay leaves, lemon juice, lemon rind, salt and pepper. Heat. Add water in which bouillon cubes have been dissolved, and simmer, covered, for fifteen minutes. Add shrimp, wine and raisins. Cook until shrimp turn pink. Serve in chafing dish. Can be served with white or saffron rice with the following condiments: chutney, shredded coconut, chopped peanuts, minced scallions and green pepper, mashed hard-cooked egg, crisp bacon crumbled or chopped ripe olives. Serves 12.

Mrs. John Brady

SHRIMP IN PATTY SHELLS

1½ cups clean boiled shrimp	⅛ teaspoon Cayenne pepper
⅓ cup chopped celery	⅛ teaspoon paprika
4 teaspoons lemon juice	4 Pepperidge Farm frozen patty
⅓ cup mayonnaise	shells
¼ teaspoon salt	grated Parmesan cheese

Heat shrimp and other ingredients over low fire, pour into patty shells. Sprinkle with Parmesan cheese and place under broiler until browned.

Mrs. Marion S. Adams, Jr.

SHRIMP JAMBALAYA

This is a recipe related by a fisherman. No proportions were given. However, if you allow one cup of rice to a pound-and-a-half (or two pounds) of shrimp, you can serve four or five people.

Using a large iron skillet, brown sliced onions in hot bacon drippings. Add peeled, raw shrimp and stir until shrimp turns red. Add salt and pepper. Stir in one cup of dry, uncooked rice and stir until rice turns brown. (Do

111

not wash rice). Now, add enough boiling water to cover all ingredients, continuing to stir while the water cooks down. Keep your kettle of boiling water handy and add more of this to rice from time to time. The rice will thicken but will not be done until the grains are tender. Add the boiling water in small amounts. Stir! After the rice is done, add seasonings to taste: salt, pepper, celery salt, paprika, Worcestershire and sherry. Keep heat very low and continue to add seasonings until you are afraid to add any more. It should be very hot and spicey. Place mixture in earthenware casserole, garnish with parsley and serve with garlic bread and green salad.

Mrs. James H. Fullton

CURRIED SHRIMP SUPREME

⅓ cup butter
3 tablespoons flour
1 tablespoon curry powder
½ teaspoon salt
¼ teaspoon paprika
¼ teaspoon nutmeg
2 cups half-and-half

2 tablespoons finely chopped
   candied ginger
1 tablespoon lemon juice
1 teaspoon onion juice
1 tablespoon sherry
dash of Worcestershire
3 cups cooked shrimp

Melt butter in double boiler top. Add flour, curry powder, salt, paprika and nutmeg. Blend until smooth. Slowly add half-and-half, and stir until mixture reaches consistency of white sauce. Add ginger, lemon juice, onion juice, sherry, Worcestershire and shrimp. Heat through and serve over fluffy rice or in patty shells. This is even better if made a day ahead.

Mrs. Francis B. Wakefield, III

COQUILLE ST. JACQUES

6 tablespoons butter
3 tablespoons flour
1 teaspoon salt
⅛ teaspoon white pepper
2 cups light cream
½ pound scallops, sliced
¼ cup onion, finely chopped

½ cup mushrooms, sliced
½ pound shrimp, cooked and
   cleaned
¼ pound white crabmeat
2 tablespoons Madeira or
   sweet sherry
3 tablespoons bread crumbs

In double boiler top, melt four tablespoonfuls butter, blend in flour, salt and pepper. Gradually add cream, over direct heat, stirring constantly, to boiling point. Return to double boiler and cook five minutes longer. Melt remaining butter in skillet, add scallops and onions and sauté. Remove

112

scallops and onions, add mushrooms and sauté for three minutes. Combine the sauce, scallops, mushrooms, shrimp, crabmeat and wine. Mix lightly and taste for seasoning. Spoon into six scallop shells or ramekins and sprinkle with bread crumbs. Bake in 400° oven for ten minutes or until delicately browned. Serve at once. Serves 6.

Mrs. Charles O. Ditmars

SHRIMP CREOLE FOR TWENTY-FIVE

1 tablespoon bacon grease	1 bottle catsup
1 stick margarine	sugar to taste
3 large onions, chopped	salt and pepper to taste
4 garlic cloves, chopped	Worcestershire to taste
2 large bell peppers, chopped	Tabasco to taste
1 celery stalk, chopped	pinch of thyme
1 bunch parsley, chopped	1 bay leaf
3 large cans tomatoes	10 pounds raw shrimp, cleaned
1 large can tomato juice	and de-veined
1 can tomato paste	

Melt bacon grease and margarine. Brown onions, garlic, peppers, celery and parsley. Add tomatoes, tomato juice, tomato paste and catsup. Let sauce cook the better part of the day. Add seasonings. Add shrimp about one hour before removing from heat. Allow to stand in sauce several hours before serving. Heat about twenty minutes.

Mrs. Vernon Dukes

SHRIMP WITH MUSHROOM SAUCE

2 tablespoons butter	½ teaspoon Worcestershire
1 cup cooked, cleaned shrimp	½ teaspoon dried dill seed
1 4-ounce can sliced mushrooms, drained	½ teaspoon paprika
	2 tablespoons lemon juice
½ cup sour cream	2 cups hot cooked rice
¾ teaspoon salt	

In small skillet, melt butter over low heat. Add shrimp and mushrooms. Mix sour cream with salt, Worcestershire, dill seed and paprika. Pour over shrimp and mushrooms. Cook, stirring, just until mixture is heated. Sprinkle with lemon juice, serve over rice. Two generous servings.

Mrs. Walter Ogburn

SHRIMP AND OYSTER CREOLE

3 heaping tablespoons flour
3 tablespoons lard
1 small can tomatoes
3 onions, grated
¾ cup hot water
1 cup chopped celery
½ cup chopped green pepper

1 tablespoon Worcestershire
dash of hot sauce
salt and pepper to taste
2 pounds large shrimp, cleaned
  and de-veined
1 pint large oysters, well
  drained

Brown flour in lard to make roux. Mash tomatoes to juice consistency. Grate onions. Add tomatoes, onion and hot water to roux. Cook until thick. In separate boiler, cook celery and pepper until well done. Add to thickened roux. Add remaining ingredients and cook all together, slowly, for one hour.

Mrs. Frank Ellis, Jr.

ALMOND SHRIMP

2 pounds small shrimp, peeled
  and de-veined
1 cup butter
1 cup slivered blanched almonds

parsley
salt and pepper to taste
sherry (optional)
croutons

Sauté shrimp in butter, with seasonings, until lightly browned. Add almonds (and sherry, if desired) and sprinkle with parsley. Turn fire very low and simmer a few minutes. Serve on croutons. Serves 4.

Mrs. Jere Austill, Jr.

SHRIMP CUTLETS

3 pounds green shrimp
12 cups water
⅓ cup sliced onion
1 bay leaf
3 celery ribs with tops
2 tablespoons salt
⅛ teaspoon Cayenne
¾ lemon, sliced

9 tablespoons butter
1 cup flour
3 cups milk
3 tablespoons chopped onion
6 tablespoons chopped parsley
6 teaspoons lemon juice
3 teaspoons Worcestershire
salt and pepper to taste

Boil shrimp in water with onion, bay leaf, celery, salt, Cayenne and lemon. Simmer fifteen minutes. Cool in this water. Drain, shell and clean shrimp.

114

Make three cups heavy cream sauce using butter, flour and milk. When sauce is smooth, add six cups shrimp, cut in halves or thirds. Add onion, parsley, lemon juice, Worcestershire, salt and pepper. Spread in a large platter and refrigerate overnight.

6 cups whole wheat bread crumbs	6-8 tablespoons water home-made mayonnaise
salt and pepper	a few tablespoons capers
4 eggs	

Next day, shape mixture into about fourteen cutlets. Roll in bread crumbs seasoned with salt and pepper; then, in eggs diluted with water; and again in bread crumbs. Dry the cutlets about two hours in refrigerator. Fry in deep fat (390°) about two minutes. Drain on paper. Serve with mayonnaise (beaten fluffy) to which capers have been added. Chopped stuffed olives may also be added to mayonnaise.

Mrs. Ernest L. Brown

SEAFOOD CASSEROLE

1 pound crabmeat	½ teaspoon salt
1 pound shrimp (cooked, shelled and de-veined)	1 tablespoon Worcestershire sauce
1 cup mayonnaise	2 cups crushed potato chips
¼ cup finely chopped onion	paprika
1 cup finely chopped celery	

Combine crabmeat, shrimp, mayonnaise, onion, celery, salt and Worcestershire. Pour into buttered 2½-quart casserole. Top with potato chips. Sprinkle with paprika. Bake at 400° for 25 minutes until thoroughly heated. Serves 6.

Mrs. William E. Drew

SHRIMP RAMEKINS

¼ pound butter or margarine	2 teaspoons salt
1½-2 pounds raw shrimp (cleaned and de-veined)	½ teaspoon paprika
1 can mushrooms	1 teaspoon Worcestershire
¼ pound cream cheese	dash of Cayenne
1 cup sour cream	2 teaspoons chopped parsley
¼ teaspoon pepper	½ cup grated Parmesan cheese
	2 tablespoons dry sherry

115

Melt butter in skillet; add shrimp and sauté for two minutes. Add mushrooms. Cook slowly, turning frequently. Beat cream cheese until light and add to shrimp. Add sour cream gradually and bring to a boil. Add remaining ingredients. Fill six or eight ramekins. Sprinkle with cheese and place under broiler until lightly browned. (If liquid is needed, add mushroom juice.)

Mrs. Harry Partridge

SHRIMP AND ARTICHOKES

2 tablespoons butter	3 tablespoons lemon juice
2 tablespoons flour	3 tablespoons sherry
½ teaspoon pepper	1 can artichokes, sliced
¼ teaspoon Cayenne	2 pounds shrimp, cooked and
1 pint half-and-half	cleaned
1 tablespoon tomato catsup	1 cup grated New York cheese
1 tablespoon Worcestershire	

Melt butter. Add flour, pepper and Cayenne. Mix well. Add half-and-half. Cook over low heat until thick and well blended. Add catsup, Worcestershire, lemon juice and sherry. Blend. In baking dish, alternate layers of artichokes and shrimp. Pour sauce over these layers; top with grated cheese and bake in 400° oven about thirty minutes.

Mrs. J. M. Hull

STUFFED PEPPERS WITH SHRIMP

1 teaspoon salt	2 tablespoons grated onion
3 cloves garlic	2 tablespoons butter
6 medium size green peppers	1 pound fresh or 2 (5-ounce)
½ cup uncooked rice	cans shrimp
1 (10 ounce) can cream of	1 teaspoon finely chopped parsley
mushroom soup	1 cup grated Swiss cheese
juice of 1 lemon	6 pats of butter
black pepper to taste	paprika

Add salt and split garlic cloves to two quarts of water in a pan. Boil. Cut tops off green peppers. Scoop and drop cleaned peppers into boiling water. Cook ten minutes. Boil rice. Heat mushroom soup. Add lemon juice, black pepper, onions and butter to soup and stir over low heat until butter melts. Add rice and cleaned, boiled shrimp to sauce. Add parsley. Stuff pepper almost to top and add cheese and a pat of butter to each. Sprinkle with paprika. Place peppers in baking dish with a small amount of warm water. Bake in 250° oven for forty minutes.

Mrs. W. B. Shields

BAKED SHRIMP

1 pound shrimp	½ teaspoon salt
6-8 individual baking shells	¼ teaspoon Tabasco
1 cup chopped lettuce	1 teaspoon celery salt
½ cup chopped green onions	2 garlic cloves, minced
2 (12-ounce) packages	½ cup chopped parsley
frozen spinach, cooked	½ cup dry bread crumbs
½ cup butter	Parmesan cheese (½ cup)
1½ teaspoons Worcestershire	2 tablespoons olive oil
2 teaspoons anchovies	

Clean and de-vein raw shrimp and place in the bottom of baking shells. Combine all ingredients—lettuce through parsley—and place on top of shrimp. Place shells on ice-cream salt in large baking pan. Sprinkle with bread crumbs, cheese and, lastly, olive oil. Bake in 350° oven thirty to forty minutes, until brown.

Mrs. Frank Sauer

SHRIMP AND EGGPLANT

3 medium eggplants	2 cans tomatoes, No. 2½
1 stick margarine	1 tablespoon salt
3 tablespoons bacon grease	fresh ground pepper
4 pounds shrimp, peeled and	Cayenne
de-veined	¼ cup brown sugar
3½ cups chopped onion	2 eggs
3½ cups chopped green pepper	1½ cups bread crumbs
2 garlic cloves, pressed	

Peel and dice eggplant. Cook in boiling water until tender, drain. Melt butter and bacon grease. Add shrimp, onions, peppers and garlic. Add un-drained mashed tomatoes, salt, pepper, Cayenne and brown sugar. Cook until shrimp are done and juice has cooked down. Remove from heat. Add eggplant, beaten eggs and bread crumbs. Bake in moderate oven approximately thirty minutes. Serves twenty-five.

Mrs. Dewitt King
Mobile Country Club

EGGPLANT WITH SHRIMP

1 large or 2 medium eggplants	pinch of thyme
2 tablespoons butter	pinch of Cayenne
¾ cup milk	salt and pepper to taste
¾ cup grated cheese	¾ cup bread crumbs
1 finely chopped onion	½ pound boiled shrimp
1 small green pepper, chopped	2 beaten eggs
2 tablespoons chopped parsley	

Cut eggplant into halves. Cut out the pulp. Boil pulp in salted water. When tender, drain, mash and add milk and grated cheese. Melt butter in frying pan and sauté onion and green pepper. Add parsley, thyme, Cayenne, salt, pepper and a little brown sugar. Add eggplant mixture, bread crumbs, boiled shrimp and beaten eggs. Stuff shells. Cover with bread crumbs and dot with buttter. Bake in moderate oven until brown and bubbly. Suitable for casserole instead of shells.

Mrs. Ben Radcliff

EGGPLANT WITH SHRIMP STUFFING

1½ pounds fresh shrimp or 2 cans shrimp (4½ ounces each)	1 cup canned tomatoes
	2 whole bay leaves
	1 teaspoon salt
½ cup chopped onion	½ teaspoon pepper
¼ cup chopped green pepper	⅔ cup shrimp liquid
½ cup chopped parsley	3 tablespoons butter or
2 garlic cloves, chopped	margarine
⅓ cup melted shortening	¾ cup dry bread crumbs
1 large eggplant	

Drain shrimp, saving liquid. Sauté in shortening until tender: onions, green pepper, parsley and garlic. Wash and cut eggplant in half, lengthwise, and scoop out pulp, leaving about ¼ inch thickness around shell. Turn shells upside-down in a pan of cold water to prevent discoloration. Chop pulp. Add tomatoes, seasoning, shrimp liquid and chopped eggplant to onion mixture. Cover and simmer ten minutes or until eggplant is tender. Remove bay leaves. Add shrimp. Combine butter and crumbs. Fill shells with alternate layers of shrimp mixture and crumbs. Place in baking pan, adding a little hot water to prevent sticking. Bake in 400° oven 35 to 40 minutes or until brown. Six generous servings.

Mrs. Ferrell McBroom

Fowl and Game

GAME AND FOWL

WILD DUCK I

Debone three ducks, keeping breast and leg intact. Brown duck in one stick margarine, remove duck and sauté one half cup diced onion and one cup sliced mushrooms in same margarine until limp. Remove onions and mushrooms, add another stick of margarine and enough flour to thicken. Add one cup chicken broth, one fourth cup white wine and three table-spoonfuls cognac. Stir until smooth, add duck, onions and mushrooms to sauce and simmer for two hours. Serves 6.

Mrs. Norman Hutchings, Jr.

WILD DUCK II

1 wild mallard (canvas-back, gray, teal). If small, use two ducks. (Serves 2)	1 onion, sliced
	2 bay leaves
	1 cup dry sherry
salt and pepper	2 tablespoons flour
paprika	juice of one orange
1 onion, sliced	2 tablespoons orange marmalade
1 lemon, sliced	¼ cup brandy
4 tablespoons butter	

Wash and dry duck, season with salt, pepper & paprika. Stuff with one sliced onion and one sliced lemon. Either sew or use toothpicks to prevent stuffing from falling out. Brown duck well in 4 tablespoons butter on top of stove. Add sliced onion to butter while duck is browning. Add enough water to almost cover duck. Cover pot and simmer either on top of stove or in 350° oven for 1½ hours. Add 2 bay leaves, 1 cup dry sherry, and

119

cook for another ½ to ¾ hour (do not worry about cooking too much— it simply makes the duck juicier and more tender.) Remove duck from gravy. Carefully rub 2 tablespoons flour into the gravy, add orange juice and marmalade and brandy. Put duck back in gravy, heat thoroughly, and serve. Slice duck quite thinly.

Mrs. Marion Adams, Jr.

CAJUN STYLE WILD DUCK

Clean duck thoroughly. With a sharp knife, cut a slit about three inches long between the breast meat and breast bone on both sides, thus making a pocket on both sides. Salt and pepper inside and out and in pockets. Insert a large onion slice in each pocket, or garlic, if desired. Pour one cup of cooking oil into a deep skillet, fry duck until brown on all sides, taking about thirty minutes. When ducks are brown, add two cups hot water and simmer, covered, about one hour, adding water as needed. Cut duck in half and serve. Remaining juices in skillet can be cooked down and is called red eye gravy to use with rice or potatoes.

Mrs. M. B. McMurphy

DUCKS

1 teaspoon poultry seasoning	1 stalk celery and leaves, cut
1 teaspoon salt	in small pieces
¼ teaspoon black pepper	½ green pepper, cut in small
1 small onion, quartered	pieces
4-5 sprigs parsley	½ apple

Combine ingredients, stuff two ducks. Rub salt and pepper all over duck. Place a strip of raw bacon on duck and place in 350° oven until duck begins to brown. Reduce oven temperature to 300° and cook until done.

Mrs. J. P. Courtney, Jr.

WILD DUCK (WITHOUT WILD FLAVOR)

Cover duck with salted water to which has been added one teaspoon soda. Soak for thirty minutes to one hour. Rinse duck and place in a pan of fresh water with a quartered potato and half an onion. Boil gently thirty to forty-five minutes. Pour out water, wash duck thoroughly. Season the cavity heavily with salt and red and black pepper. Insert one fourth onion, a cooking apple cut in quarters and a sprig of celery leaves. Place duck in

120

roaster in one inch of water. Squeeze juice of one half orange over duck and lay a strip of bacon over the breast. Salt and pepper outside. Cover and cook in 275° oven for three and a half to four hours, basting often, about every thirty minutes. Remove cover the last half hour of cooking time to brown duck. Allow one half duck per person.

Mrs. Conrad Armbrecht

ROAST PHEASANT WITH DRESSING

FRESH DRESSED DRAWN PHEASANT:

Pheasant may be prepared in all ways that chicken is prepared. However, roasting brings out the flavor best. If roasted, they should be stuffed with wild rice dressing. The wild rice should be soaked overnight before preparing dressing.

WILD RICE DRESSING:

4 ounces wild rice	2 tablespoons melted butter
⅓ teaspoon salt	finely chopped celery
¼ teaspoon pepper	finely chopped onion
¼ teaspoon sage	(or onion juice)
¼ teaspoon thyme	

Wash rice until water is clear; soak overnight. Drain off old water and add fresh water to cover, sprinkle with salt, simmer ten to fifteen minutes. Do not boil severely, do not stir. Mix two cups wild rice with salt, pepper, sage, and thyme. Add melted butter, celery and onion. Four ounces of dry wild rice will make sufficient dressing for two birds.

ROAST PHEASANT:

With tips of fingers, rub skin with fat and a little flour, seasoned slightly with salt and pepper. Place dressing in bird. If there is an excess of dressing, just place it in the pan beside the pheasant. After placing the pheasant and dressing in the pan add about one half cup boiling water, sear. Cover and bake in 350° oven for two hours, basting occasionally with juices or with hot water and melted butter.

Mrs. C. R. Gottlieb

DOVES, COUNTRY STYLE

Wash birds, lightly flour, salt and pepper. Brown in bacon grease in heavy skillet. When brown, add water, a little Kitchen Bouquet (very little), salt and pepper and cook, covered, very slowly until tender, at least an hour and a half. Squirrel may be prepared in the same way, after skinning.

Mrs. D. Binion Cochran

BROILED DOVES

Split doves down back, wash thoroughly. Salt and pepper both sides generously. Grease bottom of broiler pan with butter or margarine, place doves in pan, breast side down. Put a large piece of butter on each dove. Start cooking doves in cold broiler on high temperature. Brown on both sides, add a cup of water, turn broiler temperature down as low as possible. Continue broiling for another hour, basting frequently with drippings and adding water as needed. Gravy is delicious with rice or grits.

Mrs. H. C. Slaton, Jr.

DOVES AND GRAPES

8 doves, cleaned and dressed	1 cup seedless white grapes
salt and pepper to taste	juice of 1 lemon
flour, sifted	½ cup slivered blanched almonds
1 stick butter	decrusted toast squares

Salt and pepper doves inside and out and sprinkle liberally with flour, inside and out. Melt butter in skillet, brown doves on all sides, add a cup of water. Cover and cook very slowly until tender. Do not let water evaporate, add more if your fire is too high. Add white grapes and cook about twenty minutes longer. Remove birds and keep warm. Add lemon juice and almonds, simmer a few minutes and pour over doves. Serve doves on toast with sauce spooned over.

Mrs. Jere Austill, Jr.

LONG ISLAND DUCKLING

1 duckling	⅓ cup chopped celery
salt and pepper	1 teaspoon chopped onion
½ orange, quartered	½ teaspoon salt
½ apple, quartered	2 tablespoons chopped parsley
2 celery stalks, cut up	¼ teaspoon pepper
Giblets, cooked (reserve liquid)	1 egg
8-9 bread slices, broken in pieces	orange juice

122

Salt and pepper duckling (does not require as much salt as turkey or hen), fill with combined orange, apple and celery. Bake in 325° oven until bird begins to brown. Remove from oven, remove filling from bird and stuff with dressing made as follows. Remove three to four tablespoons fat from pan and pour over bread, celery, onion, parsley, salt and pepper which have been mixed together. Add some giblet liquid and mix well. Beat egg and add to dressing. (Giblets may be cut up and added now or saved for gravy.) Stuff dressing into bird or cook in separate pan thirty-five to forty minutes. Pour two or three tablespoonfuls of orange juice over duckling. Baste with orange juice several times as duckling cooks. Cook the length of time noted on wrapping.

Mrs. Robert D. Hays

CHAFING DISH BIRDS

1 dozen small birds (partridges)
6 small red peppers, cut fine
salt and pepper to taste
12 one inch squares of butter
½ cup stock or hot water

2 tablespoons Worcestershire
juice of 1 lemon
2 cans small mushrooms
1 teacup cream

Split birds open as for broiling, sprinkle with peppers. Place birds in chafing dish, breast down and sprinkle with salt. On the back of each bird place a square of butter, add stock, cover and steam until butter has melted. Combine Worcestershire and lemon juice and add to birds. After cooking one half hour add mushrooms. If birds are young, two hours cooking time is required. When done and just before serving, add cream.

Mrs. Leon McVay, Jr.

DOVES

12 doves
1½ cups salad oil
½ cup vinegar
½ cup red wine
2-3 bay leaves
1 medium onion, sliced
1 garlic clove, minced fine
½ teaspoon Worcestershire
1 teaspoon salt

1 teaspoon pepper
1 teaspoon Beau Monde
    seasoning
½ stick butter
3 tablespoons flour
1 medium onion, chopped
2 bouillon cubes
2 cups boiling water
salt and pepper to taste

123

Combine ingredients, salad oil through Beau Monde seasoning and marinate doves seven to eight hours. Brown doves in butter over very hot fire, remove when browned on all sides. To drippings in pan, add flour (more butter may be needed) and onion, stirring until flour is very brown. Dissolve bouillon cubes in boiling water, slowly add to roux stirring until smooth. Add salt and pepper. Put doves and gravy in electric skillet, set at 225° and cook three and a half to four hours, basting frequently.

Mrs. John Brady

QUAIL FOR TWO

Wash and dry six quail (or four large ones). Sprinkle with salt and flour, then sauté in ½ stick butter. Remove and place in a casserole dish. In butter left in pan sauté:

¼ to ½ cup chopped onion   2 tablespoons parsley
½ cup chopped mushrooms

Pour over birds. Add ½ cup white wine and enough water to almost cover birds. Cook covered in a 350° oven an hour to an hour and a half, basting frequently. Add ½ cup cream about ten minutes before serving.

Mrs. Marion Adams, Jr.

BROILED WILD TURKEY BREASTS

Remove breasts whole from turkey and slice into steaks about one inch thick. Salt and pepper and soak in heavy cream. Melt butter in skillet and pan broil steaks until lightly browned. Alternate: steaks may be lightly dipped in flour after soaking in cream, then broiled.

Mrs. Ben Stimpson

VENISON STEAK

1 venison steak   monosodium glutamate
seasoned salt   juice of 1½ lemons
seasoned pepper   ½ cup butter

Sprinkle venison steak generously with seasoned salt, seasoned pepper and monosodium glutamate on both sides. Squeeze lemon juice on both sides, let stand for one hour. Broil steak in heavy skillet to desired degree of doneness. When steak is done, remove to a hot platter and keep warm. Serve with the following sauces.

HOT WINE SAUCE:

2 tablespoons butter	1 teaspoon salt
½ cup currant jelly	Cayenne pepper
juice of ½ lemon	½ cup red wine
½ cup water	

Simmer butter, jelly, lemon juice, water, salt and pepper together with drippings in pan. Blend into a smooth gravy. Remove from fire, add wine and serve over steak.

GRITS GRAVY:

2 tablespoons flour	1 tablespoon Worcestershire
1 cup water	2 tablespoons tomato catsup
salt and pepper to taste	

To drippings in pan add all ingredients. Simmer together until thickened.

Mrs. Jere Austill, Jr.

VENISON ROAST

Salt and pepper roast, rub with garlic or insert garlic. Mix half and half combination of flour and dry mustard with vinegar to make sufficient paste to cover entire roast. Cook twenty minutes in 500° oven in shallow, uncovered pan. Lower oven temperature to 350° and add two cans of tomatoes, several celery stalks, one halved onion and a bay leaf. Baste often and cook slowly until done.

Mrs. Manning McPhillips, Jr.

VENISON POT ROAST

3 pound venison shoulder	2 bay leaves
1 cup vinegar	¼ teaspoon whole cloves
1 tomato, diced	¼ teaspoon peppercorns

Place roast in mixture of combined ingredients and enough water to cover roast, refrigerate eight to ten hours. Remove meat and cover with mixture of:

125

| ¼ cup flour | 1 teaspoon salt |
| ½ teaspoon pepper | ½ teaspoon allspice |

Brown roast in skillet containing:

| 4 tablespoons margarine | 1 onion, chopped |

Put in covered roaster or casserole, add one and a half cups of the liquid the meat was marinated in, more water if necessary, to almost cover roast. Bake in 350° oven two and a half hours. Add six crushed gingersnaps to gravy, season with additional salt if necessary and serve. Serves 4.

Mrs. Marion Adams, Jr.

VENISON AND EGGPLANT CASSEROLE

½ pound ground venison	½ teaspoon paprika
1 medium sized eggplant	1 teaspoon salt
1 onion, chopped	½ teaspoon pepper
3 tablespoons chopped parsley	cornflakes
1 (8 ounce) can tomato sauce	

Have the butcher grind for you a venison sirloin or round steak (or you may use venison hamburger). Peel eggplant, dice and mix with venison and other ingredients, except cornflakes. Pour into 1½ quart casserole, cover with cornflakes and bake in 350° oven for one hour. Serves 4.

Mrs. Marion Adams, Jr.

HOW TO PREPARE VENISON ROAST

1. Place meat in large enamel pan or earthen crock and pour over it the following mixture so that the meat is submerged a little over half.
2. The mixture to consist of 2 cups wine vinegar and 2 cups water. For about 5 pound roast, use 1 large onion, 2 teaspoons salt, 1 tablespoon peppercorns, 1 bay leaf, several red peppers, 1 teaspoon cloves and 2 celery stalks, chopped.
3. Allow roast to remain in mixture in cool room, turning several times, twelve to twenty-four hours.
4. Take meat out and pat dry with towels.
5. Brown thoroughly in bacon drippings in Dutch oven.
6. Add cup or more of mixture, reduce to low fire and cook slowly until tender or cook in oven in aluminum foil. Baste with cup of beef stock or bouillon instead of mixture, if you want gravy.

126

7. Cook about thirty minutes per pound. If cooked in oven, remove foil and brown last thirty minutes.

Mrs. Mark Lyons, Jr.

TURKEY SMOKED IN DOUGH

Use favorite bread or biscuit dough. Roll dough ¼ inch thick, preparing enough to cover turkey. Salt and pepper turkey inside and out. Rub entire turkey, including cavity with butter or margarine. Lightly flour top of rolled dough and wrap or cover turkey completely with dough. Stuff cavity with one onion, quartered, about two or three leafy celery stalks, one apple, quartered, two or three big parsley sprigs, thyme or sage if desired. Place a cookie sheet on outdoor smoke oven and place turkey on this. Cook four to six hours or until dough is brown. Crack dough away. Do not eat dough. Turkey meat will be pink. (Hickory chips on fire add to flavor)

Mrs. James Ogden

FIRE FOR SMOKED TURKEY

Use a lot of LUMP charcoal, allow to get very hot. Soak handful of hickory chips in water while preparing fire. Before putting turkey on fire, put top on cooking unit and open both dampers for about five minutes in order to get fire under control. Grill should not be over the fire at this time, but should be placed over fire just before placing turkey. Spread hickory chips on coals and then put turkey on grill. Turn turkey after five minutes and every fifteen minutes thereafter. Cook ten minutes per pound.

SMOKED TURKEY

| 13 pound broadbreasted turkey | 3 celery stalks |
| 2 medium onions | salt and pepper |

Salt and pepper neck and chest cavities well. Quarter onions and cut celery stalks into nine pieces. Stuff neck cavity with two quarters of onions and three pieces of celery. Stuff chest cavity with remaining pieces of onion and celery. Skewer cavities and secure legs and wings by tying to bird. Salt and pepper very generously over outside of turkey, place on grill. Turn every fifteen minutes to keep sides from burning. Cook ten minutes per pound. Meat around leg, when pulled away from turkey may look rare, but it will be done and bird will be juicy.

Mrs. Jere Austill, Jr.

CORNISH HEN A LA FRANCAISE

6 cornish hens
cooked wild rice
mushrooms
parsley
bouquet garni
savory
rosemary
butter
6 ounces carrots, cut

5 ounces turnips, cut
10 small white onions, sliced
5 ounces diced celery
hen stock or 3 ounces
   chicken stock
3 ounces truffles
½ cup white wine
rice pilaf

Pan roast cornish hens until light brown. Stuff with wild rice seasoned with mushrooms and herbs. Place in a cocotte (casserole). In butter, in tightly sealed pan, cook carrots, turnips, onions and celery, until tender. Garnish chicken with these. Bake in 350° oven about forty-five minutes. Add hen stock or chicken stock. Truffles, sliced, may be added the last five minutes as a garnish. White wine should be added for last five to fifteen minutes of baking time. Serve with rice pilaf. This dish stays well if serving is delayed.

Mrs. Barbara Cowan Butler

CORNISH HEN IN WINE

Cornish hens
butter
salt
pepper
paprika
lemon juice
Worcestershire
Tabasco

thyme
garlic clove, split
chicken stock or consommé
½ cup white wine
sautéed mushrooms
white grapes
chopped ripe olives or truffles
¼ cup white wine

Rub each hen with butter, salt, pepper, lemon juice, Worcestershire, Tabasco, thyme and split garlic clove. Place in roaster with about one inch of stock or consommé, bake covered in 275° oven for two to two and a half hours. When half done add one half cup white wine. About a half hour before removing from oven add mushrooms, grapes, olives or truffles and additional wine. If more liquid is needed during cooking, add wine. Remove cover before cooking time is completed to speed cooking and also to brown hens.

Mrs. Edward B. Baumhauer

CORNISH HEN IN CHERRY SAUCE

3 Cornish Hens	2 cups chicken broth
salt and pepper	¾ cup red wine
½ cup butter	1 can pitted bing cherries
4 tablespoons minced onion	4 tablespoons cornstarch
3 bay leaves	salt and pepper to taste

Split and clean hens thoroughly. Salt and pepper both sides. Brown halves in butter in iron skillet, then place in shallow roasting pan. Bake in 325° oven about one hour. Meanwhile, pour all but four tablespoonfuls butter from skillet in which hens were browned. Sauté onion and bay leaves for a few minutes, do not brown. Add broth, red wine, juice from cherries and corn starch, stirring and simmering until thickened. Add a teaspoonful salt and ground pepper to taste. When sauce thickens add cherries. Pour over hens and serve. Serves 6.

Mrs. Jere Austill, Jr.

CORNISH HENS—STUFFING FOR TWELVE

1 box wild rice, cooked	1 cup onion, chopped and
1 small box curried rice, cooked	sautéed in butter
1½ cups white rice, cooked	1 small can sliced almonds
1 cup celery, chopped and	garlic salt
sautéed in butter	Worcestershire
2 cans white grapes	poultry seasoning

Mix all ingredients together, stuff twelve hens. Brown hens on top in butter and cooking oil. When brown, place in roaster with two cups of sherry and bake an hour and a half in 350° oven.

Mrs. Lowell Friedman

CHICKEN OR QUAIL WITH WINE SAUCE

20 large pieces of chicken (breasts and short thighs) or 20 quail	10 tablespoons parsley
bony pieces of above chicken	3 medium cans mushrooms
1 stick butter	5 tablespoons flour
10 green onions	8 tablespoons Rhine wine

Boil bony pieces of chicken to make broth, or use canned chicken broth. Sauté onions, parsley and mushrooms in butter, adding flour by sprinkling to avoid lumping. Simmer until done, add 1 cup broth, remove from heat,

129

add wine. Broil chicken pieces until seared, place in casserole. Pour gravy over chicken and bake in 300° oven one hour. Serve with wild rice.

Mrs. Wilson Gaillard, Jr.

SHERRIED CHICKEN WITH HERBS

1 fryer (or deboned breasts)	pinch of savory
1 teaspoon monosodium	pinch of thyme
glutamate	pinch of rosemary
½ teaspoon salt	pinch of marjoram
½ teaspoon paprika	1 tablespoon parsley, minced
¼ cup butter	1 bay leaf
1 can sliced mushrooms	pepper to taste
½ cup sherry	

Sprinkle chicken with monosodium glutamate on both sides, salt, pepper and paprika. Melt butter and brown chicken. Drain mushrooms, adding liquid and sherry to chicken. Sprinkle with herbs and parsley, add bay leaf, cover and simmer until tender. Add mushrooms last ten minutes of cooking time.

Mrs. Hunter Boulo

CHICKEN FROM THE TROPICS

2 cut up fryers, or equivalent	4-5 sliced green onions and tops
in parts	1 green pepper, cut in strips
salt, pepper, paprika and flour	½ cup dry white wine
½ cup melted butter and salad oil	1 tablespoon brown sugar
(½ and ½)	½ cup diced, blanched almonds
1 (30 ounce) can sliced pineapple	

Season chicken parts with salt and pepper. Shake in bag with flour to which generous amount of paprika has been added. Turn chicken in melted butter and oil until completely coated. Place in single layer, skin side down in glass baking dish. Bake in 400° oven for thirty minutes. Turn chicken. Cut ½ pineapple in bite size pieces. Leave remaining pineapple in half slices. Combine pineapple and syrup, onions, green pepper, wine, brown sugar and a dash of salt. Pour this mixture over and around chicken. Sprinkle with almonds. Bake in 375° oven until brown and tender, about 45 minutes longer. Baste occasionally. Serve with hot, fluffy rice. Serves eight.

Mrs. H. C. Hitchcock

HERB CHICKEN

4 chicken breasts
salt and pepper
¼ cup olive oil
¼ cup dry white wine
1 teaspoon marjoram

1 teaspoon thyme
1 teaspoon parsley
1 tablespoon chopped
   green onion tops
1 tablespoon cognac
1 teaspoon grated lemon rind

Wash and dry chicken breasts. Prepare sauce by combining remaining ingredients, except cognac. Brush chicken well on all sides with sauce. Pour sauce over chicken, reserving a little to add later. Bake in 350° oven one hour. Baste and add cognac and remaining sauce during last fifteen minutes of cooking time. Serves 4.

Mrs. Laura Jackson Corley

CHICKEN BREAST BAKED IN WINE

4 large chicken breasts
juice of one lemon
salt and pepper to taste
1 large onion, grated
1 teaspoon dry mustard

4 teaspoons parsley, fresh
   or dried
1 stick butter
paprika
½ cup white wine

Place chicken breasts in open baking pan, skin side up. Sprinkle with lemon juice, salt and pepper, grated onion, dry mustard and parsley. Dot with butter. Sprinkle with paprika and bake in 350° oven for one hour or more. When nearly done add wine and baste with juices in pan. Do not overcook. This is delicious with rice.

Mrs. Ernest L. Brown

CHICKEN BREASTS COOKED IN WINE

1 stick butter
1 onion, chopped
6 chicken breasts
salted flour

½ pint cream
1 cup white wine
   (port or sauterne)

Melt butter in pan, add onion, sauté and remove onion. Dredge chicken in salted flour, brown lightly in butter. Put chicken in baking pan, pour butter drippings over chicken and also rinse pan with small amount of water and pour over chicken with the butter. Cover with one cup white wine. Cover with foil. Bake in 350° oven for 45 minutes. Add cream, cook covered 15 minutes, uncover and cook 5 minutes.

Mrs. Robert F. Kirkpatrick

SMOTHERED CHICKEN

1 two to three pound fryer	1 large can mushrooms
garlic	¾ cup water
salt, pepper and flour	⅔ cup sherry
3 tablespoons olive oil	1 tablespoon dried
1 stick butter	parsley flakes

Cut chicken in pieces and rub with garlic. Sprinkle with salt, pepper and flour. Melt oil and butter in skillet, brown chicken. Remove chicken and place in casserole. Add mushrooms, water, sherry and parsley. Bake in 350° oven for one hour or until tender. Baste, adding more water, if needed. Serves 4.

Mrs. Thomas A. Horst, Jr.

CHICKEN SAUTERNE

1 broiler or six chicken breasts	1 (5 ounce) can chestnuts
flour, salt and pepper	(drained and sliced)
1 stick margarine	1 (3 ounce) can mushrooms,
1 can cream of chicken soup	undrained
¾ cup cooking sauterne	2 tablespoons green pepper

Lightly dredge chicken pieces in flour, salt and pepper. Sauté, until brown on both sides in margarine, remove chicken to baking dish. To margarine, add soup, sauterne, chestnuts, mushrooms and green pepper. Pour mixture over chicken, cover with foil and bake for twenty-five minutes in 350° oven. Remove foil and cook 20-25 minutes longer.

Mrs. Walter Ogburn

CHICKEN JUBILEE

4 fryers, quartered	½ cup brown sugar
2 teaspoons salt	1 teaspoon garlic (optional)
¼ teaspoon pepper	2 medium onions, sliced
½ cup melted butter	1 (12 ounce) bottle chili sauce
1 cup water	1 (16 ounce) can bing cherries
½ cup raisins	1 cup sherry

Place chicken in shallow roasting pan, skin side down. Season with salt and pepper and dribble with melted butter. Broil under medium heat until golden brown. Combine remaining ingredients except cherries and wine, mix thoroughly. Pour sauce over chicken and cover entire pan with aluminum foil, bake about 1½ hours in 325° oven. Fifteen minutes before serving remove foil, add cherries and wine. Place on hot platter and spoon sauce over chicken. Serves 16.

Mrs. Jack Hyman

ORANGE GLAZED CHICKEN

SAUCE: (make the day before)

¼ cup olive oil	dash of pepper
1½ pounds mushrooms, sliced	2 garlic cloves, crushed
6 yellow onions	2 bay leaves
2 or 3 teaspoons salt	

Sauté above ingredients until tender. Add the following and simmer five minutes:

1 teaspoon oregano	¼ teaspoon nutmeg
1 teaspoon powdered savory	1½ cups orange juice
½ teaspoon basil	½ cup dry wine

Salt and pepper chicken, two pieces per person and shake in herb flour.

HERB FLOUR:

1½ cups flour	1 teaspoon savory
1 teaspoon oregano	½ teaspoon nutmeg
1 teaspoon basil	½ teaspoon rosemary

Brown chicken in olive oil. Lay browned chicken on bed of cooked rice (can use 1 box of Minute Rice), 1 cup of chopped pecans and one half of the sauce, mixed all together. Pour remaining sauce over chicken. Cover with foil and bake one and a half to two hours at 300°. Serves 12.

Mrs. Jerry Curran

DELA'S CHICKEN

1 fryer	salt and pepper to taste
½ pint whipping cream, whipped	boiled, steamed rice
½ teaspoon mustard	1 teaspoon dry curry powder
3 tablespoons Worcestershire	1 cup partially cut chutney

Cut and broil chicken in oven. Arrange chicken in baking dish. To cream add mustard, Worcestershire, salt and pepper. Pour over chicken and cook in oven until brown. Serve with rice flavored with curry powder and chutney.

Mrs. Gillette Burton

GAME AND FOWL

COUNTRY CAPTAIN

2 pound frying chicken, cut in
   pieces
seasoned flour
¼ cup shortening
1 onion, chopped
1 bell pepper, chopped
1 clove garlic, minced
1 teaspoon salt

½ teaspoon black pepper
½ teaspoon curry powder
¼ teaspoon thyme
3 tablespoons currants
1 cup blanched almonds, slivered
1 tablespoon chopped parsley
2 (No. 2) cans tomatoes
1 cup cooked rice

Dredge chicken in seasoned flour, brown in shortening, arrange in casserole. Sauté onion, pepper and garlic until golden in shortening in which chicken was browned. Add seasonings and tomatoes to onion mixture. Add to chicken and bake in 325° oven about one hour or until tender. Serve over hot rice. Serves 4.

Mrs. Charles R. Hicks

CHICKEN AND OKRA

1 fryer, cut up
½ cup cooking oil
2 pounds small okra, cut in
   pieces

2 medium onions, chopped
1 small can tomatoes
1 can tomato sauce
4 cups water

Brown fryer in oil. Remove chicken and brown okra. Remove okra and brown onion. To onion, add tomatoes, tomato sauce and water, simmer thirty minutes. Add okra and chicken and simmer one hour. Serve over rice.

Mrs. John Blacksher

SOUTHERN STEWED CHICKEN

1 2½-3 pound broiler or fryer,
   quartered
3 tablespoons bacon drippings
2 tablespoons flour
¼ green pepper, diced
1 tablespoon chopped parsley

¼ cup chopped onion
⅛ teaspoon pepper
1 teaspoon Worcestershire
1 can tomatoes
dash of Cayenne

Wash and dry chicken pieces and sauté in bacon drippings until golden. Remove from pan. Make a roux by blending flour into the drippings and cook until dark brown, stirring constantly. Add green pepper, parsley and

134

onion. Season with salt, pepper and Worcestershire. Add tomatoes and Cayenne. Cover and simmer until chicken is tender, about twenty-five minutes. Serves 4.

Anne Goode

FRIED CHICKEN

Place cut up fryers in pan or dish and pour milk over all, but not enough to cover. Soak chicken about thirty minutes, turning often. Dip in flour, shaking off excess and fry in oil or shortening. Sprinkle with paprika while frying for a golden brown color. Salt and pepper while frying or add salt and pepper to flour. This method does not call for the fat to be extremely hot.

Mrs. Ernest L. Brown

BATTER FOR FRIED CHICKEN

2 whole eggs   1 cup flour
juice of 2 lemons   2 cups milk

Mix all ingredients into a batter. Salt and pepper chicken. Dip chicken in batter, then in flour. Fry chicken to a golden brown.

Mrs. E. Ward Faulk, Jr.

CHICKEN AND BROCCOLI CASSEROLE

2 packages frozen broccoli or
    1 bunch fresh broccoli
4 chicken breasts, cooked and
    boned
2 cans cream of chicken soup
    (undiluted)
1 cup mayonnaise

1 teaspoon lemon juice
¾ teaspoon curry powder
½ cup shredded sharp
    American cheese
½ cup toasted bread crumbs
1 tablespoon butter or
    margarine, melted

Cook the broccoli and drain, arrange in a greased baking dish. Place the chicken on top. Mix the soup, mayonnaise, lemon juice and curry powder together and pour over chicken. Sprinkle with cheese. Combine bread crumbs with melted butter and sprinkle on top of cheese. Bake in 350° oven thirty minutes or until thoroughly heated. This dish can be fixed the day before and kept in refrigerator. Allow a little extra heating time in this case.

Mrs. William Porter

135

CHICKEN BARBECUED WITH A SPANISH FLAIR

¼ cup onion, chopped	1 cup tomato juice
1 tablespoon brown sugar	¼ cup wine vinegar
1½ teaspoons paprika	¼ cup water
½ teaspoon salt	½ cup sliced stuffed olives
½ teaspoon dry mustard	flour
¼ teaspoon chili powder	salt and pepper
½ teaspoon soy sauce	3 pounds chicken breasts
½ teaspoon Worcestershire	¼ cup butter or margarine

Combine all ingredients, onion through water, and mix well. Cook over low heat for ten minutes, then add olives. Dredge chicken in flour seasoned with salt and pepper. Brown dredged chicken in melted butter. Add sauce and cook, covered over low heat, forty-five minutes, or until tender.

Mrs. Mac Greer

CHICKEN DIVAN

2 packages frozen broccoli	1 can cream of chicken soup
6 boned chicken breasts	1 cup sour cream
garlic salt	3 tablespoons milk
butter	1 cup grated cheese, or more
grated American cheese	3 tablespoons sherry
toasted slivered almonds	paprika

Cook broccoli according to package directions. Place a layer of broccoli and a layer of chicken pieces in casserole, sprinkle all over with garlic salt and chunks of butter. Cover lightly with grated cheese, sprinkle with almonds. Mix soup, sour cream, milk, cup of grated cheese and sherry together and heat. Pour over chicken and broccoli. Sprinkle with almonds and paprika. Bake in 375° oven for forty-five minutes.

Mrs. Frank Frazer

CHICKEN MORNAY

1 hen (4-6 pounds)	1 cup grated cheese
1 can mushrooms	1 teaspoon Worcestershire
butter	dry toast
1 cup white sauce	1 can asparagus

Cook chicken, bone and cut in small pieces. Sauté mushrooms in butter for ten minutes. Add cheese to white sauce, add Worcestershire. Place

136

toast in bottom of baking dish, cover with layer of chicken then layer of asparagus, cheese sauce and finally mushrooms. Bake in 350° oven for twenty-five minutes.

Mrs. Edward Brinson

CHICKEN AND ASPARAGUS CASSEROLE

1 five pound hen	2 cups chicken broth
1 teaspoon salt	1 cup salad dressing
6 tablespoons butter	1 teaspoon lemon juice
½ cup flour	½ teaspoon curry powder
1 cup milk	2 large cans asparagus

Half cover hen with water, add salt, and cook until tender. Cool in broth. Remove meat from bones in large pieces. Melt butter in saucepan, blend in flour, gradually add milk, then broth. Cook over low heat until thick and smooth, stirring constantly. Remove from heat, add salad dressing, lemon juice, curry powder. Mix well. Arrange one can asparagus in bottom of shallow baking dish, place chicken on top, pour part of sauce over chicken, add other can of asparagus and rest of sauce. Bake in 400° oven for twenty minutes or until it bubbles and is very hot. Garnish with slivered almonds and pimento strips. Serves 8.

Mrs. Marion Adams, Jr.

CHICKEN SPAGHETTI I

4 pound hen	3 celery stalks, chopped
1 garlic clove	1 green pepper, chopped
1 onion	2 tablespoons oil
celery leaves	1 large can tomatoes
salt	1 can tomato paste
1 package spaghetti	1 large can mushrooms
1 onion, chopped	grated cheddar cheese

Cover hen with water and cook with garlic, onion, celery leaves and salt until tender. Cool and cut into pieces, larger than one inch. Cook spaghetti in chicken broth. Sauté chopped onion, celery, and green pepper in oil until tender. Add tomatoes, tomato paste and mushrooms. Simmer thirty to forty-five minutes. Add chicken to sauce and cook another thirty minutes, stirring often. Pour over spaghetti and sprinkle with cheddar cheese.

Mrs. Ernest Brown

CHICKEN SPAGHETTI II

1 medium hen
2 boxes spaghetti
chicken stock
1 large onion, chopped
2 tablespoons bacon fat
2 tablespoons flour
1 medium can tomatoes

1 bunch celery, chopped
1 large green pepper, chopped
salt and pepper to taste
1 tablespoon Worcestershire
5 drops Tabasco
horseradish to taste
1 pound American cheese, grated

Steam hen until tender and shred as for salad. Boil spaghetti in chicken stock. Brown onion in bacon fat, remove onion and add flour, stirring. Add one cup chicken stock gradually, stirring until mixture is smooth. Replace onions and add tomatoes, celery and green pepper. Season with salt and pepper, Worcestershire, Tabasco and horseradish. Add chicken to the sauce. This sauce can be mixed with spaghetti and served on a large platter or can be put in alternate layers in a casserole. Grate cheese on top if platter is used, between layers in casserole.

Mrs. Ben F. King

CHICKEN LIVER TOMATOES

6 firm tomatoes
1 cup finely chopped, cooked
    chicken livers
¼ teaspoon grated onion
¼ teaspoon dried basil

2 tablespoons melted butter
½ cup finely dried bread crumbs
salt, pepper, garlic salt to taste
1 tablespoon parsley

Remove slice from top of tomato and gently scoop out pulp. Drain and salt inside of tomato shell. Mix pulp with remaining ingredients and return to tomato shell. Bake in 325° oven for about twenty minutes or until shells are soft.

Mrs. Ernest Brown

GREEN NOODLE CHICKEN

4 pound hen
1 stick margarine
1 cup chopped green pepper
1 cup chopped onion
1 cup chopped celery
½ pound Velveeta cheese, cubed

1 small jar stuffed olives
1 large can sliced mushrooms
1 can cream of mushroom soup
1 pack (4½ ounces) artichoke
    noodles
cheese crackers

138

Boil hen until tender in as little water as possible. Reserve stock for later use. Cut chicken in bite size pieces. Sauté green pepper, onion and celery in margarine until tender. Add cheese and stir gently until cheese is melted. Add to this the olives, sliced mushrooms and chicken. Blend well. Then add the soup (melted). Boil noodles in chicken stock. As these noodles take longer than the regular kind, taste to make sure they are tender, but not mushy. Mix all ingredients, thinning sauce with stock if necessary. Top with cheese crackers which have been "swished around" with melted butter. Heat and brown top slightly.

Mrs. J. H. Friend, Sr.

HOT CHICKEN SALAD

2 cups coarsely diced chicken   ¼ teaspoon pepper
2 cups diced celery   2 teaspoons grated onion
½ cup toasted almonds   1 cup mayonnaise
¾ teaspoon salt   ½ cup grated American cheese

Mix all ingredients, pour into casserole, crush potato chips on top and bake in 400° oven for forty minutes. Serves 6-8.

Mrs. Frank DuValle

ALMOND CHICKEN DISH

1 (5 pound) chicken   pinch of thyme
1 large onion   pinch of marjoram
2 celery stalks   red pepper to taste
1 small bay leaf   one large can mushrooms
salt   1 medium can pimento, chopped
2 tablespoons butter   large jar ripe olives
3 heaping tablespoons flour   1 large can toasted almonds,
dash of Worcestershire   cut in large pieces
dash of monosodium glutamate   Chinese noodles
½ teaspoon paprika   almonds

Into cavity of uncooked chicken place the onion, celery, bay leaf and salt. Add water, using an adequate amount to have at least four cups liquid for later use. Cook chicken until tender, cool and cut into bite size cubes. In skillet add flour to butter and stir until smooth. Slowly add about three cups of chicken stock, diluting with a little milk if stock is too rich. Add

Worcestershire, monosodium glutamate, paprika, thyme, marjoram and red pepper. Add mushrooms, pimento and olives, simmer 35-45 minutes, stirring constantly. This must be cooked until thick. Just before serving add almonds. Serve over Chinese noodles. (This dish can be made ahead and frozen, but almonds should not be added until serving time.) Serves 8.

Mrs. Walter Ogburn

CURRIED CHICKEN

⅓ cup butter or margarine
1 tablespoon finely chopped
  onions
⅓ cup flour
1 teaspoon salt
2 teaspoons curry powder
  (or to taste)

¼ teaspoon pepper
½ teaspoon Worcestershire
2 cups chicken stock (or with
  chicken bouillon cubes)
1 cup half and half cream
2½ cups finely chopped
  cooked chicken

This is made best and most easily in an electric skillet. Melt margarine and add chopped onions, cooking until onions appear glazed. Add flour, mixing well. Stir in seasonings, slowly add stock, stirring to blend well without lumps. Add cream and chicken. The dish can be served immediately, but develops a better flavor if simmered 30-40 minutes. Place top on skillet to simmer. Serve on hot rice. Serves 6-8.

Mrs. John Scott

CHICKEN CHOW MEIN

2 six pound hens
6 cups chicken broth
8 tablespoons chicken fat
2¼ cups thinly sliced onions
4 cups thinly sliced celery
10 tablespoons flour
2 cans Chinese vegetables

1 can bean sprouts
3 cans water chestnuts
2 large cans mushrooms
Soy sauce (about ½ bottle)
2 cans beef consommé
pinch brown sugar
⅛ teaspoon pepper

Boil chicken in salty water and save both broth and fat. Cut chicken in small pieces. Set aside. Sauté onions and celery in 8 tablespoons chicken fat until done. Set aside. Make paste of flour, ⅓ cup chicken fat in skillet. Add broth, onions and celery. Add vegetables, sprouts and thinly sliced water chestnuts that have been rinsed in cold water. Add mushrooms, consommé, brown sugar, chicken, Kitchen Bouquet to color and soy sauce to taste. Let boil well, then set aside until ready to reheat and serve. Serve on rice. Twenty-four to thirty servings.

Mrs. Manning McPhillips, Jr.

CHICKEN AND DUMPLINGS

1 large hen	2½ teaspoons baking powder
3 quarts water	4 tablespoons shortening
1 chopped onion	¾ cup cold milk
½ cup finely chopped celery	1 egg
4 teaspoons salt	¼ teaspoon pepper
2 cups flour	1 tablespoon finely chopped
1 teaspoon salt	parsley

Cut hen into pieces. Simmer in water seasoned with onion, celery, four teaspoons salt and cook until tender. (2-4 hours, depending on hen). Remove chicken from stock and keep warm. Sift flour, baking powder, pepper and salt. Cut in shortening. Add parsley. Add milk and beaten eggs all at once. Roll on lightly floured board and cut into thin strips. Drop strips into boiling stock and cook about fifteen minutes, covered. Lift from broth. Pour over chicken and serve.

Mrs. Willis R. Brown

CHICKEN 'N STUFFING SCALLOP

1 8 ounce package (3½ cups) herb seasoned or cornbread stuffing	½ cup enriched flour
	¼ teaspoon salt
	pepper to taste
3 cups cubed, cooked chicken	4 cups chicken broth
½ cup butter or margarine	6 eggs, slightly beaten

Prepare stuffing according to package directions for dry stuffing. Spread in a 13 x 9 x 2 inch baking dish. Top with layer of chicken. In a large saucepan melt butter, blend in flour and seasonings. Add cool broth, cook and stir until mixture thickens. Stir a small amount of hot mixture into eggs, return to hot mixture, pour over chicken. Bake in slow oven (325°) forty to forty-five minutes or until knife inserted half way to center comes out clean. Let stand five minutes to set, cut in squares and serve with following sauce:

141

PIMENTO—MUSHROOM SAUCE:

Mix, heat and stir until hot

1 can condensed cream of	**1 cup dairy sour cream**
mushroom soup	**¼ cup chopped pimentos**
¼ cup milk	

Serves twelve.

Mrs. Philip Atkinson

CHICKEN PIE

METHOD I

Simmer a large hen until tender. Remove chicken from broth, debone and place meat in a large casserole. Boil broth to about three cups liquid, thicken to gravy consistency and pour over chicken. Put in 350° oven and heat to boiling. Meanwhile, make biscuit (short) and drop on top of casserole which should be very hot. Brown biscuit and serve.

METHOD II

1 (5-6 pound) hen, cut up	**3 teaspoons double acting**
water to almost cover	**baking powder**
2 teaspoons salt	**1 teaspoon salt**
6 rounded tablespoons flour	**½ cup shortening**
2 cups flour	**¾ cup milk**

Simmer hen until meat begins to come loose from bones. Remove chicken from broth, debone and remove skin. Take out about one cup of broth, set aside to cool. Boil remaining broth down to about two cups. Mix six rounded tablespoonfuls flour into cup of broth (blender is the simplest way) and, stirring constantly, slowly pour flour mixture into boiling broth. Place meat in large casserole, pour thickened broth over chicken, heat to boiling in 350° oven. Sift flour, baking powder and salt together in mixing bowl. Cut shortening into flour. Make a hole in the center of mixture and add milk. Mix lightly, toss lightly on floured board, roll to half-inch thickness and cut biscuits. If excess grease has come to top of gravy in casserole, skim this off. Drop biscuits on top of hot casserole, turn oven to 425°, brown and serve. Chicken and gravy can be prepared a day or two ahead,

refrigerated. About one hour before serving, put into cold oven, turn
to 350° and top with biscuits when good and hot.

Mrs. W. J. Neely

CHICKEN POT PIE

4-5 pound hen
2 cups milk
3 tablespoons margarine
3 tablespoons flour
½ cup chicken stock
1 can English peas
2 cans mushrooms
2 very small jars chopped
   pimento
1 onion, chopped and sautéed

1 bell pepper, chopped and
   sautéed
2 celery stalks, chopped and
   sautéed
3 hard boiled eggs
salt and pepper to taste
3 cups flour
1 cup salad oil
½ cup cold milk
¾ teaspoon salt

Boil hen until tender. Remove meat from bone and cut into small pieces.
Make cream sauce with milk, margarine, flour and chicken stock. Mix in
chicken, peas, mushrooms, pimentos, sautéed onion, bell pepper, celery,
hard boiled egg, salt and pepper. Use flour, salad oil, milk and salt to make
pie crust. Line baking dish with pie crust, then a layer of chicken mixture,
a layer of pie crust, a layer of chicken, topping with pie crust. Bake in
350° oven two hours or longer, until top crust is browned. Serves 8-10 generously.

Mrs. T. M. Taul, Jr.

QUICK CHICKEN PIE

1 whole chicken
6 peppercorns
2 bay leaves
1 small onion
1 medium celery stalk
1 tablespoon parsley

1 package pie crust mix
1 can green peas
2 hard boiled eggs
1 can cream of chicken soup
chicken stock
salt and pepper to taste

Boil chicken in water with peppercorn, bay leaves, onion, celery, parsley
and salt. Remove chicken, cool and when cool, debone. Reserve stock. Line
deep baking dish with pie crust, saving enough for top. Layer chicken,

143

soup, peas, soup, and eggs in baking dish. Pour stock over all until it bubbles out of top. Place crust on top and bake in 350° oven about forty-five minutes.

Mrs. Selwyn H. Turner, Jr.

CHICKEN COQUILLE

1 large hen	2 tablespoons grated onion
salt and pepper	2 tablespoons finely chopped
¾ to 1 cup water	parsley
2 tablespoons butter or	salt and pepper to taste
margarine	½ cup sherry
2 heaping tablespoons flour	1 large can mushroom stems
1 cup cream	and pieces
1 cup chicken broth (without fat)	

Wash hen well, salt and pepper inside and out. Place in ¾ to 1 cup water in heavy pot, cover and cook slowly two to two and a half hours or until fork tests tender. Cool, save broth, pull meat from bone and cube. Melt butter in same pot, over low heat, gradually add flour, stirring until smooth. Add cream, mix, add broth, mix, add onion and parsley, mix. Heat to boiling point, but do not boil. Add seasonings, sherry, chicken and mushrooms. Can be made a day ahead, adding sherry while heating (over water rather than over direct heat). Can be served from chafing dish into patty shells. Pepperidge Farm frozen patty shells are delicious, can be baked ahead and heated for a few minutes when ready to serve.) Serves six generously.

Mrs. G. Russell Hollinger, Jr.

MY FAVORITES

MY FAVORITES

Meat Round-up

MEATS

STEAK CHARCOALED

Trim fat from steak, leaving a small amount for flavor. Marinate in red wine, garlic salt and fresh ground black pepper for several hours. Cook on grill, turning often until desired doneness and basting with the following sauce:

1 stick butter	juice of ½ lemon
1 small bottle	lemon rind
Worcestershire	Tabasco

Melt butter, add Worcestershire, lemon juice, and rind, add Tabasco and simmer about thirty minutes.

Mrs. Ernest L. Brown

GREEN PEPPER STEAK

2 pounds beef tenderloin, sliced thin	4 green peppers, cut in large strips
¼ cup margarine or cooking oil	1 pound mushrooms (preferably fresh)
salt to taste	
garlic powder to taste	¼ cup tomato paste
pepper to taste	3-4 tomatoes, quartered
1 bay leaf (optional)	¼ cup sherry
1 teaspoon oregano	

Brown meat in two tablespoonfuls margarine, add seasonings and cook until tender. Sauté pepper and mushrooms in remaining fat for five minutes. Add to meat along with tomato paste and quartered tomatoes. Heat

147

and simmer until peppers are cooked, no more than ten to fifteen minutes. Add sherry and serve. Serves 4.

Mrs. Charles O. Ditmars

CHATEAUBRIAND OF BEEF—ESPAGNOLE SAUCE

3 pounds center cut beef fillet
salt to taste
olive oil

fancy cut red pepper
parsley

Trim fat and skin from fillet and flatten with a broad blade cleaver. Sprinkle with salt, brush with oil and broil twenty minutes. Remove to platter, garnish with red pepper and parsley. Serve with Espagnole sauce:

1 onion, sliced
2 carrots, sliced
1 shallot, finely chopped
parsley
bit of bay leaf
8 peppercorns

1 whole clove
2 tablespoons butter
1 cup brown stock (bouillon or any type meat concentrate may be substituted)
3 tablespoons flour

Cook vegetables and seasonings with butter until well browned. Stir in flour and brown. Add stock, bring to boiling point, season with salt and pepper.

Mrs. James Hirs

BEEF STROGANOFF I

2 pounds beef
1 lemon
1 large onion, chopped
1 can mushrooms
½ stick butter
3 tablespoons sherry

flour
¼ cup tomato juice
salt and pepper to taste
1 bouillon cube
1 cup water
½ cup sour cream

Cut beef into small cubes and sprinkle with lemon juice, let stand. Sauté onions and mushrooms in butter. Lightly flour beef. Remove onions and mushrooms, add sherry to butter and brown beef. Add onions, mushrooms, juice, seasonings and bouillon cube, which has been dissolved in hot water. Simmer one hour. When ready to serve, add sour cream and heat through. Serve on rice. Serves 6.

Mrs. Selwyn H. Turner, Jr.

BEEF STROGANOFF II

2 small sirloin strips	1 clove garlic, minced
¼ stick butter	1 beef bouillon cube
1 onion, finely chopped	1 carton sour cream
1 can mushroom buttons	

Cut sirloin in small strips. Brown quickly in butter to medium rare. Remove from pan. Sauté onion, mushrooms and garlic in remaining butter, add bouillon, meat and sour cream. Heat, but do not boil. Serve over green noodles, salt and pepper to taste. The entire recipe, with the exception of sour cream, may be prepared a day ahead and reheated with sour cream just before serving in chafing dish. Serves 6.

Mrs. Robert A. Guthans

SPANISH STEAK

1½ pounds round steak	½ green pepper, chopped
¾ teaspoon salt	1 small can mushrooms
½ teaspoon cracked pepper	2 cans (8 ounce size) tomato
1 teaspoon Worcestershire	sauce
1 small onion	2 teaspoons lemon juice

Put beef in large iron skillet, sprinkle with salt, pepper and Worcestershire. Slice onion and place vegetables on top of meat. Pour tomato juice and lemon juice over all. Bake five minutes in 400° oven, reduce temperature to 325° and bake an hour to an hour and a half. If tomato sauce gets too thick, add one or two tablespoonfuls boiling water. Serves 4.

Mrs. R. Bruce Worley

SUKIYAKI

2 tablespoons salad oil	2 medium onions, sliced
1½ pounds steak, cut in thin strips	1 cup 1½ inch strips of celery
¼ cup sugar	1 can bamboo shoots, sliced
¾ cup soy sauce	1 can mushrooms, sliced thin
¼ cup mushroom stock (or water)	1 bunch green onions (cut in
1 green pepper, sliced in thin strips	1″ lengths, tops and all)
	½ cup sake (or sherry)

Heat oil in skillet, add meat and brown lightly. Mix sugar, soy sauce and mushroom stock. Cook half of this mixture with the meat. Push meat to one side of pan and add sliced onions, green pepper and celery. Cook a few minutes, add remaining soy sauce mixture, bamboo shoots and mushrooms. Cook three to five minutes. Add green onions, cook one minute more, then add sake, if desired. Cook one minute, stir well and serve immediately over hot rice. Serves 8.

Mrs. John T. Lutz

PEPPER BEEF

3 pounds sirloin tip roast, cut into ¼ inch slices
salt and pepper
butter
1 medium onion
2 or 3 small green onions, sliced thin
1 tablespoon butter

1 large can mushroom stems and pieces
1 large can chicken broth
2 large bell peppers
3-4 tablespoons butter
flour
salt and pepper to taste

Salt and pepper slices of meat and brown on both sides in just enough butter to keep them from sticking to skillet, set aside. In another skillet, sauté onion and green onions in a tablespoon of butter until just golden. Add mushrooms, undrained, and chicken broth. Add the meat and simmer until meat is tender, about thirty minutes. Meanwhile, cut bell peppers in strips and sauté slowly in butter until they begin to change color to dull green. Add to the meat and make a roux with butter remaining from peppers and a little flour. Add to meat, enough to thicken slightly. Don't cook dish anymore, just keep it hot, preferably about an hour before serving. Serve on fluffy rice. Add salt and pepper to taste, if desired. A good dish to prepare in electric skillet.

Mrs. John M. Scott, Jr.

CORNED BEEF

1 fancy corned brisket of beef
½ large onion, sliced
1 bay leaf

3 carrots, peeled and halved
½ stalk celery
3 whole cloves

Place corned beef in kettle and cover with cold water. Add other ingredients. Bring to a boil. Cover and simmer 3½ to 5 hours or until tender. The corned beef is best when refrigerated and then sliced into exceedingly thin slices. Serve with mustard, swiss cheese, and cabbage, cooked in the stock.

Mrs. Mac B. Greer

BOEUF EN DAUBE 85'TH STREET

3 pounds round of beef, cut in
 1½ inch pieces
½ cup flour
1 teaspoon salt
¼ teaspoon pepper
¼ cup butter
2 cloves garlic, finely chopped
2 ounces brandy
1 can beef bouillon
approximately 1 dozen small
 onions

1½ cups burgundy
1 can button mushrooms
approximately 1 dozen small
 carrots
4 whole cloves
2 bay leaves
¼ teaspoon marjoram
 (more or less)
¼ teaspoon thyme (more or less)
3 tablespoons chopped parsley
pie crust or biscuit dough

Roll beef in seasoned flour. Melt butter in heavy skillet, add garlic, add floured beef and brown on all sides. Pour in brandy and remove from heat. Place beef in casserole with tight cover. Heat bouillon and wine in skillet, stirring from bottom to loosen all brown that may adhere. Pour liquid in casserole and add onions, mushrooms, carrots and seasonings. To hold in aroma, seal casserole with pie crust or biscuit dough. Bake in 300° oven for three hours. Sprinkle each serving generously with parsley. Serves 8.

Nancy Taylor Ross

BEEF STEW

2½ pounds beef chuck,
 in 2 inch cubes
¼ cup flour
heaping ½ teaspoon salt
¼ teaspoon freshly ground
 black pepper
3 tablespoons bacon drippings
1 cup good red wine
1 cup boiling water
8 sprigs fresh parsley
1 bay leaf
1 sprig thyme

3 tomatoes (peeled, seeded
 and quartered)
2 carrots, quartered
1 white turnip, pared and cut
 into 8 pieces
3 celery stalks, halved lengthwise
 and cut into one inch strips
1 small clove garlic
10 peppercorns
1 teaspoon salt
1 more cup good red wine

Shake beef cubes in bag with flour, salt and pepper. Brown in skillet in bacon drippings over bright flame, stirring constantly with a wooden spoon. Transfer to stewpot. Pour one cup wine in skillet and deglaze carefully, pour over meat. Add boiling water, cover and bring to a boil. Boil for two

151

minutes and lower heat. Add parsley, bay leaf, thyme, tomatoes, carrots, turnip, and celery. Add garlic, peppercorns and salt. Add remaining cup of wine. Bring to a boil, lower heat and simmer very gently partially covered for at least an hour. Serves 6.

Mrs. Jack Campbell

BEEF BOURGUIGNON

3-4 pounds trimmed lean sirloin	1 teaspoon freshly ground black
6 bacon slices	pepper
2 garlic cloves	flour
2-3 parsley sprigs	red wine
sprig of thyme	½ pound mushrooms
1 leek, well washed	4 tablespoons butter
1 teaspoon salt	

Cut bacon into small pieces and fry in large, heavy skillet with tight cover or Dutch oven. Remove bacon. Roll beef (cut into ½ by 4 inch strips) in flour and sauté in bacon drippings, browning evenly on all sides. Add salt, pepper, leek, thyme, parsley, garlic and bacon. Cover with red wine, bring just to a boil and quickly lower heat. Cover tightly and simmer gently until thoroughly tender, about 1½ hours. Remove beef from pan and strain sauce. Sauté mushrooms in butter until lightly browned. Add to beef and strained sauce. Sauce may be thickened with small balls of butter and flour kneaded together if desired. Add more salt if needed. Serves 6.

Anne L. Goode

BEEF RAGOUT

1 pound round steak, cut in cubes	¼ teaspoon herb blend for meat
1 heaping tablespoon flour	1 large bay leaf
2 cups beef stock	⅛ teaspoon salt
1 teaspoon kitchen bouquet	⅛ teaspoon freshly ground black
1 teaspoon tomato paste	pepper
1 medium onion, chopped	1 can mushrooms
2 tablespoons sherry	

Brown meat in butter, add flour, stir until smooth. Add stock, kitchen bouquet and tomato paste, bring to a boil, reduce heat. Add onion, sherry, herbs, salt and pepper. Cook slowly, covered, until meat is tender. Add mushrooms, cook five minutes more. Serve over rice. Serves 2.

Mrs. Vance E. Thompson, Jr.

OLD-FASHIONED BEEF STEW

2½ pounds boneless beef chuck, cut in 1½ inch cubes	1 large onion, chopped
	hot water
¼ cup flour	12 small white onions
2 teaspoons salt	6 carrots, cut
¼ teaspoon pepper	6 peeled potatoes
¼ teaspoon paprika	1 cup frozen peas
pinch of thyme	parsley
3 tablespoons fat	

Before browning in fat, roll meat in mixture of flour, salt, pepper, paprika and thyme. Add onion and brown a few minutes longer. Sprinkle meat with remaining flour mixture. Add just enough hot water to cover meat. Cover, simmer two hours, or until almost tender. Add onions, carrots and potatoes, cook thirty-five minutes longer. Sprinkle with chopped parsley. Serves 6.

Mrs. Amiel W. Brinkley, Jr.

POT ROAST I

Rub roast with salt and pepper. Brown in heavy pot with no water or fat. After well browned (thirty minutes or more) on all sides, add one large diced onion and a cup of water. Cook slowly, three to four hours. Add water, two ounces at a time, if needed. For gravy, remove the roast, blend in flour, water, salt and pepper.

Mrs. D. Binion Cochran

POT ROAST II

3-4 pounds beef chuck or boneless sirloin	1 cup dry red wine
	1 cup sour cream
dash of salt	4 tablespoons flour
1 teaspoon pepper	½ cup water
1 garlic clove, chopped	juice of 1 lemon
2 large onions, rings	

Rub meat with salt and pepper and brown on all sides, over high heat. Add garlic and onion rings, cook until golden. Turn meat down, heat wine and add to meat. Stir in sour cream, cover pot and reduce to very low heat. Cook about two and a half hours, testing with fork for tenderness. After removing meat to platter, add mixed flour and water and stir to thicken.

Add lemon juice. Extra red wine served with the meal makes delicious eating! (Cold sour cream toughens meat—be sure sour cream is room temperature before adding.)

Mrs. W. B. Taylor, Jr.

TAMALE PIE

1 onion, chopped	2 teaspoons salt
1 garlic clove, chopped	2 teaspoons chili powder
3 teaspoons butter	20 ripe olives, pitted
3 teaspoons olive oil	2 eggs
1 pound ground meat	1 cup corn meal
½ pound pork sausage	1 cup milk
1 can tomatoes (No. 2½)	Parmesan cheese
1 can corn (No. 2½)	

Sauté and brown onion, garlic, butter, olive oil, meat and sausage. Simmer tomatoes, corn, salt and chili powder in saucepan for twenty minutes. Combine meat and tomatoes. Add olives and pour into large baking dish. Beat eggs, add corn meal and milk. Pour evenly over filling, sprinkle with Parmesan cheese. Bake one hour in 350° oven, slice and serve.

Mrs. W. B. Erickson, Jr.

HOMINY PIE

1½ pounds ground beef	1 can big hominy (No. 2)
1 tablespoon flour	1 medium onion, chopped
2 cups canned tomatoes	¼ pound grated American cheese
1 teaspoon chili powder	salt and pepper

Brown meat lightly in fat. Add flour, tomatoes and seasonings. Brown hominy and chopped onion in a little hot fat, add to meat mixture. Place in greased casserole. Cover with cheese and bake for thirty minutes in 350° oven.

Mrs. Jack H. Friend

BROWNED BEEF WITH RICE

1 pound ground beef	1 teaspoon Worcestershire
2 tablespoons butter	1 teaspoon salt
1 egg	¼ teaspoon pepper
1 cup cooked rice	1 can bean sprouts

Brown meat in skillet. Remove meat and melt butter in same skillet. Break egg in and scramble gently with a fork. Add cooked rice and meat and mix well. Add Worcestershire, salt and pepper and toss well. Add bean sprouts (juice and all) and stir slowly until mixture is piping hot. Serve. This is a good side dish or main dish.

Mrs. Graham McClintock, Jr.

BEEF ENCHILADAS

1 onion, minced	3 tablespoons chili powder
1 minced garlic clove	1 teaspoon salt
3 tablespoons fat	½ teaspoon pepper
1 pound ground beef	grated onion
2 cans undrained tomatoes	grated cheese
1 tablespoon flour	tortillas

Sauté onion and garlic in fat. Add ground meat and cook until done. Add tomatoes. Make a paste of flour, chili powder, salt and pepper. Add paste to sauce and cook forty-five minutes to an hour. Dip tortillas in hot grease to make limp enough to roll. Roll a tablespoonful of sauce in each tortilla. Place in baking pan. Cover with remaining sauce, sprinkle with grated onion. Spread cheese over top. Bake in moderate oven until cheese melts.

Mrs. Kenneth M. Hannon

PIZZA PIE

1½ teaspoons garlic salt	1 teaspoon salt
1½ cups biscuit mix	⅛ teaspoon pepper
½-⅔ cup milk	½ teaspoon ground sage
1 pound ground meat	1 cup grated cheese
¼ cup finely chopped onion	2 cups drained canned tomatoes
2 tablespoons cooking oil	

Add garlic salt to biscuit mix. Add milk gradually and stir until flour is moistened and dough follows fork. Knead lightly on a floured board and roll in about ⅛ inch thickness. Fit into nine inch pie pan or shallow casserole. Cook ground meat and chopped onion in oil until meat is brown and onion is tender. Add salt, pepper and sage. Spread meat mixture over dough, sprinkle with cheese and arrange tomatoes on top. Bake in 425° oven for 20 to 25 minutes. Can be made ahead and refrigerated.

Margaret Horn Hixon

155

GRANDMOTHER'S GROUND ROAST BEEF PATTIES

1 onion, chopped	¼ teaspoon salt
1 celery stalk, chopped	¼ teaspoon pepper
1 tablespoon chopped bell	1 pound leftover roast beef,
pepper	ground
¼ teaspoon parsley	2 potatoes, cooked and mashed
¼ teaspoon chervil (optional)	1 egg, beaten
2 tablespoons butter	corn flake crumbs

Sauté onion, celery, bell pepper and spices in butter. Remove and add to meat, mashed potatoes and egg. Roll in crumbs and fry until golden brown.

Mrs. Selwyn H. Turner, Jr.

CHEESEBURGER DELUXE

2 pounds ground beef	½ teaspoon pepper
¼ cup evaporated milk	1 cup grated cheddar cheese
2 teaspoons Worcestershire	¼ cup crumbled blue cheese
1 teaspoon salt	1 tablespoon grated onion

Combine beef, milk, Worcestershire, salt and pepper. Make sixteen thin patties. Mix cheeses together with onion and spread on eight patties. Cover with remaining eight patties and press edges together. Grill over medium heat, turning once.

Mrs. Wiliam Rowell, Jr.

LASAGNA I

½ pound ground pork	1 can tomato paste
1 pound ground beef	2 bay leaves
½ cup olive oil or salad oil	2 cups water
1 ounce butter	lasagna noodles
1 teaspoon oregano	Parmesan or Romano cheese,
1 teaspoon chopped parsley	grated
2 medium onions, chopped	Mozzarella cheese, sliced
1 garlic button, minced	salt and pepper to taste
2 cans tomato sauce	

Brown meat in oil, add butter and seasonings. When golden brown add tomato sauce, tomato paste and bay leaves. Dissolve in water and simmer slowly for two hours. If sauce gets too thick, add beef stock or water. Cook noodles. Grease a baking dish well with butter, place a layer of noodles in the bottom, sprinkle with grated cheese. Add some sauce, then thinly sliced cheese. Season with salt and pepper. Continue layers until pan is filled. Cover the top layer with slices of Mozzarella and top with sauce. Bake in 250° oven for forty-five minutes, until cheese is completely melted.

Mrs. Frank S. Stone

LASAGNA II

1 pound ground beef	1 teaspoon oregano
1 small onion, chopped	1 garlic clove
1 can tomato paste	sharp cheese
2 cans tomato sauce	Recotta (or 1 pint Cottage cheese)
1 teaspoon salt	Mozzarella cheese
¼ teaspoon pepper	1 package lasagna noodles

Brown beef and onion in skillet. Add tomato sauce, tomato paste, salt, pepper, oregano and garlic. Simmer one hour. Line baking pan or casserole with cooked noodles. Make alternating layers of meat sauce, sharp cheese, Recotta, Mozzarella and noodles, ending with meat sauce topped with Mozzarella. Bake in 350° oven thirty minutes. Serve hot. Serves four.

Mrs. Graham McClintock, Jr.

HAMBURGERS WITH BARBECUE SAUCE

2 pounds ground meat	4 tablespoons Worcestershire
2 cups soft bread crumbs	4 tablespoons vinegar
1½ cups milk	1 teaspoon salt
1 teaspoon salt	½ teaspoon black pepper
4 tablespoons sugar	2 cups catsup

Mix meat, bread crumbs, milk and 1 teaspoon salt and make into patties. Mix remaining ingredients thoroughly and pour over meat as it cooks.

Mrs. Jack C. Gallalee

CABBAGE ROLLS I

8 large cabbage leaves	2 cups tomatoes
1 pound ground meat	1 onion, chopped
salt and pepper to taste	2 tablespoons vinegar
juice of 1 small onion	2 tablespoons sugar
¾ cup cooked rice	

157

Boil cabbage leaves in salted water a few minutes to tenderize. Combine meat, salt, pepper, onion juice and rice. Make into eight balls. Roll one ball in each leaf, fastening with a toothpick. Place in a kettle with remaining ingredients, add a little water and simmer until tender and browned, about an hour and a half.

Mrs. Ben M. Radcliff

CABBAGE ROLLS II

1 pound good ground beef
¼ pound ground smoked sausage
   or ¼ pound pork sausage
1 cup cooked rice
salt and pepper to taste

a little onion
1 loose cabbage head
canned sauerkraut
1 large can tomatoes

Mix ground beef and sausage with rice. Add salt, pepper and onion. Cut core out of back of cabbage head and steam about five minutes, until leaves are pliable. Put spoonful of meat on large cabbage leaf, turn sides in and roll up. In dutch oven or roaster alternate layers of cabbage rolls and canned sauerkraut. Crush tomatoes and pour over all. Cover and bake slowly in 300° oven for two to two and a half hours. If recipe is doubled bake three hours. Serves 6-8.

Mrs. Carter Luscher

HOT TAMALE PIE

1 large onion, chopped
3 tablespoons shortening
1 pound ground beef
2 cups thick tomato soup

1½ teaspoons salt
2 teaspoons chili powder
¼ teaspoon pepper
2 cups corn meal

Sauté onion in shortening until brown. Add beef and cook until red color disappears. Add soup and cook for fifteen minutes, adding salt, chili powder and pepper. Drain off and measure the liquid; add enough boiling water to make six cups liquid in all. Pour corn meal slowly into boiling liquid, cook fifteen minutes over low heat, stirring constantly. Mixture should be very thick. Place layer of corn meal mush in greased baking dish, then a layer of meat. Alternate layers with mush on top. Bake in 350° oven thirty minutes. Serves ten.

Mrs. N. Q. Adams

TOURNEDOS OF BEEF TENDERLOIN

½ cup sherry	½ pound butter, melted
8 egg yolks	12 slices filet mignon,
juice of 1 lemon	¾ inch thick
½ teaspoon tarragon	12 whole mushrooms, fried

Place sherry in shallow pan over low heat. Add well beaten egg yolks slowly. Then slowly add lemon juice and tarragon. Simmer for one minute. Place pan in double boiler to keep mixture hot while adding melted butter, stir constantly. Place steaks in broiler or pan and broil to taste. When done place one tablespoonful sauce mixture on each steak and top with a fried mushroom. Serves 6.

Mrs. James H. Coil, Jr.

MEAT LOAF

2 cups day old bread crumbs	1 tablespoon salt
¾ cup minced onion	1 teaspoon dry mustard
¼ cup green pepper, minced	¼ cup milk
2 eggs	¼ cup catsup
2 pounds lean chuck, ground	½ cup catsup
6 teaspoons horseradish	

Prepare bread crumbs, first removing crust from bread. Mince onion and pepper. In large bowl, beat eggs slightly, add ground meat and toss lightly. Add remaining ingredients, except last amount of catsup, and shape meat into an oval loaf in a greased baking pan, spreading ½ cup catsup on top. Bake in 400° oven for forty minutes.

Mrs. T. S. Cowan

EASY MEAT BALLS

1½ pounds ground beef	⅛ teaspoon garlic salt
½ cup bread or cracker crumbs	⅛ teaspoon celery salt
½ cup water or milk	⅛ teaspoon nutmeg
1 small onion, finely chopped	⅛ teaspoon pepper
(or 2 teaspoons instant)	1 can mushroom soup
1 teaspoon Worcestershire	⅓ can water
½ teaspoon salt	3 tablespoons sherry

Mix thoroughly ground beef, bread crumbs, water, onion and seasonings. Shape into balls, roll in flour and brown in two tablespoonfuls fat. When brown, pour soup and water over them. Cover and simmer twenty to thirty minutes. Add sherry last five minutes. A dash of Kitchen Bouquet may be added also. Good served with bread crumbled noodles. Excellent made in miniature and served from chafing dish for hors d'oeuvres.

Mrs. George Hitchcock

SPAGHETTI SAUCE

1 pound ground beef
2 medium onions, chopped
½ stick butter
salt and pepper to taste
2 tablespoons parsley
2 teaspoons Worcestershire
1 "family size" can tomato sauce
1 can tomatoes (No. 2)
1 green pepper, chopped

1 can mushroom slices
3 tablespoons catsup
½ teaspoon cloves
½ teaspoon nutmeg
¼ teaspoon sage
¼ teaspoon marjoram
2 bay leaves, broken
¼ teaspoon oregano
2 tablespoons lemon juice

Brown meat and onion in butter after sprinkling with salt, pepper, parsley and Worcestershire. Add tomato sauce, tomatoes, green pepper, mushrooms and catsup. Add herbs and then lemon juice. Cook two to three hours over low heat or 200°-250° in electric skillet. If sauce gets too thick, add one small can tomato sauce and equal amount boiling water.

Mrs. R. Bruce Worley

DIVINE CASSEROLE

1 large package small egg noodles
2 pounds ground beef
2 cans tomato sauce
1 tablespoon Worcestershire
1 carton cream style cottage
    cheese

salt to taste
1 large package Philadelphia
    cream cheese
½ pint sour cream
3 or 4 green onions, chopped
1 stick butter or margarine

Boil, drain and rinse noodles under hot water. Brown meat well, add tomato sauce, Worcestershire and salt. Mix cottage cheese, cream cheese, sour cream and onions. Melt butter. Grease two two-quart casseroles. Place one-fourth noodles in each casserole, pour a little melted butter over noodles, add one-half cheese mixture to each casserole. Add remaining noodles, more butter and top with meat mixture. Bake in 350° oven for thirty to forty-five minutes. Freezes well.

Mrs. Robert A. Guthans

COMPANY CASSEROLE

1 large green pepper, chopped fine	salt to taste
1 large onion, chopped fine	pepper to taste
4 celery stalks, chopped fine	2 pounds ground meat (enough
1 stick butter	for 2 casseroles)
¼ cup water	1 can mushrooms
1 can tomatoes	1 package thin spaghetti
Tabasco to taste	2 garlic pods
	cheddar cheese

Sauté peppers, onion and celery in butter until tender, add water. Add tomatoes and season with Tabasco, salt and pepper to taste. Salt and pepper ground meat and drop pinches of meat into skillet with sauce until meat is done. Continue cooking and add mushrooms and spaghetti sauce. Put garlic pods on small toothpicks or small skewers and add to sauce. Cook spaghetti, season and drain when done. When meat sauce is done, remove garlic, and layer in greased casserole with spaghetti. Top with cheddar cheese and place in moderate oven until cheese is bubbly. Good with sliced boned ham, salad and French bread.

Mrs. Jere Austill, Jr.

SMOTHERED LIVER

Use medium thick calves liver slices. Dip lightly in flour and shake off excess. Brown in two tablespoonfuls oil. Drain off any excess fat or oil and add small amount of water and one large onion sliced and the rings separated. Sprinkle over each slice: mushroom powder, Worcestershire, dried parsley, dried celery, salt and seasoned pepper. Cover and simmer about five minutes. Add not more than one-fourth cup red wine. Cover and simmer until tender. Add fresh mushrooms, if in season.

Mrs. Ernest L. Brown

PAN BROILED CALVES LIVER

Rub liver with cut end of lemon. Season with salt and pepper and dip lightly in flour. Sauté in butter with minced onion over high heat. Remove liver from pan with onions and place on heated platter. Remove fat from pan and replace over high heat. Melt butter, add 1 tablespoon parsley and dry red wine, mix. Pour over liver.

Mrs. H. Manning McPhillips

VEAL PARMESAN

1-1½ pounds veal cutlets	2 cups milk
1 egg	½ cup grated Parmesan cheese
1 cup bread crumbs	½ cup Munster cheese
4 tablespoons butter	1 teaspoon salt
4 tablespoons flour	1 teaspoon pepper

Pound and flatten veal cutlets. Dip cutlets into beaten egg, then into bread crumbs. Fry in butter until brown and cooked through. Melt butter, blend in flour, add milk and stir until thick and smooth. Add Parmesan cheese and seasonings and blend thoroughly. Place cutlets in baking dish, cover with sauce and top with strips of Munster cheese. Place under broiler for five minutes.

Mrs. Norman A. Nicholson

LAMB ROAST

Rub lamb with vinegar, oil, salt and pepper. Cut a slit in fat and insert small garlic slice. Allow to sit overnight. Roast in 325° oven until done, about thirty to forty minutes per pound.

Mrs. B. Franklin King

SHISH—KEBABS

2 teaspoons salt	½ teaspoon pepper
2 large garlic cloves, sieved	½ cup olive oil
1 large onion, chopped	⅔ cup sherry
2 teaspoons oregano or	handful parsley, finely chopped
marjoram	6 pound leg of lamb

Mix all ingredients and marinate bite size pieces of meat overnight, turning once or twice. Next day, add about two small parboiled onions per person, two halves of green pepper and two halves of large tomato or two small whole tomatoes. Marinate all together until cooking time. Raw mushrooms may also be added if desired. Have ready four or five metal skewers and alternate ingredients on skewers, allowing a little space between each for ˙orough cooking. Brown over hot coals for about fifteen to twenty minutes, ˙ng tomatoes during last half of cooking time for best results. Baste ˙arinade as you cook.

Mrs. H. Manning McPhillips, Jr.

162

LAMB STEW

1 pound left over lamb roast, cubed	1 medium orange, thinly sliced
½ cup lamb gravy	1 small onion, sliced
¼ cup catsup	1 pared, cored, sliced apple
¼ cup water	½ teaspoon powdered ginger
1 (5½ ounce) can tomato juice	1 tablespoon brown sugar
	salt and pepper to taste

Combine and cook for one hour. Serve over hot, fluffy rice.

Mrs. Joseph M. Courtney

GLAZED ROAST PORK

5-6 pound pork roast	1 cup cider (or sauterne)
1 teaspoon salt	1 jar red currant jelly (10 ounces)
¼ teaspoon pepper	1 cup consommé

Wipe roast with a damp cloth, trim off excess fat. Season with salt and pepper and place in open roasting pan. Roast in 325° oven, allowing thirty-five to forty minutes per pound, or until meat thermometer registers 185°. About an hour and a half before meat is done, remove from oven and pour all fat from pan. Heat cider with jelly until blended and pour over meat. Continue roasting, basting frequently. To serve, remove meat from pan and skim excess fat from sauce. Stir in consommé, bring to a boil and serve this delicious gravy with roast.

Mrs. B. F. King, III

SPARE RIBS

4 pounds spare ribs	1 teaspoon pepper
1 cup vinegar	1 bottle A-1 sauce
1 cup water	1 bottle of Worcestershire
½ cup lemon juice	½ bottle lemon juice
1 teaspoon salt	

Over low charcoal fire baste spare ribs with sauce made of vinegar, water, lemon juice, salt and pepper every ten minutes for about forty minutes. During remaining cooking time, about twenty minutes, baste with remaining ingredients, combined.

Mrs. Julian Gewin

163

PORK CHOPS APRICOT

6 pork chops	shortening
salt and pepper	1 can apricot halves (No. 303)
flour	1 medium onion, finely chopped

Flour, salt and pepper pork chops, brown in small amount of shortening. Add apricots and juice with onion. Simmer until juice thickens, about forty-five minutes to an hour, covering the first fifteen or twenty minutes. Can be prepared ahead of time, always a hit with guests.

Mrs. D. M. Mullins

BAKED PORK CHOPS SOUTHERN STYLE

6 extra thick center cut pork chops	½ cup uncooked rice
2 tablespoons shortening	salt and pepper to taste
2 medium onions, sliced	1 (No. 2½) can tomatoes

Brown pork chops on both sides in shortening. Place in a baking dish and cover with onion slices. Sprinkle rice over dish and season well with salt and pepper. Cover with tomatoes and bake two hours in preheated 300° oven.

Mrs. H. L. Clarke

BARBECUED SPARERIBS

3-4 pounds spareribs	2 teaspoons each, vinegar and
2 small onions, sliced	Worcestershire
1 teaspoon salt	1 teaspoon each, paprika and
½ teaspoon each, red and black	chili powder
pepper	¾ cup each, catsup and water

Have spareribs cut into serving pieces. Season with salt and pepper. Place in baking pan and brown in 450° oven. Cover with onions, combine re-ʼining ingredients and pour over meat. Cover tightly and bake in 350° about an hour and a half. Baste occasionally, uncover last fifteen to brown. Serves 6.

Mrs. L. Randall Hollinger

164

SWEET AND SOUR RIBS

4 pounds ribs (cut in finger length
    pieces)
soy sauce
1 cup sugar
1 cup vinegar
2 tablespoons soy sauce

1 green pepper, cut in strips
1 tablespoon cornstarch
1 tablespoon preserved ginger,
    chopped fine
1 cup pineapple chunks, drained

Brush ribs with soy sauce and roast in 350° oven until crisp, about one hour
and fifteen minutes. Heat together in sauce pan the sugar, vinegar, soy
sauce and green pepper. Bring to a boil and add cornstarch, mixed with a
little cold water, stirring constantly until thick and transparent. Add ginger
and pineapple and spoon over hot ribs.

Mrs. K. E. Granger

SWEET AND SOUR PORK

8 lean, center cut pork chops
    or
6 butterfly pork chops (preferred)
flour, seasoned with salt, pepper
juice from canned pineapple
vinegar and brown sugar to taste

cornstarch
2 large cans chunk style pineapple
3 large carrots, sliced thin,
    crosswise
1 large bell pepper, slivered
soy sauce

Cut pork into thin slices, bite size. Roll in seasoned flour and brown in
hot cooking oil. Let meat simmer until tender and well cooked, cover after
browning. Remove meat, pour off grease. Add pineapple juice to drippings
in frying pan, then vinegar and brown sugar and soy sauce to taste. Thicken
with corn starch mixed with water. Return meat to sauce. Just before
serving add carrots and bell pepper, heat. Vegetables are supposed to be
crisp. Serves 10 to 12 over hot rice.

Mrs. Vernon M. Dukes

PORK FRIED RICE

5 or 6 lean pork chops
½ cup sliced green onions
    and tops

½ cup sliced mushrooms
3½ cups cold cooked rice
soy sauce

Cut fat from chops into tiny cubes. Fry in skillet until brown and crisp.
Push to side of skillet and fry chops until lightly done, but not too dry

165

Cool and cut meat into narrow strips, discarding bones. Leave two table-spoons fat in skillet, add meat, brown fat cubes, rice, onion and mush-rooms. Fry on high heat, stirring constantly and drizzling soy sauce on mixture until brown, in color, but not soupy (about ⅓ of a 5 ounce bottle). This dish may be prepared in advance, placed in a casserole and heated in oven.

Mrs. Jack H. Friend

STUFFED PORK CHOPS

4 double loin chops
1 medium onion, finely chopped
3 tablespoons butter
⅓ cup finely chopped mushrooms
thyme

2 tablespoons chopped parsley
½ cup toasted rolled crumbs
salt and pepper
1 egg, lightly beaten

Slit each pork chop to make a pocket for stuffing. Sauté onion in butter until transparent. Add mushrooms, a few thyme leaves, parsley and crumbs, mix thoroughly. Remove from heat, add salt and pepper to taste and stir in egg. Salt and pepper chops lightly. Stuff the pocket of each chop, secure with toothpicks. Roast, uncovered, in oven (325°) for one hour or until tender and nicely browned.

Mrs. John M. Morrissette, Jr.

PORK ROAST

Salt and pepper roast, add garlic by piercing meat and inserting thin slices, if desired. Make a paste of flour with just enough margarine to hold to-gether and thickly coat roast with this mixture. Roast in 350° oven in open pan about thirty to thirty-five minutes per pound. Half way through cook-ing time scrape mixture from roast, add as much water as you think neces-sary. Don't worry about lumps, but do mix as well as possible with a wooden spoon. Continue cooking, adding more water to gravy as needed. This paste seems to hold juices in and makes a delicious gravy. This method rks equally well on a beef roast which you plan to cook until well done. xtra piece of fat secured to top with toothpicks is suggested. Also beef cook in 325° oven.

Mrs. Jessie H. Murray

166

PORK CHOP OR CHICKEN CASSEROLE

enough red potatoes for 4	3 tablespoons fat
salt and pepper	1 medium onion, chopped
pork chops or chicken for 4	1 can cream of celery soup
flour	1 cup milk

Peel and cut (the round way) potatoes for four. Boil in water with salt and pepper until well done. Meanwhile brown meat which has been floured, salted and peppered, in fat. Sauté onion until slightly brown. The potatoes should be done by now. If so, drain well, but do not rinse. Combine in a saucepan soup, milk and sautéed onion, heat a minute or so, until mixture is smooth and well blended. Place potatoes in the bottom of a flat casserole dish, add soup mixture, mix well with potatoes. Place meat on top, cover and bake in 350° oven forty-five minutes. This casserole can be made well ahead of time and for a delicious potato dish, follow the recipe eliminating meat. Cream of chicken soup may be substituted for celery soup.

Mrs. Jessie H. Murray

ROASTED FRESH PORK HAM

Sliver two garlic pods and insert in meat in several places. Salt and pepper meat well. In shallow uncovered roasting pan place meat fat side up, preferably on rack. Roast in 300° oven approximately thirty to thirty-five minutes per pound. Should be well done.

Mrs. Frank Terrell

HAM AND BROCCOLI CASSEROLE

2 packages frozen broccoli	1 cup white sauce
thickly sliced ham	½ cup sharp Cheddar cheese

Cook broccoli in salted water until tender, drain. Place in casserole dish. Put a layer of sliced ham over broccoli. Make white sauce, add cheese and stir until cheese melts completely and sauce is smooth. Pour sauce over ham and bake in 300° oven about thirty minutes. This may also be served cold.

Mrs. Roger J. Geil

CANADIAN BACON

½ cup brown sugar	1 tablespoon cider vinegar
½ teaspoon dry mustard	pineapple juice
2 tablespoons bread crumbs	

167

Make a paste of the above ingredients and spread over desired amount of Canadian bacon. Bake in 325° oven for one hour. Baste with pineapple juice every fifteen minutes.

Mrs. William E. Drew, Jr.

BAKED SLICE OF HAM

1 large slice of ham, about 1 inch thick	1½ teaspoons whole cloves
1 tablespoon prepared mustard	4 pineapple slices or 1 cup canned apricots
3 tablespoons brown sugar	1 cup juice from fruit

Remove skin from ham. Spread with mustard and sugar. Stick cloves around the edge. Place in a flat pan. Add ½ cup fruit juice. Cook in hot oven for twenty minutes. Lower heat and cook one hour. Place fruit on ham long enough to heat thoroughly. Serve immediately. 8 adequate servings.

Mrs. Maude Luttrell

TENNESSEE HAM

1 ham	⅓ cup mustard
1 pound brown sugar	1 pound brown sugar
8 green apples, quartered	sherry wine

Soak ham for twenty-four hours, changing water three times during soaking. Wash and scrub ham with a stiff brush. Cover ham with water in a large kettle. Add one pound brown sugar and apples. Simmer eighteen minutes per pound or until iliac bone (near the shank) can be loosened. Remove skin and excess fat. Mix mustard and remaining pound of brown sugar and add sherry until pastey. Spread paste over the fatty portions of ham and roast in 350° oven until crust browns. Baste while roasting. Serve chilled.

Mrs. Barbara C. Butler

HAM AND PINEAPPLE DISH

1 tablespoon butter	2 tablespoons vinegar
1 tablespoon flour	½ teaspoon dry mustard
½ cup brown sugar	dash of pepper
1 No. 2 can crushed pineapple	1½ pounds sliced ham

Melt butter and stir in flour, add all other ingredients except ham and cook over low heat until slightly thickened and sugar is dissolved. Sauté ham lightly on both sides and place in a greased shallow baking dish. Pour sauce over ham and bake in 350° oven for thirty minutes, basting several times.

Mrs. L. Randall Hollinger

HAM WITH BRANDY CHERRY SAUCE

Cook tenderized ham as directed, but an hour before baking time is over, remove rind, score fat in diamonds. Sprinkle with one cup brown sugar and four tablespoonfuls good brandy. Pour syrup from a can of sour cherries, seasoned with 1½ tablespoons dry mustard into the pan. Finish roasting ham, basting often with syrup. Serve hot, garnished with cherries.

Mrs. Amiel W. Brinkley, Jr.

COLD HAM LOAF

2 envelopes gelatin
4 cups ground ham
1 small jar pimentos
1 small bunch celery
4 hard cooked eggs

1 small onion
½ cup mayonnaise
juice of 2 lemons
¾ cup bread crumbs

Dissolve gelatin in ½ cup cold water, then add to one cup boiling water. Mix ham, pimentos, celery, eggs, onion, all chopped. Then add mayonnaise, lemon juice, bread crumbs and boiling water with gelatin. Grease a loaf pan (or two). Turn mixture into pan and refrigerate. Good for lunch or Sunday night supper. Serves 12.

Miss Bessie Mayers

HAM LOAF WITH CHERRY SAUCE

1½ pounds ground smoked ham
1 pound ground fresh pork
2 eggs, beaten
1 cup wheat flakes or 1 cup
   Pepperidge Farm Dressing

2 tablespoons chopped green
   pepper
2 tablespoons chopped onion
½ cup milk

Combine all ingredients, mix well and put into lightly greased loaf pan. TOPPING:

¼ cup brown sugar   ¼ teaspoon powdered cloves
1 tablespoon prepared mustard

Combine ingredients and spread on top of loaf. Bake in 350° oven one and a half hours. Drain well and invert on platter. Cool in refrigerator. (Must be made the day before needed.)

CHERRY SAUCE:

2½ cups red tart pitted cherries   2 tablespoons cornstarch
    (reserve liquid)   ½ teaspoon cloves
½ cup sugar

In double boiler mix sugar, cornstarch and cloves and gradually stir in cherry liquid. Cook, stirring constantly, until mixture thickens. Add ¼ teaspoon red food coloring. Thin with sherry. Serve hot over cold thinly sliced loaf.

Mrs. David B. Freeman, Jr.

SWEDISH HAM BALLS IN BROWN SAUCE

1 pound ground ham   1 cup brown sugar
1½ pounds ground pork   1 teaspoon dry mustard
2 cups bread crumbs   ½ cup vinegar
2 eggs, well beaten   ½ cup water
1 cup milk

Combine meats, crumbs, eggs and milk, mixing well. Form into balls and place in pan. Combine remaining ingredients and stir until sugar dissolves. Pour over meat balls and bake for one hour in 325° oven, basting frequently. Makes 16 balls.

Mrs. Frank P. Ellis, Jr.

HAM LOAF

2 teaspoons butter   2 tablespoons tomato catsup
1 medium onion, chopped   2 teaspoons Worcestershire
2 cups ground, cooked ham   sauce
2 eggs, well beaten   ¼ teaspoon prepared mustard
½ cup bread crumbs   salt and pepper to taste

Melt butter in frying pan. When hot add chopped onion, fry until not quite brown. Add to ham, which has been mixed with all the remaining ingredients, and shape into a loaf. Place in well greased baking pan in a

170

moderate oven (350°) for about forty minutes. Turn out on a hot platter and serve with raisin sauce, or serve with prepared horseradish which has been mixed with whipped cream. Serves 4.

RAISIN SAUCE:

1 cup apple cider	¼ cup seeded raisins
2 tablespoons flour	pinch of salt
2 tablespoons butter	

Melt butter in sauce pan. Add flour and salt and brown slightly. Add cider gradually, stirring constantly to make smooth sauce. Add raisins, serve hot.

Mrs. George Irvine

MY FAVORITES

MY FAVORITES

VEGETABLE FIESTA

ARTICHOKE AND MUSHROOM CASSEROLE

1 (No. 2) can artichoke hearts	heavy cream to cover mushrooms
1 (No. 2) can mushrooms	salt and pepper to taste
2 tablespoons butter	Parmesan cheese

Cut artichoke hearts and place in greased casserole. Saute mushrooms in butter, add cream to cover mushrooms. Cook over low fire until much of cream is absorbed, salt and pepper to taste. Pour mixture over artichokes and sprinkle with a generous amount of grated Parmesan cheese. Bake until good and hot. Serves 4.

Mrs. Henry R. Luscher, Jr.

BOILED ARTICHOKES

Cut off stems, the tough bottom leaves and snip thorny tops. Soak in salted water for about thirty minutes. Place in large pot and fill with salted water to cover. Bring to a boil and cook about forty-five minutes. Drain and serve with melted butter, mayonnaise or hollandaise sauce.

Mrs. Kenneth Hannon

ARTICHOKES IN LEMON-HERB BUTTER

½ cup finely minced onion	¾ cup canned chicken broth
½ clove garlic	3 tablespoons lemon juice
2 tablespoons butter	1½ teaspoon salt
2 (15 ounce) cans artichoke hearts	½ teaspoon oregano
	½ teaspoon grated lemon rind

173

VEGETABLE FIESTA

In a saucepan, sauté onion and garlic in butter, until tender. Add chicken broth and artichoke hearts. Add seasonings and rind. Simmer about ten minutes. Serves six.

Mrs. F. L. DuValle

ARTICHOKES STUFFED

4 large or 6 medium artichokes
¼ pound butter or margarine
1 cup water
1 package Pepperidge Farm
    seasoned bread dressing
juice from 2 garlic pods

4 ounces Roquefort cheese
olive oil
vinegar
salt to taste
pepper

Parboil artichokes or cook until not quite tender enough to each and still firm enough to handle without separating. Put aside to cool. Melt butter in water. Mix this into bread dressing, add garlic juice. Break roquefort into small pieces and toss all together. Beginning at the outside bottom leaves, pack a small amount of the mixture in and around each layer of leaves. Place in large pot or Dutch oven on a rack over a small amount of water. Dribble Italian sauce of olive oil, vinegar, salt and pepper over and around the artichokes taking care to get a good part around the heart section. Cover and steam until leaves are easily removed.

Mrs. Charles McEnry

FRESH ASPARAGUS

Wash well and pare off triangular points up sides. Soak in cold water. Tie together and cut stems off to bright green on bottom. Place, standing up, in old coffee pot or deep pot. Fill one third way up with water and add salt. Turn on high heat until water boils, reduce to medium heat. Cover and steam until tender when tested with sharp fork, cooking time depends on desired crispness. Serve with lemon juice, butter and pepper. One pound is usually needed for two people.

Mrs. Ernest L. Brown

ASPARAGUS WITH HORSERADISH SAUCE

1 cup sour cream
3 tablespoons horseradish sauce
3 tablespoons butter

¾ cup soft bread crumbs
2 packages frozen or 2 cans
    green asparagus

174

Heat sour cream in double boiler over hot, not boiling, water. Add horseradish. Melt butter and fry bread crumbs until crisp and golden. Cook asparagus according to directions. Place asparagus in serving dish, or preferably a chafing dish, and serve. Sprinkle with paprika. Serves 6.

Mrs. W. B. Taylor, Jr.

ASPARAGUS LOAF AU GRATIN

1 (1 pound) can asparagus tips
pimento strips
2 tablespoons butter
4 tablespoons flour
1 cup milk
¼ cup liquid from asparagus

½ teaspoon salt
⅛ teaspoon pepper
2 cups grated cheese
1¾ cups fine soft bread crumbs
2 eggs, slightly beaten

Grease a loaf pan and alternate asparagus and pimento strips across bottom. Make cream sauce with butter, flour, milk and asparagus liquid, cook until thick. Add salt, pepper and cheese, stir until cheese melts. Stir in crumbs. Add to eggs and fold in remaining asparagus tips, cut up. Pour into loaf pan and place in a pan of hot water. Bake in 325° oven for one hour or until firm.

Mrs. Marshall J. Demouy

ASPARAGUS CASSEROLE

2 cans asparagus spears
3 tablespoons butter
3 teaspoons flour
¾ cup asparagus juice
¼ cup milk
salt to taste
Worcestershire to taste

Tabasco to taste
pepper to taste
garlic salt to taste
onion salt to taste
1 cup sharp cheese, grated
bread crumbs

Drain asparagus, reserving juice. Melt butter, add flour, asparagus juice and milk. Cook as white sauce until thickened, add salt. Add remaining seasonings. Add grated cheese to sauce, stirring slowly. Alternate layers of asparagus spears and sauce, top with crumbs. Bake in 400° oven until sauce bubbles.

Mrs. James Coil, Jr.

ASPARAGUS AND EGG CASSEROLE

2 tablespoons butter or margarine	1 cup grated cheese
2 tablespoons flour	1 small can pimento, chopped
salt and pepper to taste	1 (No. 1) can green asparagus tips
1 cup liquid (mixed asparagus juice and milk)	3 hard boiled eggs
	grated almonds (optional)

Melt butter and heat to bubbling point, add flour, salt and pepper. Add liquid gradually and cook until thick. Add cheese and pimento. In a greased baking dish arrange a layer of asparagus, then a layer of eggs, then sauce. Repeat. Grated almonds may be sprinkled on top if desired. Bake in 350° oven long enough to heat thoroughly. Can be made the day before using.

Mrs. Ben F. King

BAKED BEANS

1 quart pea beans	½ teaspoon dry mustard
½ pound salt pork	1 medium onion
2 teaspoons salt	2 bay leaves
¼ cup molasses	½ cup heavy cream

Wash beans and soak overnight in cold water. In the morning, drain, cover with fresh water and simmer until skins break. Scald the pork for one minute in boiling water, add to beans. Add salt, molasses, mustard and press in among the beans. Add onion and bay leaves. Add boiling water to cover. Cover and bake in 250° oven for about eight hours without stirring. Add water as necessary and uncover during last half hour of cooking time. Dribble cream over beans and let brown for thirty minutes. Remove onion and bay leaf and serve.

Mrs. Hunter Boulo

SPICED BEETS

1 can tiny whole beets (8 ounces)	2 tablespoons sugar
	2 tablespoons vinegar

Drain beet juice into saucepan. Add sugar and vinegar. Bring juice to a boil, simmer ten minutes. Slice beets into thin slices. Add sliced beets to juice and simmer ten to fifteen minutes. These are also good chilled and served as a salad with sour cream. Serves three or four.

Mrs. H. C. Slaton, Jr.

176

VEGETABLE FIESTA

HARVARD BEETS

1 onion, cut fine	3 tablespoons vinegar
1 tablespoon butter	juice from canned beets
2 tablespoons flour	salt and pepper to taste
½ cup water	1 can sliced beets
1 tablespoon sugar	

Cover onion with cold water and simmer until tender. Melt butter, add flour, water, sugar, vinegar, juice from beets, salt and pepper. Add onion and beets. Best if prepared ahead and reheated several hours later. Serves 6.

Mrs. Marion Adams, Sr.

BEETS AND PINEAPPLE

1 No. 2 can pineapple chunks	1 No. 303 can sliced and diced
liquid from canned pineapple	pickled beets
2 tablespoons cornstarch	1 teaspoon vinegar
juice from canned beets	¾ teaspoon salt

Drain pineapple chunks, reserving syrup. Blend two tablespoons of syrup with cornstarch. Drain beets, mix beet juice with one-half cup pineapple syrup and cornstarch mixture. Heat juices, stirring constantly until thickened. Add vinegar, salt and drained pineapple chunks to the beets. Heat through.

Mrs. Robert Meador

DUTCH GREEN BEANS

1 package frozen whole green beans	½ tablespoon grated onion
2 tablespoons butter	2 tablespoons white vinegar
¼ cup ale	1 tablespoon flour
1 teaspoon celery salt	2 tablespoons brown sugar
	½ cup crumbled, cooked bacon

Cook beans over low heat in butter and ale. Drain, reserving liquid. Stir salt, onion and vinegar into liquid. Mix flour with sugar and stir into mixture. Cook, stirring constantly, over low heat until mixture thickens. Add beans and bacon to sauce and serve hot. Serves 4.

Mrs. T. G. St. John, Jr.

177

GREEN BEANS WITH ONIONS

2 packages French cut frozen green beans	2 teaspoons chopped garlic
	3 tablespoons dry white wine
½ cup sweet butter	½ teaspoon salt
½ cup slivered almonds	¼ teaspoon pepper
2 tablespoons brown sugar	1 large jar small onions

Cook beans according to directions. Drain. Melt butter in skillet with tight lid. Stir in almonds, sugar, garlic, wine and seasonings. Add drained onions and simmer twenty to thirty minutes, coating onions well. Pour over hot beans. Serves 6.

Mrs. Charles Rutherford

GREEN BEANS WITH WATER CHESTNUTS IN SOUR CREAM

Cook 1 cup drained water chestnuts in 3 tablespoons butter for three minutes. Cook 3 cups of green beans until barely tender. Drain. Stir in ½ cup sour cream and ¼ teaspoon salt. Add water chestnuts and heat vegetables thoroughly over very low heat. Serve at once.

Mrs. Robert Meador

BEANS HARRIGAN

French cut green beans (frozen, 1 package for three people)	dash of cream (optional)
	water chestnuts (4-6 cans for 12 people)
ham hock	
cream sauce (or mushroom soup, 1 can per package of beans)	whole almonds
	toasted bread crumbs
salt and pepper to taste	butter
white wine (optional)	

Cook beans slowly with ham hock. Mix cream sauce, add salt and pepper to taste. White wine or cream may be added now to thin sauce. Layer beans in casserole, add sauce, layer water chestnuts, sauce, beans, etc. until full. Add almonds and toasted bread crumbs. Dot with butter and bake in 350° oven twenty-five minutes.

Kay Harrigan Woods

FRENCH GREEN BEAN CASSEROLE

1 large onion, thinly sliced
¾ stick butter or margarine
2 cans French cut green beans
  or 2 packages frozen, cooked
1 can bean sprouts

1 can water chestnuts
1 can cream of mushroom soup
2 cups sharp cheese, grated
2 cans French fried onion rings
½ cup sherry wine (optional)

Sauté onion in butter until transparent. Drain beans, bean sprouts and water chestnuts. Mix vegetables with soup, add wine, mix well. Grease 9 x 13 x 2 inch baking dish with one-fourth stick butter. Pour entire mixture in dish, cover with grated cheese, then onion rings. Bake in 350° oven thirty-five minutes. This dish can be made a day ahead, adding cheese and onion rings when ready to bake. The dish can be prepared a week ahead, frozen without cheese and onions.

Mrs. Robert Doyle

STRINGBEAN CASSEROLE

2 packages frozen French cut
  string beans
1 can mushrooms
1 medium onion, chopped
½ stick margarine
1 tablespoon flour
1 cup milk

⅓ cup medium sharp cheese,
  grated
½ teaspoon Tabasco
2 teaspoons soy sauce
salt and pepper to taste
½ can water chestnuts
sliced almonds, sautéed

Cook beans according to package direction. Sauté mushrooms and onion in margarine. Sprinkle in flour, then slowly add cheese, Tabasco, soy sauce, salt and pepper. Let thicken, add water chestnuts. Mix beans with sauce and turn into greased casserole. Sprinkle almonds over top. Bake fifteen to twenty minutes in 375° oven.

Mrs. Inman P. Ellis

GREEN BEANS

2 packages frozen French cut
  green beans
2 tablespoons butter
2 tablespoons lemon juice

½ teaspoon white pepper
¼ cup slivered almonds
1 teaspoon Beau Monde

179

VEGETABLE FIESTA

Cook according to package directions, drain and season with remaining ingredients.

Mrs. Julian Gewin

FRESH BROCCOLI

Pare stems and cut off bottoms. Wash well in cold water. Tie together, stand up in wide boiler. Cover and steam in salted water until stems are fork tender. Serve with favorite dressing.

Mrs. Ernest L. Brown

BROCCOLI—RICE—CHEESE CASSEROLE

3 packages frozen chopped
   broccoli
2 tablespoons chopped onion
2 tablespoons margarine
1 can cream of chicken soup

1 8 ounce jar Cheese Whiz
½ cup rice (Uncle Ben's long
   grain) cooked in 1½ cups
   water

Cook broccoli. Sauté onion in margarine, add soup and one can water. Add broccoli, cheese and cooked rice. Mix thoroughly. Put in casserole, sprinkle with paprika and bake for twenty to twenty-five minutes in 350° oven. Serves 12.

Mrs. E. S. Greer

BROCCOLI AND BACON

Cook frozen broccoli according to directions on the package. Make white sauce (about ½ cup per broccoli pack). Fry bacon slices (ten to fifteen per broccoli pack) as crisp as possible. Drain well and allow to cool. Crumble between fingers until completely pulverized. Hard boil one egg per broccoli pack. Mash with fork to pulverize. Mix bacon and egg. Pour white sauce over broccoli, sprinkle egg and bacon on top. Serve immediately.

Mrs. Frank Ellis, Jr.

180

BROCCOLI AU GRATIN

6 tablespoons butter
6 tablespoons flour
1½ teaspoon salt
¼ teaspoon dry mustard
2¼ cups milk
¾ cup diced cheese

3 packages chopped broccoli,
  cooked
Parmesan cheese
paprika
slivered almonds

Melt butter, add flour, salt and mustard. Cook until bubbly, add milk and cook until thick and smooth. Add cheese and stir until melted. Add drained broccoli, pour into greased casserole, sprinkle with cheese, paprika and almonds. Bake in 350° oven thirty minutes. Serves eight.

Mrs. Marion S. Adams, Jr.

BRUSSEL SPROUTS

1 quart Brussel sprouts
5 tablespoons butter
2½ tablespoons tarragon vinegar

½ cup shredded blanched
  almonds slightly toasted

Cook Brussel sprouts in boiling salted water ten to twelve minutes. Drain well. Melt butter and let brown, remove from heat. Add tarragon vinegar and almonds. Heat to boiling point and pour over sprouts.

Mrs. Frank Sauer

CABBAGE CASSEROLE

1 cabbage
at least 1 cup cream sauce

¾ cup sharp cheese, grated

Shred cabbage as for slaw, boil in salted water to blanch, strain in collander. Layer cabbage and cream sauce in baking dish, top with strong grated cheese and bake in 325° oven until cheese melts. Before serving, top with chopped pimento.

Mrs. Frank Ellis, Jr.

CARROT CROQUETTES

1 bunch carrots (small)
1 egg
salt to taste

2 tablespoons sugar
flour
1 teaspoon baking powder

Cook carrots until done and mash through a sieve. Beat egg and add salt to taste. Mix with carrots, then add sugar and enough flour to hold together. Add baking powder. Shape into croquettes and fry in deep fat until brown, roll in sugar and serve.

Mrs. Ernest Brown

CARROT SOUFFLÉ

1 cup carrots	Cream sauce (about 1 cup)
3 to 5 eggs	salt, pepper and butter

Cook carrots until done. Mash. Separate eggs. Make cream sauce. Fold in egg yolks, then carrots. Beat egg whites until stiff, fold into mixture. Add salt and pepper to taste. Turn into lightly greased casserole, dot with butter and bake 30 minutes in preheated 350° oven. Serve at once. Serves 6.

Mrs. H. M. McPhillips, Jr.

CARROT RING

1 large bunch carrots	½ teaspoon sugar
1 cup thick cream sauce	dash of grated nutmeg
¼ teaspoon salt	

Boil carrots until tender and mash. Pour cream sauce over carrots; season with salt, sugar and nutmeg. Blend mixture and place in a greased ring mold. Set in a shallow pan with an inch of water in bottom and bake for about thirty minutes in 300° oven. Turn out on a platter and fill center with creamed peas and mushrooms, if desired.

Mrs. Leon McVay, Jr.

CAULIFLOWER

Boil and drain cauliflower. Melt two sticks of butter with one half teaspoon anchovy paste, pour over cauliflower and sprinkle with chopped chives.

Mrs. Frank Sauer

CAULIFLOWER SAUTÉ

2 tablespoon butter	½ cup dry white wine
1 medium cauliflower	1 tablespoon Mu Yen seasoning
1 cup celery, chopped very fine	(optional)
1 tablespoon grated onion	½ teaspoon salt
1 tablespoon chicken stock base	½ teaspoon black pepper

Melt butter in skillet, slowly add cauliflower, celery and onion. Combine chicken stock base with wine, Mu Yen, salt and pepper, pour into cauliflower, cook quickly, turning constantly with pancake turner. Cook until vegetables are tender and clear, eight to ten minutes. Serve at once.

Mrs. Harry Partridge

CAULIFLOWER AU GRATIN

4 ounces elbow macaroni	1½ cups milk
3 tablespoons butter	1 cup grated American cheese
3 tablespoons flour	1½ cups steamed cauliflower
1½ teaspoons salt	¼ cup buttered bread crumbs
½ teaspoon paprika	

Cook macaroni in boiling salted water ten minutes, drain and rinse. Melt butter, stir in flour, salt and paprika. Gradually add milk, stirring until thickened. Add cheese and steamed cauliflower. Fold in macaroni. Pour into greased casserole, sprinkle with bread crumbs. Bake fifteen minutes in 350° oven. Serves 4.

Mrs. Willis Brown

CORN PUDDING I

1 (303) can cream style white corn	½ teaspoon salt
	⅛ teaspoon pepper
2 eggs, beaten	1 tablespoon minced onion

Combine in greased baking dish, dot with butter and bake in 325° oven about fifty minutes. Serves 3.

Mrs. William Drew

VEGETABLE FIESTA

CORN PUDDING II

1 can (1 lb.) cream style corn	1 tablespoon sugar
½ cup milk	3 eggs, separated
1 tablespoon butter	

In baking dish mix corn, milk, butter, sugar and beaten egg yolks. Beat egg whites and fold into corn mixture. Bake, uncovered in 350° oven for thirty-five minutes. Serves 4 generously.

Mrs. Thomas B. Martenstein

CORN PUDDING III

3 tablespoons butter or margarine	½ teaspoon monosodium glutamate
¼ cup sugar	1½ cups milk
2 eggs	2½ cups fresh cut corn off cob
½ teaspoon salt	

Cream butter and sugar, beat in eggs. Add salt, monosodium glutamate and milk. Add corn. Bake in 350° oven 45 to 60 minutes or until pudding is firm. (knife comes out clean). Serves 6.

Mrs. John Pitman

STEWED CORN

| 6 ears fresh corn | ½ cup milk |
| ½ stick butter | 1 teaspoon salt |

Grate corn to core. With back of knife scrape juice from each cob. Place over boiling water with remaining ingredients and cook about an hour and a half, adding more milk if necessary.

Mrs. John Blacksher

DIXIE FRIED CORN

Cut fresh white corn off cob, once or twice, depending on size of kernels. Scrape milk from cob. Heat a mixture of half bacon grease and half cooking oil in iron skillet. Add corn to hot grease and fry. As corn sticks and browns turn and mash around. When about one half the corn is brown lower heat and add a cup of boiling water and salt and pepper to taste. Cover and simmer to desired thickness. More water may be added, if desired.

Mrs. Ernest L. Brown

184

CORN AND SOUR CREAM

2 tablespoons chopped onion
2 tablespoons butter
2 tablespoons flour
1 teaspoon salt
1 cup sour cream

2 cans (12 ounces each) whole
   kernel corn
½ pound bacon
1 tablespoon parsley, chopped

Cook onion in butter until soft, blend in flour and salt. Cook bacon and drain. Add sour cream to first mixture gradually, stirring constantly. Heat to boiling, add corn, bring to boil, fold in ½ cup crumbled bacon. Turn into serving dish, garnish with remaining bacon and parsley.

Mrs. Hunter Boulo

FRENCH FRIED EGGPLANT STICKS

1 (1 pound) eggplant
¾ cup fine dry bread crumbs
6 tablespoons grated Parmesan
   cheese

2½ teaspoons salt
¼ teaspoon freshly ground pepper
2 eggs, beaten
2 tablespoons milk

Peel and cut eggplant into crosswise slices one half inch thick. Cut each slice into one half inch strips, soak in water for fifteen minutes. Combine bread crumbs, cheese, salt and pepper. Beat eggs with the milk. Dip eggplant sticks into egg mixture, then into bread crumbs. Fry sticks in deep fat or oil preheated to 375°. Sprinkle with celery salt. Drain on brown paper or paper towel. Serve hot. Serves 6.

Mrs. Norman A. Nicolson

EGGPLANT CASSEROLE

1 eggplant
hard cooked egg
buttered bread crumbs

grated cheese
cream sauce

Peel eggplant and cook in boiling, salted water until tender. Drain. Place layer of eggplant, slice hard cooked egg and grated cheese in baking dish. Over this pour cream sauce, repeat. Top with buttered bread crumbs and grated cheese. Bake in 375° oven for fifteen minutes.

Mrs. Walter Ogburn

185

CREOLE EGGPLANT

1 large eggplant	seasoned bread crumbs
1 onion, chopped fine	1 tablespoon dried parsley
½ bell pepper, chopped fine	pinch of oregano
1½ fresh tomatoes, chopped	3 tablespoons Parmesan cheese
salt and pepper to taste	butter
1 large egg (or two small)	

Peel, slice and soak eggplant in cold salted water for fifteen to twenty minutes. Simmer onion, bell pepper and tomato in small amount of water until done. Drain eggplant slices and cook with salt and pepper until done. Mash or whip until fluffy. Drain onion mixture and mix with eggplant. Beat egg and add to eggplant with enough bread crumbs to keep mixture from being runny. Add salt and pepper, parsley, oregano and cheese. Pour into casserole and top with bread crumbs and Parmesan cheese. Dot with butter. Bake in 300° oven until top is browned. Serves 6.

Mrs. Ernest Brown

EGGPLANT—TOMATO CASSEROLE

1 large eggplant	1 onion, chopped
5 medium tomatoes	⅛ teaspoon rosemary
4 tablespoons good imported	½ teaspoon salt
olive oil (or corn oil)	Parmesan cheese
1 clove garlic	

Peel eggplant, cut into one half inch slices and boil in a small amount of salted water ten minutes or until tender. Peel and chop tomatoes; saute tomatoes, onion, garlic and seasonings in olive oil until tomatoes are cooked. Remove garlic. Drain eggplant and place in casserole, cover with tomato sauce, sprinkle generously with Parmesan cheese and bake in 350° oven thirty minutes. Serves 4.

Mrs. Marion S. Adams, Jr.

BAKED EGGPLANT

1 medium or large eggplant	4 slices toasted bread
1 cup chopped celery	2 eggs
¾ cup chopped onion	1 can minced clams
½ stick butter or margarine	salt and pepper to taste

186

Parboil eggplant about eight minutes. Cut in half and scoop out pulp. Sauté celery and onion in butter, but do not brown. Make a dressing with celery, onion, toasted bread, eggs, pulp of eggplant and clams. Bake in greased casserole in 250°-300° oven for forty-five minutes.

Mrs. Norman Pitman

MUSHROOM SAUTÉ

1 pound fresh mushrooms
½ stick butter or margarine
2 cloves pressed garlic

1 tablespoon onion, finely
 chopped
½ cup red wine or sherry

Wash mushrooms, leaving buttons whole and chopping stems. Saute in butter, adding garlic and onion. When tender add wine. Delicious addition to any red meat.

Mrs. Frank E. Stone

CHESTNUT AND MUSHROOM CASSEROLE I

5 lbs. fresh mushrooms
2½ cans chestnuts (chestnuts packed
 in water 2 pound can)
2 cups milk (or half milk-half cream)
4 heaping teaspoons flour
1 can mushroom soup, 12 ounces

New York state cheese, grated
1 stick butter
1 scant teaspoon granulated
 bouillon cube
½ teaspoon salt
½ teaspoon white pepper

Put mushrooms and chestnuts in three quart casserole. Make white sauce using milk, flour, butter, bouillon cube, salt, pepper and soup. Pour over chestnuts and mushrooms. Top with grated cheese. Bake in 350° oven twenty-five minutes. Serves 20.

Mrs. Basil McNeely

CHESTNUT AND MUSHROOM CASSEROLE II

½ pound chestnuts
½ pound mushrooms

Sharp cheddar cheese, thinly sliced
rich cream sauce

Boil and peel chestnuts. Wash and slice raw mushrooms. Place layer of each in casserole with thinly sliced cheese between. Pour cream sauce over all. Top with grated cheese. Bake in moderate oven about thirty minutes.

Mrs. Robert Mudd

VEGETABLE FIESTA

FRIED OKRA

Slice okra thin and roll in corn meal with salt and pepper. Fry in hot grease until brown. Grease or oil may be added as needed. Drain on paper.

Mrs. Ernest L. Brown

OKRA AND TOMATOES

2 medium to small onions, chopped	1 large can tomatoes
cooking oil	salt
1 package cut frozen okra	freshly ground black pepper
	2 small bay leaves

Sauté onions in as little oil as possible until slightly done. Add frozen okra or the equivalent in fresh okra. Turn heat very low and cook for five minutes after okra has thawed. If fresh okra is used, simply cook five minutes. Add tomatoes, salt and pepper to taste and bay leaves. Cook on top of stove over extremely low heat until thick, about forty-five minutes to an hour. This dish is especially good with pork.

Mrs. Jessie H. Murray

GREEN PEAS

Simmer 2 cups fresh peas in ¼ cup water with 4 lettuce leaves, one small onion sliced, 2 tablespoon butter, I sprig parsley, ¼ teaspoon sugar, pinch of thyme and salt and pepper to taste. Cover tightly and cook about 30 minutes until peas are tender. Serves 4.

Mrs. Frank Frazer

GREEN PEAS AND MUSHROOMS

Combine:

1 can green peas	1 hard cooked egg, chopped
½ can mushroom soup	1 tablespoon butter
1 small can sliced mushrooms	salt and pepper
2 tablespoons chili sauce	

Heat in double boiler and serve.

Mrs. Frank P. Ellis, Jr.

VEGETABLE FIESTA

GREEN PEA CASSEROLE

medium cream sauce	1 small jar of sliced pimentos
1 large can green peas	sharp cheese, grated
3 hard boiled eggs	butter, salt and pepper

Prepare cream sauce, of medium thickness. Drain green peas and put them in a casserole dish. Pour in cream sauce and coarsely chopped hard boiled eggs. Add salt, pepper and a little butter. Add pimentos and cover dish with a generous amount of grated cheese. Bake in moderate oven until cheese is thoroughly melted.

Jesslynn Johnson

ENGLISH PEAS AND WATER CHESTNUTS

2 packages frozen English peas   1½ cups cheese sauce
1 can water chestnuts, chopped

Cook peas until almost done. In casserole, place a layer of peas and a layer of cheese sauce, then a layer of water chestnuts. Top with cheese sauce. Bake in 350° oven until bubbly, thirty to forty minutes. Serves 6.

Mrs. John H. Wilson

POTATO BALLS

2 cups creamed potatoes   1 teaspoon baking powder
1 well beaten egg   flour
¾ teaspoon salt

Rub creamed potatoes through a sieve, add egg, salt, baking powder. Add enough flour to make the mixture stiff enough to mold into small balls. Fry in smoking fat, drain and serve hot.

Mrs. Paul Sheldon

SOUR CREAM GRILLED POTATOES

1½ cups sliced, cooked potatoes   1 package onion soup mix
salt and pepper   ¼ cup light cream
1 pint sour cream   broiler foil

Place sliced potatoes in center of a fourteen inch square of foil. Season with salt and pepper. Combine sour cream, onion soup mix and cream and pour over potatoes. Seal foil and place on grill for twenty minutes.

189

Serves 6. (Sliced raw potatoes may be used—cook forty-five minutes to an hour.)

Mrs. Wallace S. Clark, II

POMMES DE TERRE SOUFFLÉS

Peel potatoes. Cut into ⅛ inch slices, lengthwise, place in a wire basket and run under cold water to remove excess starch. Dry potatoes. Have two kettles of fat, one of moderate temperature, the other very hot. Place some of the potatoes in frying basket in moderately hot fat and cook until they rise to the top and the edges show slight signs of puffing. (If the puff does not develop, start again.) When puffing appears, transfer immediately to hot fat, cook until fully puffed and browned. Drain, salt and serve immediately.

Mrs. Leon McVay, Jr.

AU GRATIN POTATOES

8 medium potatoes	1½ cups grated sharp cheese
1 large onion, chopped	salt and pepper to taste
½ green pepper, chopped	about 2 tablespoons parsley
6 tablespoons butter	(fresh or dried)
6 tablespoons flour	thin cheese slices
3 cups milk	paprika

Boil potatoes and set aside to cool. When cool, peel and cut up, as for salad. Simmer together until tender the onion and green pepper, drain and set aside. Make three cups cream sauce using butter, flour, milk and adding grated cheese. Add onions, pepper, salt and pepper. Add parsley to sauce and mix well with potatoes. Transfer to baking dish, cover with sliced cheese, sprinkle with paprika and bake in 300° oven for thirty minutes. Serves 10.

Mrs. Ernest Brown

POTATO CASSEROLE

5 cups freshly cooked mashed pota-	2 tablespoons finely grated onion
toes (about 6 medium potatoes	2½ teaspoons salt
cooked with 2 teaspoons salt)	¼ teaspoon pepper
3 cups cream style cottage cheese	melted butter
1 cup commercial sour cream	½ cup toasted almonds

190

VEGETABLE FIESTA

Mash potatoes thoroughly using no milk or butter. Buzz cottage cheese in blender. Mix warm mashed potatoes and cheese. Add sour cream, onion, salt and pepper. Spoon into shallow buttered 2 quart casserole. Brush surface with melted butter. Bake in 350° oven for ½ hour. Place under broiler for a few minutes to brown lightly. Sprinkle with toasted almonds.

Mrs. John D. Brady

PENNSYLVANIA DUTCH POTATO DRESSING

8 medium potatoes	2 celery stalks, chopped
salt and pepper to taste	1 small bell pepper, chopped
butter	1 medium onion, chopped
milk	½ stick margarine
½ stick margarine	1 cup fresh bread crumbs

Peel and boil potatoes in salted water until done. Drain, mash and add salt, pepper, milk and butter to taste, as for creamed potatoes. While potatoes are cooking sauté celery, bell pepper and onion in one-half stick margarine. When vegetables are limp, add one-half stick margarine and bread crumbs and sauté until bread is brown. Fold into creamed potatoes and turn into greased one and a half quart casserole. Dot with butter and bake in 325° oven until brown. This can be made ahead. Serves 8 to 10.

Mrs. Kenneth Hannon

ARNAUD'S PINEAPPLE AND LOUISIANA YAMS FLAMBEÉ A LA GERMAINE

Boil 2 yams and slice. Roll 4 slices pineapple and sliced yams in flour, then in milk, then roll in flour again. Fry pineapple and yams in oil or shortening until golden brown. Place cherry in the center of each pineapple. Place pineapple and yams in oven dish and cover freely with sugar. Bake in moderate oven for five minutes. When ready to serve, pour rum over mixture, light with match and then, pour sherry wine over all. Serves 4.

Mrs. Frank Webb

DRAMBUIE YAMS

4-6 yams or sweet potatoes	2 tablespoons brown sugar
⅛ pound butter	2 ounces Drambuie
3 tablespoons honey	

Steam potatoes until tender, but not soft. Cool slightly and peel. Arrange whole potatoes in a baking dish. Spread honey, brown sugar, chunks of butter and 1 ounce Drambuie over potatoes. Bake in 350°-375° oven for fifteen to twenty minutes. Approximately five minutes before removing from oven pour remaining Drambuie over potatoes. Cut potatoes in half before serving. 4-6 servings.

Mrs. James Coil, Jr.

YAM CROQUETTES

5 medium sweet potatoes	2 teaspoons lemon juice
2 tablespoons sugar	6 marshmallows, halved
2 eggs, separated	3 cups crushed corn flakes
2 tablespoons butter	

Boil, peel and mash sweet potatoes, add sugar, egg yolks, butter and lemon juice; mix well. Shape around marshmallow halves into twelve balls, chill. Dip in slightly beaten egg whites, coat with corn flakes. Fry in deep fat (375°). Serves six.

Mrs. Browne Mercer

SHUMP'S SWEET POTATO PONE

4 large sweet potatoes	cinnamon to taste
pinch of salt	nutmeg to taste
sugar to taste	milk
2 eggs	1 teaspoon baking powder

Grate sweet potatoes. Add salt, sugar, eggs, spices and enough milk to make corn bread consistency. (about one cup milk). Add baking powder. Grease casserole well with one cooking spoon full lard, pour mixture into casserole and bake in 350° oven until mixture begins to set and brown. Add butter the size of an egg, stir in well. Bake, stirring occasionally, until cooked through, about one hour. Serves six and is delicious.

Mrs. T. M. Taul, Jr.

SWEET POTATO CASSEROLE

3 large baked sweet potatoes	2 tablespoons marmalade
½ cup orange juice	1 small package or ¼ cup raisins
¼ cup brown sugar	2 tablespoons butter
1 teaspoon cinnamon	

192

Mash pulp of potatoes thoroughly. Add remaining ingredients and place in greased casserole. Bake in preheated 350° oven twenty minutes. Liquor of your choice may be added, being careful about too much liquid.

Mrs. Jere Austill, Jr.

DELICIOUS SPINACH

3 pounds prepared raw spinach   1 tablespoon grated onion
piece of butter the size of an egg   ¼ pint heavy cream

Place spinach in boiling water for three minutes. Place butter in an iron pan or skillet and when bubbling shake in onion and brown, being careful not to burn. Add chopped spinach and heavy cream, heat and serve. Serves 10.

Mrs. Frank Terrell

SPINACH SOUFFLE

4 tablespoons butter   1 cup milk
4 tablespoons flour   ½ cup grated cheese
1 teaspoon salt   1 egg
½ teaspoon pepper   1 cup cooked spinach

Melt butter, remove from heat, blend in flour and seasonings. Mix until smooth, gradually stirring in milk and mixing until well blended. Cook over low heat, stirring constantly until thick and smooth. Stir in cheese and egg, mix until cheese is dissolved. Add spinach, mixing well. Pour into greased casserole and bake for forty-five minutes in 350° oven. Serves 4.

Mrs. Jere Austill, Sr.

SPINACH MOLDS

2 cups milk   ⅛ teaspoon pepper
1½ cups bread crumbs   4 eggs
(2½ slices)   2 cups cooked spinach
4 tablespoons butter   1 teaspoon onion
1 teaspoon salt   1 tablespoon vinegar

Scald milk, add bread crumbs, butter, salt and pepper, blend well. Add slightly beaten eggs. Combine with well drained, finely chopped spinach to which onion and vinegar have been added. Fill greased molds, bake in a pan of hot water in 350° oven forty to forty-five minutes or until knife

193

comes out clean when inserted. Unmold, serve with well seasoned cheese sauce and hot asparagus. Serves twelve.

Mrs. James Irby

SQUASH CASSEROLE

2 pounds tender yellow squash
1 medium onion
1 bay leaf
1 tablespoon parsley flakes
1 tablespoon sugar
2 teaspoon salt

1½ cups hot, rich cream sauce
2 egg yolks, well beaten
6 tablespoons grated Swiss cheese
fine toast crumbs
salt and Cayenne pepper to taste

Combine first six ingredients and boil until tender. Remove bay leaf and strain excess liquid. Add to cream sauce, add well beaten egg yolks and 4 tablespoons grated cheese. Place in buttered casserole and top with remaining grated cheese mixed with toast crumbs. Dot with butter and bake in 350° oven for forty minutes or until browned on top. Serves 8.

Mrs. Jack Campbell

BAKED SQUASH

8 white squash
1 tablespoon grated sharp
cheese for each squash
(8 tablespoons)

salt and pepper to taste
2 raw eggs
juice of 1 onion

Boil squash until tender. Carefully cut outside hull on stem end and scoop out pulp. To this mixture add salt, pepper, eggs, juice and grated cheese. Place mixture back in squash shells and sprinkle with more grated cheese. Bake about thirty minutes in 350° oven. This can be prepared a day in advance.

Mrs. Robert T. King

BAKED YELLOW SQUASH WITH FRESH TOMATOES

2 pounds yellow squash
3 medium tomatoes, peeled and
sliced
2 small onions, sliced paper thin

1½ teaspoons salt
fresh ground pepper to taste
3½ tablespoons butter or
margarine

Wash squash and slice. Place layer of sliced squash in greased casserole, add layer of tomatoes and cover with a layer of onions. Sprinkle with half the

194

VEGETABLE FIESTA

salt and pepper. Build up casserole until all vegetables are used, dot with butter. Cover and bake in 350° oven about 45-50 minutes. Serves 8. (If desired, sprinkle either crisp bacon or Parmesan cheese on top and run under broiler.)

Mrs. John Pitman

YELLOW SQUASH CASSEROLE

1 pound yellow squash	1 can cream of chicken soup
1 large onion	pepper to taste
2 tablespoons bacon grease	bread crumbs (3 bread slices)

Cut squash after washing, into skillet with diced onion. Sauté in bacon drippings very slowly in covered skillet, stirring often. Cook only until tender. Pour into casserole, adding soup and pepper, topping with bread crumbs. Dot with butter and bake thirty minutes in 350° oven. Serves 6.

Mrs. J. Tyler Turner

SQUASH AND CELERY CASSEROLE

2 pounds yellow squash	salt and pepper to taste
1 can undiluted cream of	½ cup diced Swiss cheese
celery soup	butter
onion powder to taste	Parmesan cheese

Wash and slice squash, boil until tender. Grease baking dish with butter and add in layers; squash and cream of celery soup mixed with seasonings, Swiss cheese and butter. Repeat layers and top with Parmesan cheese. Bake in 350° oven twenty minutes. Serves 6.

Mrs. Norman Hutchings, Jr.

ZUCCHINI SQUASH ITALIAN

1½ pounds zucchini squash	½ teaspoon poppy seed
1 onion, chopped	½ teaspoon garlic salt
1 egg	½ teaspoon black pepper
1½ tablespoon butter	Parmesan cheese

Scrub and slice squash. Boil gently in salted water with onion until tender. Drain in colander. Add egg, butter, poppy seed and seasoning, mix together and place in baking dish. Sprinkle all over with grated Parmesan cheese. Bake in 375° oven for thirty minutes. Serves 6.

Mrs. Frank Frazer

195

ZUCCHINI SQUASH

Par boil the desired number of squash (at least one per person). Cut lengthwise and scoop out pulp. Mix with salt, pepper, one tablespoonful scraped onion, one egg (beaten), Parmesan cheese and bread crumbs to hold together and make a dry, dressing type filling. Put this back in squash hulls and mound. Sprinkle with Paprika and dot with butter. Run in the hot oven until butter melts and squash is heated through.

Mrs. Ernest L. Brown

BAKED STUFFED TOMATOES

1 tablespoon butter or margarine	1 teaspoon celery salt
½ cup finely chopped onion	(or chopped celery)
1 garlic bud, minced	salt to taste
8 toast slices	pepper to taste
8 hard boiled eggs	8 medium tomatoes
16 slices cooked bacon, crumbled	1 cup sharp, grated
⅛ teaspoon Cayenne	cheese

Melt butter in skillet, cook onion and garlic until tender. Wet toast with enough water or milk to moisten, crumble with a fork. Combine remaining ingredients, except tomatoes and cheese, add to onions and cook over medium heat until almost a stuffing consistency. Put this mixture in tomatoes, which have been halved, pulped and drained. Top with grated cheese, bake ten minutes in 350° oven.

Mrs. W. B. Taylor, Jr.

STUFFED TOMATOES WITH RICE

6 large tomatoes	1 tablespoon chopped parsley
1½ cups cooked rice	2 tablespoons melted butter or
¼ pound sharp cheese, grated	margarine
1 teaspoon Worcestershire	

Cut a thin slice from the stem end of each tomato and scoop out pulp, leaving one fourth inch walls. Turn upside down to drain. Toss remaining ingredients lightly and fill tomatoes with this mixture. Bake in 350° oven about fifteen minutes.

Mrs. Hunter Boulo

TOMATOES STUFFED WITH YELLOW RICE

1 package yellow rice	Cheese Whiz
1 can beef consommé	chopped parsley
tomatoes	chopped pimento

Cook yellow rice according to package directions, adding at least one half can consomme. Scoop out tomatoes and put a little Cheese Whiz in the bottom of each. Add parsley and pimento to rice and stuff into tomatoes. Top with a very small amount of Cheese Whiz and more parsley, if desired. Place in baking pan with a small amount of water in bottom and bake in 350° oven until tomatoes are tender.

Mrs. Frank P. Ellis, Jr.

SPINACH IN TOMATO CUPS

2 packages frozen chopped	¼ cup broken almonds
spinach	salt and pepper to taste
½ cup Cheese Whiz	6 fresh tomatoes
2 tablespoons Worcestershire	

Cook spinach with no water added. Add Cheese Whiz, Worcestershire, Nut meats and seasonings. Hollow out 6 tomatoes, fill with spinach mixture, top with dot of Cheese Whiz. Cook in 350° oven for twenty minutes.

Mrs. Norman Hutchings, Jr.

BROILED TOMATOES I

6 tomatoes	1 tablespoon minced parsley
salt and pepper to taste	1 garlic pod, minced
½ cup bread crumbs	olive oil

Cut tomatoes in half, salt and pepper. Spread tops with bread crumbs mixed with minced parsley and minced garlic. Sprinkle with olive oil and broil 10 to 15 minutes until soft and golden brown.

Mrs. Frank Sauer

BROILED TOMATOES II

Slice fresh tomatoes in half. Place in broiling pan with a little water. Sprinkle tops with salt, pepper and brown sugar, dot with butter. Broil about fifteen minutes until soft and bubbly.

Mrs. Ben M. Radcliff

197

TURNIP GREENS

2 large bunches of young turnip greens	½ pound lean salt pork
	2 tablespoons bacon grease

Wash greens well to remove dirt. Put small leaves in pot and strip larger leaves from stems. While washing greens, put one quart cold water in large pot. Cut salt pork into slices about one fourth inch thick and drop them into pot of water. Add bacon grease. Bring above ingredients to a boil and simmer for about thirty minutes, then add washed greens. Cover pot and heat to boiling again. Turn greens in pot so as to allow those on top to go to the bottom of pot. After this has been done press the leaves down to be covered by water. Lower heat after boiling point has been reached and cook over lowered heat about two hours, the longer, the better. Should more water be needed to keep leaves covered, add boiling water. Actual cooking time depends on age and tenderness of greens. Small turnips can be cut up and cooked along with greens.

Mrs. Jere Austill, Jr.

WILD RICE

1 cup wild rice	1 can mushroom stems and pieces
6 bacon strips	butter
1 medium onion	4 tablespoons cream

Wash rice well, cook forty-five to fifty-five minutes until very tender in heavily salted water. Rinse rice and steam one hour or more. Fry bacon crisp, remove from pan and saute chopped onion in bacon grease until tender. Saute mushrooms in butter. Crush bacon in rice, add onion and mushrooms and mix well. Just before serving add cream.

Mrs. J. P. Courtney, Jr.

WILD RICE CASSEROLE I

1 cup wild rice	1 can mushroom pieces
1 stick butter	¾ medium onion, chopped

Cook rice as directed. Sauté mushrooms and onion in butter. Combine with rice and mix well. Turn into greased casserole and heat until butter bubbles. Delicious with wild game. Serves 8.

Mrs. John S. McClelland

WILD RICE CASSEROLE II

1 pound sausage
1 large can sliced mushrooms (or
   1 pound fresh mushrooms)
1 cup sliced onions
2 cups wild rice
¼ cup flour
½ cup heavy cream
2½ cups condensed chicken
   broth

1 teaspoon monosodium
   glutamate
pinch of oregano, thyme, and
   marjoram
salt and pepper to taste
½ cup toasted almonds or pine
   nuts

Sauté sausage, drain and break into small pieces. Sauté mushrooms and onions in sausage fat (or butter). Add sausage. Cook rice in boiling, salted water ten to twelve minutes. Drain. Mix flour with cream until smooth. Add chicken broth and cook until thickened. Add seasonings. Combine rice with sausage mixture. Pour into casserole and bake 25-30 minutes in 350° oven. Sprinkle nuts around rim of casserole before serving. (If prepared in advance, rice will absorb liquid so add a little more chicken broth before baking.) Serves 18.

Mrs. Autry D. Greer

RICE PILAF

4 tablespoons chopped onion
3 ounces butter
1 pound rice

4 cups chicken bouillon
3 ounces butter

Lightly brown onion in butter and add unwashed rice. Shake in the skillet until rice turns milky white, add bouillon. Cover and bake in 250° oven about thirty minutes. After baking pour the rice into a cocotte and mix in remaining butter, broken into pieces. Serve with chicken, fish, shellfish, etc. This may be kept warm in the oven for a long period of time. Do not cover. Serves 12.

Mrs. Barbara Cowan Butler

PILAF

1 heaping teaspoon minced onion
1 generous tablespoon butter
1 teacupful raw rice
1 pint tomatoes
1 pint boiling water

salt to taste
red and black pepper to taste
1 pint boiling water
two cups minced, cooked meat

199

Sauté onion in butter in saucepan. Add rice and parch until light brown, stirring constantly. Add tomatoes and one pint boiling water, season and stew for 25-30 minutes. Add another pint boiling water and meat. Serves 12.

Miss Bessie Mayers

DIRTY RICE

1 pound minced gizzards	1 pound chicken or duck liver
½ pound minced hearts of	cut in small pieces
chicken or duck	1 cup rice
1 large onion, chopped	salt to taste
1 cup cooking oil	black pepper to taste
2 bell peppers, minced	2 cups minced green onion
1 onion, minced	1 cup parsley, chopped fine

In large skillet add gizzards, hearts and onion to cooking oil. Sauté until brown, adding a little hot water from time to time. This takes about an hour and a half. In another pan with water place bell peppers, onion and liver. When gizzards and hearts are brown and tender add to bell pepper mixture. Boil together for thirty minutes. Add rice and more water if necessary. Add black pepper and salt. When nearly done, add green onions and parsley and cook at least ten minutes over a low fire, covered. Serve immediately.

Mrs. M. B. McMurphy

BAKED RICE

1 medium onion, diced	1 small can mushrooms
¼ pound margarine	1 bay leaf
1 beef bouillon cube	parsley
1 can consommé	salt and pepper to taste
1 can water	dash or 2 of Worcestershire sauce
1 cup rice (raw & rinsed)	

Sauté onions in margarine, crumble (Bouillon) cube, stirring well. Add consommé, water, rice and other ingredients. Bake in covered casserole for one hour in 350° oven. Serves 8.

Mrs. J. Tyler Turner

RICE CASSEROLE I

medium onion, chopped
¾ stick of butter
1 cup rice

2 cups beef consommé
2 small cans sliced mushrooms

Sauté onion in butter, but do not brown. Add uncooked rice, mushrooms and consomme. Put in casserole, cover and bake for 45 minutes in 325° oven. Serves 10-12.

Mrs. J. E. Brown, Jr.

RICE CASSEROLE II

1 cup rice
½ stick butter
1 can chicken consommé
1 can onion soup

garlic salt
2 teaspoons Parmesan cheese
dash of Cayenne
slivered almonds

Stir rice and butter together over low fire until light brown. Add remaining ingredients. Bake in covered dish in 325° oven for one hour.

Mrs. Peter F. Beville

GREEN RICE

2½ cups cooked rice
½ cup melted butter
2 cups sharp cheese, grated
1 cup milk
1 cup chopped parsley

1 large egg, beaten
1 medium onion, chopped fine or to taste
salt, Worcestershire sauce and garlic to taste

Mix all ingredients together, reserving ½ cup cheese. Place in buttered baking dish, top with cheese, bake in 350° oven for forty-five minutes.

Mrs. Phillip Sapp

MY FAVORITES

Cheese and Egg Lessons

CHEESE & EGG LESSONS

GARLIC GRITS

1 cup grits, cooked
1 stick butter
1½ tablespoons Worcestershire
    sauce

¾ pound grated American cheese
½-1 clove garlic
Tabasco sauce to taste
2 egg whites

To hot grits add all remaining ingredients except egg whites. Cool. When cool, add stiffly beaten egg whites and bake twenty minutes in 400° oven. Serves 6.

Mrs. Charles O. Ditmars

EGGS VIEUX CARRÉ

2 English muffins, halved
    lengthwise
4 slices grilled ham

1 pack frozen artichoke hearts
4 eggs, poached
1 cup Hollandaise sauce

Split and toast muffins, spread with butter. On each muffin half lay a slice of ham and ¼ of the artichokes. Top with a poached egg (eggs stay compact while poaching if a little vinegar is added to the cooking water.) Spoon sauce over each.

HOLLANDAISE SAUCE:

2 egg yolks
¼ teaspoon salt
    dash Cayenne pepper

½ cup melted butter
1½ teaspoons lemon juice
1½ teaspoons tarragon vinegar

Beat egg yolks until thick and lemon colored. Add salt and cayenne. Add very slowly ¼ cup melted butter, beating constantly. Then combine re-

203

maining melted butter with lemon juice and vinegar, adding slowly and beating after each addition.

Variations: Use rye bread or whole wheat or Holland rusk instead of English muffins. Use tomato slices instead of artichokes.

Mrs. Mac B. Greer

EGG ROLLS

3 eggs
pinch of salt
1½ cups flour
1-1½ cups water
3 spring onions, chopped
1 cup cooked pork, finely chopped
1 cup cooked chicken, finely
    chopped

1½ cups chopped bean sprouts
3 dried Chinese mushrooms,
    chopped
1 egg
pinch of salt
soy sauce to taste
(minced shrimp can be substituted
    for pork and chicken)

Make a light pancake batter with eggs, salt, flour and water. Heat small frying pan, add a little grease. Pour in a tablespoonful of thin dough mixture, in center of pan, let run evenly over pan. Leave until quite dry, peel off. Repeat until all are done. Prepare filling. Fry spring onions, pork, chicken, bean sprouts and mushrooms. Add egg, salt, and soy sauce. Place two tablespoonsful across center of each fried pancake. Fold both ends first, then sides. Seal with water and fry in deep fat about four minutes. (They fry better if cold or frozen.)

MUSTARD SAUCE:

Stir equal parts of dry mustard and cold water to a smooth paste.

SWEET AND SOUR SAUCE:

5 tablespoons marmalade
1 teaspoon vinegar

½ teaspoon Worcestershire
⅓ teaspoon salt

Mrs. J. W. Hartman

SCRAMBLED EGGS WITH CREAM CHEESE

1 package (3 ounces) cream
    cheese
6 tablespoons heavy cream
1 tablespoon butter or margarine
6 eggs

1 teaspoon salt
dash fresh cracked black pepper
dash Cayenne pepper
1 teaspoon finely chopped chives
    or parsley

204

Work cheese with two tablespoons cream until soft and creamy. Melt butter or margarine in double boiler. Beat eggs, remaining cream, salt, both kinds of pepper and chopped chives or parsley until well mixed. Pour into melted fat, cook over boiling water, stirring frequently, until eggs are set. Now stir in cream cheese mixture and cook a minute or so longer, just enough to heat mixture. Spoon over hot toast. Serves 4.

Mrs. T. Potter Yeend

CHEESE 'N RICE

¼ cup mushroom stems and pieces
1 tablespoon chopped onion
¼ cup chopped blanched almonds
1 tablespoon butter
½ cup uncooked rice

2 tablespoons parsley, finely chopped
½ cup shredded cheese
1¾ teaspoons salt
1 teaspoon meat extract
1½ cups boiling water

Drain mushrooms, reserving liquid. Lightly brown mushrooms, onions and almonds in butter. Add rice, parsley and cheese, mix well. Place mixture in baking dish, add salt and meat extract mixed with water and mushroom liquid, by pouring over rice. Cover and bake in 375° oven for one hour.

Mrs. Stewart Thames

TALLIARINE

1 large onion, chopped fine
2 heaping tablespoons butter
1 can tomato soup
1 cup water
salt and pepper to taste

2 heaping cups uncooked noodles
1 can of corn
1 can ripe olives
1 cup diced cheese
butter
1 pound ground beef

Sauté onions in butter until brown, add soup and water with seasoning, when boiling, add noodles. Stir and cook until noodles are done, fifteen to twenty minutes. More water should be added, if stiff. Remove from heat, add browned meat, corn and olives. Pour into buttered casserole, mix in cheese, dot with butter. Bake in 350° oven forty-five minutes. Serves 6.

Mrs. J. P. Turner

WELSH RAREBIT

1 tablespoon butter	1 cup beer
1 pound dried Cheddar cheese	1 beaten egg
1 teaspoon dried mustard	salt, if needed
1 teaspoon paprika	6 slices freshly made toast

In double boiler melt butter over hot water, add cheese. As cheese melts, using wooden spoon, slowly stir in mustard, paprika and beer, mixing well. Stir in beaten egg and taste for salt. Pour over toast slices and serve at once.

Mrs. Frank Sauer

CHEESE NOODLE CASSEROLE

1½ pounds noodles	¼ teaspoon salt
1 cup cottage cheese	¼ teaspoon pepper
1 (6 ounce) cream cheese	⅓ cup chopped chives or scallions
1 cup sour cream	½ cup grated Parmesan cheese

Cook noodles according to package directions. Blend cottage cheese, cream cheese and sour cream in blender, remove from blender and mix with noodles. Season with salt, pepper and chives or scallions. Turn into generously buttered two quart baking dish. Sprinkle Parmesan cheese over all and dot with butter. Bake in 350° oven for thirty minutes. Serves 18.

Mrs. Robert T. Clark

CHEESE SOUFFLÉ I

¼ cup butter	1 cup milk
¼ cup flour	½ pound nippy cheese, grated
½ teaspoon salt	4 eggs, separated

Melt butter in double boiler, add flour and salt, blend. Add milk and stir constantly until sauce is thick and smooth. Add cheese, cover and let stand over boiling water until cheese melts. Beat egg yolks and add to cheese mixture. Fold in stiffly beaten egg whites. Pour into greased casserole which should be ⅔ full. Bake in 325° oven for one hour. Serves 4.

Mrs. Randall Hollinger

CHEESE SOUFFLÉ II

3 tablespoons butter	4 egg yolks
3 tablespoons flour	pinch of salt
1 cup hot milk	dash of Cayenne
1 cup diced camembert cheese	6 egg whites

206

To make smooth sauce cook butter, flour and milk over low heat for about five minutes, stirring constantly. Add cheese and stir until almost melted. Remove from heat and stir in lightly beaten egg yolks. Add salt and Cayenne. Cool mixture. Fold in stiffly beaten egg whites and pour into buttered soufflé dish. Bake in 350° oven for thirty to forty minutes. Serve at once. Serves 8-10.

Mrs. Frank Sauer

CHEESE SOUFFLÉ III

4 tablespoons butter	Cayenne pepper
4 tablespoons flour	½ pound cheddar cheese,
1½ cups milk	finely grated
pinch of salt	4 eggs, separated
dash of Worcestershire sauce	

In a saucepan melt butter over low heat and add flour. Stir with a wire whisk until mixture is smooth. Meanwhile bring milk to a boil and vigorously add all at once to the flour-butter blend. Continue stirring until mixture is thick and smooth. Add salt, Worcestershire sauce and Cayenne. Turn off heat and let mixture cool for two or three minutes. Add cheese and stir until cheese has melted. Beat in the egg yolks, one at a time. Cool. Beat egg whites until they hold a peak, but do not overbeat. Cut and fold egg whites into basic mixture. Turn into a two quart casserole dish and bake in a moderate oven (375°) for thirty to forty-five minutes. Serves six generously.

Mrs. William J. Hearin, Jr.

CURRIED EGGS

1 can cream of chicken soup	6 hard boiled eggs sliced
½ cup milk	4 ounce can Chow Mein noodles
½ teaspoon curry powder	

Combine soup, milk, and curry powder, let come to a boil. Add eggs, simmer two or three minutes. Serve over noodles. Serves four.

Mrs. Trotter Jones

MACARONI AND CHEESE

1 cup macaroni	¼ teaspoon paprika
1½ cups sharp cheese, grated	salt and pepper
1 egg, beaten	dash of Tabasco
⅔ cup milk	½ cup corn flake crumbs

Cook and drain macaroni. Put in layers in casserole with one cup cheese. Mix egg, milk and seasonings and pour over macaroni. Mix remaining cheese with crumbs and sprinkle over top. Bake at 375° until brown.

Mrs. John Morrissette, Jr.

CHINESE OMELETTE ROLL

1 medium onion	dash pepper
1 small can mushrooms	1 teaspoon cornstarch
3 tablespoons butter	1 tablespoon water
¾ pound ground beef	4 eggs
1 teaspoon salt	

Chop onion and mushrooms very fine. Melt one tablespoon butter in a saucepan, toss in chopped vegetables and cook until wilted—no longer. Stir in beef and cook until lightly browned. Season with ½ teaspoon salt and a dash of pepper. Make a smooth paste of cornstarch and water, stir into meat mixture and cook until thick. Beat eggs together with remaining salt and another dash of pepper. Heat remaining two tablespoons butter to a foamy stage in large skillet, pour in egg mixture, stirring a few times with the back of a fork. Cook until eggs are set. Now spread beef on top of eggs and roll up the omelette with the side of your fork. Remove from pan to a warm platter and serve in slices. Serves four.

Mrs. Rockne Lee

MY FAVORITES

MY FAVORITES

Breads...

with

a

Southern Accent

BREADS

BUTTERMILK BISCUITS

2½ cups flour   2 teaspoons baking powder
1 teaspoon salt   3 tablespoons shortening
½ teaspoon soda   1 cup buttermilk

Sift dry ingredients together. Work in shortening, add buttermilk slowly, mixing well. Roll out on lightly floured board, cut into desired shape and bake in 425° oven ten to twelve minutes.

Mrs. Rae Crowe

BISCUITS SUPREME

2 cups sifted flour   2 teaspoons sugar
4 teaspoons baking powder   ½ cup shortening
½ teaspoon salt   ⅔ cup milk
½ teaspoon cream of tartar

Add milk to dry ingredients and mix well. Knead gently ½ minute. Pat and roll ½ inch thick. Bake on ungreased cookie sheet for 10 to 12 minutes in 450° oven. Sixteen medium biscuits.

Mrs. Norman A. Nicolson

BISCUITS

2 cups flour   1 teaspoon sugar
4 teaspoons baking powder   ¼ cup Wesson Oil
½ teaspoon salt   ⅔ cup buttermilk
¼ teaspoon baking soda

211

Sift dry ingredients together. Add oil and milk. Mix thoroughly. Roll out to desired thickness and cut with biscuit cutter. Bake at 450° for 12 to 15 minutes. Three dozen biscuits.

Mrs. Tom Horst, Jr.

BEATEN BISCUITS

3 cups sifted flour
1 teaspoon salt
1 tablespoon sugar

2 tablespoons butter
2 tablespoons shortening
½ cup cold milk

Sift dry ingredients. Cut in butter and shortening. Add milk, a little at a time and mix to a very stiff dough. (May not require full ½ cup milk.) Place on floured board, marble or tile. Beat with wooden ice mallet or rolling pin until perfectly light, turning and folding as you beat. Beat until dough blisters and is very white. Roll ⅓ inch thick and cut with small biscuit cutter. Place on ungreased baking sheet, prick with fork. Bake in 450° oven for 15 to 20 minutes (until brown).

Mrs. Robert D. Hays

HUSH PUPPIES

1 egg
1 cup milk
1¼ cups corn meal
¾ cup flour

5 teaspoons baking powder
salt to taste
finely chopped onion, to taste

Beat egg and add milk to egg. Add remaining ingredients and stir well. Drop by ice teaspoonfuls into deep boiling fat. Remove when golden brown and drain well before serving.

Miss Margaret Smith

BRAN MUFFINS

¾ cup sifted flour
2 teaspoons baking powder
½ teaspoon soda
¼ teaspoon salt
2 tablespoons sugar

1 egg, beaten
¾ cup buttermilk
3 tablespoons melted shortening
1½ cups bran flakes
½ cup chopped nuts

Sift flour, measure, add baking powder, soda, salt and sugar, sift again. Combine egg and milk. Add to flour mixture, add shortening and mix only

212

enough to dampen flour. Fold in cereal and nuts. Fill greased small size muffin tins half full. Bake in 425° oven twelve to fifteen minutes.

Mrs. James J. Duffy, Jr.

ORANGE-HONEY MUFFINS

1½ cups sifted flour
½ cup sugar
2 teaspoons baking powder
½ teaspoon salt
¼ cup softened shortening

2 eggs
½ cup milk
1 thinly sliced orange with rind
honey

Sift dry ingredients, blend in shortening. Add milk and eggs together and stir until all ingredients are moistened. Place in each well greased muffin cup one slice of orange and one teaspoon honey. Add batter and bake 20 minutes at 400°. Turn out upside down. Yield 18 muffins.

Mrs. Albert Reynolds, Jr.

BLUEBERRY MUFFINS

¼ cup shortening
⅓ cup sugar
1 egg, beaten
2⅔ cups flour

½ teaspoon salt
4 teaspoons baking powder
1 cup milk
1 cup blueberries

Cream shortening and sugar. Add beaten egg, mix well. Reserve ¼ cup flour to sprinkle over blueberries. Sift rest of flour with salt, baking powder. Add dry ingredients, alternating with milk. Add blueberries and stir carefully so as not to crush berries. Fill greased muffin pans and bake at 400° for 35 minutes.

Mrs. Frank Courtney

HERB ROLLS

¾ cup butter
1 teaspoon sweet basil
1 teaspoon tarragon

½ teaspoon chopped parsley
12 brown and serve rolls

Soften butter, season with basil, tarragon and parsley. Mix and mix and mix more. Slice rolls in quarters, but only half way through, separating slices a little and spread on both sides with herb mixture. Heat until rolls are lightly browned.

Mrs. Robert L. Meador

213

REFRIGERATOR ROLLS

1 cup Crisco	2 eggs, beaten
1 cup sugar	2 envelopes yeast
1½ teaspoon salt	1 cup warm water
1 cup boiling water	6 cups unsifted flour

Pour boiling water over shortening, sugar and salt; blend and cool. Add eggs, dissolved yeast cake (following package directions), sift in flour. Blend well, cover and place in refrigerator for at least four hours, using large bowl as dough will rise slightly. About three hours before using rolls, roll into desired shape, using minimum amount of flour in handling. Place in greased pans and allow to rise until almost double in size. Bake in 425° oven for twelve to fifteen minutes.

Mrs. Robert L. Meador

MARTHA'S ROLLS

2 tablespoons shortening	1 cup sifted flour
1 tablespoon sugar	1 egg
1 tablespoon salt	2 cups flour
1 yeast cake	melted butter
1 cup milk	

Cream shortening, sugar and salt. Dissolve yeast cake in one half cup of the lukewarm milk. Add remaining milk, very hot, to creamed mixture. Add one cup flour and egg, beat well. Add dissolved yeast mixture and two cups flour. Let rise two hours or until double in size. Roll and shape into rolls, using as little flour as possible. Grease tops with melted butter and allow rolls to rise another hour. Mixture may be kept in refrigerator covered and made into rolls as desired. Bake in hot (425°) oven ten to twelve minutes.

Mrs. Marion S. Adams, Sr.

YEAST ROLLS

1½ cups milk	2 yeast cakes
1 tablespoon shortening	½ cup lukewarm water
1 tablespoon sugar	4½ cups flour
1 teaspoon salt	1 egg

Heat milk until lukewarm (hot enough to melt shortening). Add shortening, sugar and salt. Dissolve yeast cakes in lukewarm water. Add one and a

214

half cups flour to make a thin batter dough, then add well beaten egg. Add yeast and remaining flour. Mix well and place in a greased bowl in a warm place. When dough has risen to double it's original size (about an hour) roll out on floured board, cut and make into rolls. Let rise again and bake in 400°-425° oven.

Mrs. C. D. Wilson

ICE BOX ROLLS

1 yeast cake	1 cup sugar
¾ cup water	1 teaspoon salt
1 cup hot mashed potatoes	1½ cups milk
1 cup shortening	6-7 cups flour

Dissolve yeast cake in water. In large bowl mix potatoes, shortening, sugar, and salt. Mix yeast with potato mixture. Add alternately milk and flour. Cover dough with cloth and refrigerate until double in size. If using immediately make into desired shape and allow to rise until double in size—about three hours. Will keep in refrigerator about two weeks. Bake in 350° oven until brown.

Mrs. Frank Courtney

POTATO RUSKS

1 cup Irish potatoes, creamed	4 eggs, beaten
1 cup sugar	1 teaspoon salt
1 yeast cake	4-5 cups flour
½ cup tepid water	confectioner's sugar
1 cup shortening	

At night cream potatoes and while hot add one cup sugar. Dissolve one yeast cake in tepid water. When both have cooled mix well and cover with cloth until morning. For one o'clock luncheon make up dough at 7:00 A.M. as follows. To shortening add eggs, salt and yeast. Add flour to make like tea cake dough and set aside to rise. Three hours before serving make into rolls. Bake in 350° oven for about twenty minutes or until golden brown. When ready to serve brush with butter and sprinkle with confectioner's sugar. Yield—about three dozen rolls. (Note: Handle rolls gently. Do not use any more flour or handle any more (when rolling out to cut) than absolutely necessary. In warm weather two to two and a half hours are required for rising before baking.)

Mrs. J. F. Maury, Jr.

215

FRENCH ICE BOX ROLLS

1 yeast cake	1 egg, beaten
½ cup lukewarm water	4 cups flour
½ teaspoon salt	sugar and cinnamon
¼ cup sugar	raisins
½ cup butter	2 tablespoons butter
(¼ pound margarine)	brown sugar
1 cup boiling water	

Soak yeast in lukewarm water. In large bowl combine salt, sugar and one half cup butter. Pour boiling water over this mixture, add beaten egg and yeast, mixing well. Add flour, using a little more than called for if mixture is real sticky. Cover bowl and let mixture rise for one hour. Refrigerate for at least four hours and for no longer than four days. Remove from refrigerator and let dough rise for two hours, then sprinkle with flour. Knead and cut batter in half. Spread each half, one at a time, out lengthwise and wide. Sprinkle all over with sugar and then with cinnamon. Sprinkle raisins over all. Roll up across the width of dough and cut into one inch slices. Melt one tablespoon of butter in each of two tins, sprinkle with brown sugar and place rolls in tin. Allow rolls to rise two hours at room temperature. Bake in 425° oven for about twenty minutes. Turn out on plate immediately and serve warm.

Mrs. C. M. A. Rogers, Jr.

QUICK ORANGE MUFFINS

2 cups flour	5 tablespoons shortening
1 tablespoon baking powder	2 tablespoons grated orange rind
½ cup sugar	1 egg, well beaten
¾ teaspoon salt	½ cup orange juice

Sift dry ingredients, cut in shortening. Add orange rind. Combine beaten egg and orange juice and add to first mixture, stirring only until flour is moist. Fill greased muffin tins ⅔ full. Bake 15 to 20 minutes at 425°. Yield 12 muffins.

Mrs. Randall Hollinger

COTTAGE CHEESE ROUNDS

1 cup flour	1 cup small curd cottage cheese
½ teaspoon baking powder	1 teaspoon salt
½ cup butter or margarine	1 egg yolk, beaten

216

Sift and measure flour, sift with baking powder and combine with butter, cottage cheese and salt. Mix thoroughly with a spoon until well blended, shape into a ball, place on lightly floured board and knead about ten times. Roll one half inch thick and cut in rounds, two inches in diameter or smaller. Brush top with egg yolk. Place on greased baking sheet in a hot oven for twelve to fifteen minutes. Serve hot. Makes 18. Can be made ahead and baked when needed.

Mrs. A. S. Guerard

ICE BOX WAFFLES

3 eggs	1 teaspoon salt
2 cups milk	1 tablespoon meal
2 cups flour	½ cup oil
1 tablespoon sugar	6 teaspoons baking powder

Beat eggs and milk, add dry ingredients, add oil. Refrigerate and add baking powder before using.

Mrs. Randall Hollinger

BUCKWHEAT CAKES

1 cup buckwheat	1 tablespoon molasses
1 tablespoon corn meal	1 tablespoon melted lard
1 teaspoon salt	1 cup milk
½ yeast cake	1 beaten egg
1 cup tepid water	1 teaspoon baking powder

Sift buckwheat and corn meal with salt. Add yeast cake dissolved in a little water. Add tepid water, beat well and put in a warm place. Next morning, add molasses, lard, milk, egg and baking powder.

Mrs. John Van Aken

HOME-MADE WAFFLES

3 eggs, separated	1¾ cups flour
1 cup salad oil	4 teaspoons baking powder
1 cup milk	4 teaspoons sugar
½ teaspoon salt	

Beat egg yolks in large mixing bowl. Add oil and milk. Sift salt, flour and baking powder and gradually add to liquid mixture. If too thick add milk.

217

Beat egg whites in separate bowl, adding sugar gradually until whites form stiff peaks. Fold into waffle batter. Make about 12 squares.

Mrs. G. Russell Hollinger

DOUGHNUTS

3 tablespoons shortening
1 cup sugar
2 eggs, well beaten
3½ cups flour
¼ teaspoon nutmeg
1 teaspoon salt
¼ teaspoon cinnamon
4½ teaspoons baking powder
1 cup milk
about ½ cup additional flour

Cream shortening and sugar together until well blended, add eggs. Sift flour with remaining dry ingredients; add to egg mixture alternately with milk. Beat well, then add additional flour to make a soft dough that can be handled easily. Roll to three-eights inch thickness and cut into desired shapes. Fry in deep fat (370°) until golden brown. Roll in powdered sugar, if desired. Makes about five dozen doughnuts.

Mrs. Tom Horst, Sr.

HOME-MADE DOUGHNUTS

1 cup milk, scalded
2 tablespoons butter
1 tablespoon sugar
1 tablespoon brown sugar
1 package yeast
3 cups flour
1 teaspoon salt
½ teaspoon nutmeg
1 egg
confectioner's sugar

Pour milk over butter and sugars, stir until melted and cool to lukewarm. Add yeast, stirring until dissolved. Sift flour, salt and nutmeg. Gradually add half the dry mixture to milk, add egg and beat well. Add remaining flour and leave dough in warm place for one hour. Knead gently, roll to quarter inch thickness and cut into diamonds. Allow to rise thirty minutes to an hour. Fry in deep fat (385°) and dust with confectioner's sugar.

Mrs. Taylor Morrissette

MUSTARD BREAD

1 small loaf French bread
¼ cup butter
½ cup chopped green onions
(including some of tops)
2 tablespoons prepared mustard
2 tablespoons parsley flakes or finely chopped parsley
2 tablespoons sesame or poppy seeds

218

Cream butter. Blend in onions and parsley. Split the loaf lengthwise. Spread the loaf with butter mixture, then with mustard. Top with seeds. Cut bread diagonally in inch and a half slices not quite through crust. Heat in 350° oven for twelve minutes or until lightly browned. Serves 4.

Mrs. Joe Peck

OATMEAL NUT BREAD

2 eggs	1 teaspoon salt
1 cup sugar	1 teaspoon baking powder
⅔ cup dark syrup	1 teaspoon soda
2 cups buttermilk	1½ cups oatmeal
3 cups sifted flour	1½ cups chopped pecans

Beat eggs until light, add sugar gradually and beat well. Stir in syrup and buttermilk. Sift dry ingredients together and add to egg mixture. Add oatmeal and nuts, stirring only enough to combine. Grease with butter two loaf pans 4½ x 8½ inches, line with waxed paper and grease again. Bake in preheated 350° oven for one hour.

Mrs. G. R. Irvine, Jr.

SALLY LUNN

3 tablespoons sugar	3 large eggs or 4 small, separated
2 teaspoons salt	1 cup tepid milk
1 quart flour	1 yeast cake dissolved in
1 cup lard and butter mixed	½ cup luke warm water

Add sugar and salt to flour. Melt shortening and pour into beaten egg yolks. Add the milk, yeast, shortening, flour and stiffly beaten egg whites. Beat thoroughly and set aside in a warm place until double in size, about three hours. Then beat, beat, beat. Pour into greased cake pan and let rise again, one and a half to two hours. Bake in a moderate oven about forty-five minutes and serve with melted butter. Start oven at 325°, when half done increase to 375°. Twelve servings.

Mrs. Leon McVay, Jr.

OLD VIRGINIA SPOON BREAD

1 cup corn meal	4 eggs
½ teaspoon salt	1 cup cold milk
3 tablespoons butter, melted	

219

Stir corn meal into two cups boiling water, to which salt has been added. Cook one minute, remove from fire and add melted butter. Beat eggs and add to mixture, add milk and pour into individual hot buttered baking dishes. Bake approximately 25 minutes in 425° oven.

Mrs. William Rowell

SOUTHERN SPOON BREAD

1 pint sweet milk	1 teaspoon salt
½ cup white corn meal	3 eggs, separated
½ teaspoon baking powder	3 tablespoons butter

Scald milk and slowly stir in corn meal. Cook over low heat until consistency of soft grits. Add baking powder and salt and well beaten egg yolks. Add melted butter. Fold in stiffly beaten egg whites. Bake in greased casserole for thirty minutes in 275° oven. Serve immediately. Serves 8.

Mrs. Manning McPhillips, Jr.

SPOON BREAD

1 pint milk	1 teaspoon salt
¾ cup corn meal	3 egg yolks, beaten
1 tablespoon butter	3 egg whites, beaten stiff
1 tablespoon sugar	

Scald milk, gradually add corn meal and cook slowly until thick and smooth, about five minutes, stirring constantly. Cool slightly and add butter, sugar and salt. Add egg yolks then fold in whites. Bake in greased baking dish in 275° oven for thirty minutes. Serve immediately with plenty of butter. Serves 8.

Mrs. Thomas E. McCown

A MAN'S FAVORITE—SPICE BREAD

½ cup shortening	½ teaspoon allspice
1 cup sugar	½ teaspoon nutmeg
1 egg	½ teaspoon salt
1 cup seedless raisins	2 cups flour
1 cup sweetened applesauce	1 teaspoon soda
½ cup walnuts	2 tablespoons hot water
1 teaspoon cinnamon	

Blend shortening, sugar, and egg thoroughly in one operation. Add raisins, applesauce and walnuts. Sift the spices and salt with flour and add in several portions. Before the last addition, stir in soda, dissolved in hot water, beat well. Pour into a greased loaf pan or tube pan and bake about one hour in a 350° oven.

Mrs. John Terranova

OLD FASHIONED CORN LIGHT BREAD

1½ cups water
pinch of salt
⅔ cup corn meal
1½ cups cold water
about 2 cups corn meal

½ cup sugar
scant ½ teaspoon soda
1 teaspoon salt
1 heaping teaspoon shortening

Put water in double boiler and let come to a boil. Add salt and stir in two thirds cup corn meal and cook into mush. Remove from fire and stir in cold water. Add about two cups corn meal, thick as for corn pone. Let stand overnight. Then add sugar, soda, salt and shortening. Grease square or oblong pan and heat before pouring mixture in. Bake in 425° - 450° oven until well browned. This bread should be cool or cold before slicing into half inch slivers. Delicious with barbecue meals.

Mrs. Frank Terrell

ORANGE BREAD

peeling of 2 oranges
1 cup water
1 teaspoon baking soda
⅔ cup water
1 cup sugar
1 cup sugar
2 tablespoons melted margarine

2 eggs
½ teaspoon salt
3½ cups sifted flour
3 teaspoons baking powder
1 cup chopped nuts
1 cup liquid (orange juice and milk)

Cut orange peel fine or put through food chopper. Cook peel with one cup water and baking soda for five minutes. Strain. Make syrup of sugar and water, add orange and cook until thick. Cool. Cream sugar and margarine. Add eggs, salt, flour, baking powder and nuts. Add liquid and cooled orange mixture. Pour into greased loaf pan and let rise twenty minutes in a warm place. Bake one hour in 350° oven.

Mrs. H. H. Wefel

221

APRICOT LOAF

2 cups sifted flour	¾ cup finely chopped uncooked
4 teaspoons baking powder	apricots
1 teaspoon salt	1 egg
⅔ cup sugar	1 cup milk
½ cup chopped nut meats	2 tablespoons melted shortening

Sift dry ingredients. Add nut meats and apricots. Combine well beaten egg, milk and shortening. Add liquid to dry ingredients, stirring only until flour is dampened. Turn into well greased 9 x 4 x 3 inch loaf pan. Push batter into corners of pan, leaving center slightly hollow. For well rounded loaf, allow batter to stand in pan twenty minutes before baking. Bake in 375° oven for one hour.

Mrs. Tom Cowan

DUTCH BREAD

2 tablespoons butter	1 heaping teaspoon nutmeg
1½ cups sugar	1 teaspoon cinnamon
2 eggs	1 cup buttermilk (in which
4 cups sifted flour	1 teaspoon soda has been
2 teaspoons baking powder	dissolved)
½ teaspoon cloves	1 cup nuts, chopped
½ teaspoon allspice	1 cup raisins

Cream butter and sugar, add beaten eggs. Add sifted dry ingredients. Stir in buttermilk, mix well. Add nuts and raisins. Bake in two 10 x 4½ inch loaf pans in 325° oven. Loaves wrapped in foil stay fresh about a week. Good with soft butter or cream cheese spread between slices.

Mrs. Walter J. Ogburn, Jr.

SWEET BRAN BREAD

1 cup pitted dates, sliced	1½ cups ready to eat bran
⅓ cup dried sliced apricots	1 egg, slightly beaten
1¼ cups boiling water	2 tablespoons melted butter
1½ cups sifted flour	or margarine
1 teaspoon baking powder	1 tablespoon grated orange rind
1 teaspoon baking soda	⅓ cup chopped walnuts or pecans
¾ teaspoon salt	⅓ cup orange juice
⅔ cup sugar	

222

Mix dates, apricots and boiling water, cool. Sift flour, baking powder, soda, salt and ⅓ cup sugar. Mix date mixture with bran, egg, butter and orange rind. Add sifted dry ingredients and stir until smooth. Add nuts, turn into greased loaf pan. Bake in 325° oven fifty to fifty-five minutes. Turn out. Mix remaining ⅓ cup sugar with orange juice, pour slowly over top and sides of bread.

Mrs. J. W. Hartman

CRANBERRY BREAD

Sift together:

2 cups flour	**½ teaspoon soda**
½ teaspoon salt	**¾-1 cup sugar**
1½ teaspoons baking powder	

Mix together in order given:

2 tablespoons melted shortening	**2 tablespoons hot water**
½ cup orange juice	**1 egg, beaten**

Combine the two mixtures. Do not beat. Handle carefully, mixing only until moistened. Fold in:

½ cup chopped nuts	**grated rind of two oranges**
1 large cup chopped cranberries	

Bake in 350° oven one hour and ten minutes, in greased loaf pan. Cool well before wrapping. Do not cut for twenty-four hours.

Mrs. Robert T. Clark

PORTICA—YUGOSLAVIAN EASTER BREAD

¼ cup warm water	**6 tablespoons light cream**
1 package dry yeast	**2 cups ground walnuts**
1 cup scalded milk	**⅔ cup sugar**
¼ cup sugar	**½ teaspoon salt**
¼ cup butter	**½ teaspoon vanilla**
1 teaspoon salt	**2 tablespoons butter**
3½-3¾ cups sifted flour	**2 tablespoons freshly toasted**
2 eggs, separated	**bread crumbs**

Sprinkle yeast onto warm water in small bowl and stir until dissolved. In another bowl mix milk, sugar, butter and salt, cool to lukewarm. Add two cups of flour and beat well. Beat in eggs, yeast and enough of remaining flour to make a soft dough. Knead until smooth and elastic. Place dough

223

in a greased bowl, turning once to grease surface, cover with clean towel. Let rise in warm place until double in size, about an hour and a half. When dough is doubled, punch down and again let rise until doubled, about forty five minutes. Meanwhile, grease two 9 x 3 x 3 inch loaf pans and make filling. In light cream, stir walnuts, sugar, salt and vanilla. Melt butter in saucepan, add breadcrumbs and toss together until golden, add to nut and cream mixture. Remove two tablespoonfuls from egg whites, beat remaining whites until stiff and fold into nut mixture. Punch down dough and divide into halves on lightly floured surface. Roll each half into 16 x 9 inch rectangle, spread one half the filling on each one. Roll up, jelly roll fashion. Place in loaf pan, let rise until almost double in size, thirty to forty minutes. Meanwhile, start heating oven to 375°. Bake loaves thirty five to forty minutes and remove from pans when done. Cool on racks. These loaves freeze well.

Mrs. J. W. Hartman

HERB TOASTED BUNS

1 teaspoon sweet basil	½ teaspoon thyme
½ teaspoon marjoram	1 stick soft butter

Blend herbs and butter well and spread on twice sliced hot dog buns. Place in top of moderate oven until bread is crisp.

Mrs. George Irvine

MY FAVORITES

MY FAVORITES

PICKLES, RELISHES AND JELLIES

DILL PICKLES

90-100 medium to small
  cucumbers
2 fresh dill heads per jar
½ teaspoon crushed red pepper
  per jar
15 cups water

1 large or 2 small garlic cloves
  per jar
1 cup white vinegar
1 cup salt
1 teaspoon alum
sterile jars

Wash and dry cucumbers, pack in quart jars. To each jar add dill heads, red pepper and garlic, cut in half. Put water, vinegar, salt and alum in pan on stove and bring to a roaring boil. While still boiling, pour over cucumbers in jars and seal. Pickles may cloud in time, but this does not mean they have spoiled. They will be ready to eat in about six weeks. Makes 9 quarts.

Mrs. C. D. Wilson

SWEET PICKLES

Drain juice from one gallon of large size sour pickles. Slice pickles in ¼ inch slices. Put pickles, sugar and spices in layers in the same jar, using about four pickles, 6 to 8 whole allspice, 6 to 8 cloves, 6 to 8 pieces of broken stick cinnamon, ⅛ lb. of brown sugar and one lb. of white sugar to each layer. This is for four layers. If you make more layers use the same amount of spices per layer, but do not use more than ½ lb. of brown sugar and 4 lbs. of sugar to the whole jar. You may have to press down about halfway to get all the pickles in. Finish with a layer of sugar on top. Cut two cloves of garlic in half and press about halfway down in jar on the side after jar has been filled. Let stand until all sugar is dissolved and pour

227

about ¾ cup Wesson Oil on top to seal. Takes about two weeks to make. When made, remove some of the pickles, put in a jar, refrigerate and serve cold. The large jar need not be refrigerated as oil keeps pickles fresh.

Mrs. Thomas Horst, Jr.

PICKLED OKRA

4 large onions	3½ cups sugar
2 green peppers, seeded	½ teaspoon powdered cloves
¼ cup salt	3½ teaspoons mustard seed
3½ cups vinegar	4½ pounds okra

Grind onions and peppers together in meat grinder, using coarsest blade. Mix the ground vegetables and salt in a bowl, cover with a lid or plate and weight the top. Leave for three hours, drain. Put vinegar, sugar and spices in a large pot and stir until sugar is dissolved. Cut the stems off okra, (do not cut straight across top, cone the top off), add to pot with the drained vegetables and cook over low heat until vegetables are very hot and liquid almost boiling. Do not boil. Ladle into hot, sterile jars and seal at once. Store in refrigerator or cool place for four months before using. Makes about eight pints.

Mrs. Kenneth Granger

CORN RELISH

2 pound package frozen whole kernel corn	¼ cup salt
	3 tablespoons celery seed
1 cup light brown sugar	3½ tablespoons dry mustard
4 large onions, chopped	1½-2 quarts vinegar
2 green peppers, chopped	

Mix corn with all ingredients, cook slowly for about twenty minutes in open kettle. Pack and seal in jars. Makes about 6 pints.

Mrs. John Morrissette, Sr.

GREEN TOMATO RELISH

3 quarts vinegar	1 teaspoon red pepper
5 cups sugar	1 teaspoon allspice
1 teaspoon cloves	1 peck small green tomatoes,
1 cup mustard seed	sliced
½ cup celery seed	24 small onions, sliced
1 teaspoon cinnamon	

228

Bring to a boil vinegar and all ingredients, except tomatoes and onions. When mixture reaches boiling point, add the two vegetables and cook thirty minutes. Seal in hot, sterile jars.

Mrs. Leon McVay, Jr.

HYDEN SALAD (RELISH)

cabbage	5 tablespoons prepared mustard
green tomatoes	3 ounces tumeric
bell peppers	1 tablespoon cinnamon
onions	2 tablespoons ginger
3 tablespoons sugar	1 tablespoon mace
1 ounce celery seed	1 tablespoon ground cloves

Grind in food grinder enough of the first four ingredients to make the following, one gallon cabbage, one gallon green tomatoes, one pint bell pepper and one quart onion. Sprinkle salt on above mixture and let stand several hours. Drain water off and throw away. Add remaining ingredients and cover all with vinegar. Boil until done. Put in jars and seal while hot. Makes 12—16 pints.

Mrs. G. E. Covington

RAW PEAR RELISH

4 quarts green pears	2 hot red peppers
2 quarts onions	12 dill cucumbers
8 bell peppers	2 cups salt

Quarter pears, remove core. Grind all of the above ingredients together. Add salt and let stand overnight. Squeeze water off.

Sift together:

4 tablespoons dry mustard	8 tablespoons flour
2 teaspoons tumeric	4 cups brown sugar

Make a smooth paste by adding:
2 quarts hot vinegar

Boil five minutes stirring constantly. Add pear mixture. Boil five minutes. Makes 12 pints.

Mrs. Everett Sapp

PEAR CHUTNEY

2 quarts vinegar	2 large green peppers, chopped
1 pound dark brown sugar	2 teaspoons dried, crushed
1 pound yellow sugar	red pepper
1 teaspoon Cayenne pepper	4 onions, coarsely chopped
4 teaspoons salt	2 lemons, chopped
4 garlic buds, finely chopped	2 (11 ounce) jars preserved
1 pound dark seedless raisins	ginger, chopped
2 tablespoons mustard seeds	6 pints coarsely chopped
	"sand" pears

Place vinegar, sugars, pepper, salt, garlic, raisins and mustard seed in a large boiler and cook on medium heat for twenty to thirty minutes. Add green and red peppers, onion, lemon and ginger. Cook thirty minutes. Add pears and cook until pears are done, but not mushy. Keep mixture simmering as a good amount of juice must be available. (Save ginger syrup to add last.) Pour into sterile jars and seal while boiling hot. Makes 8 or 9 pints.

Mrs. Jack Friend, Sr.

EAST INDIAN DATE CHUTNEY

2 cups cider vinegar	2 pounds coarsely chopped dates
1 cup sugar	½ teaspoon Cayenne
½ cup water	1½ teaspoon ginger
½ teaspoon instant minced garlic	¼ teaspoon salt

In saucepan mix vinegar, sugar, water and garlic. Bring to a boil and cook three minutes. Stir in dates, cayenne, ginger and salt. Cook, stirring, five to ten minutes. Pack in four hot, sterile one-half pint jars, seal.

Mrs. Leon McVay, Jr.

FIG PRESERVES I

6 pounds sugar (12 cups)	3 lemons, sliced
2 quarts water	6 quarts peeled figs

Boil sugar, water and lemons until syrup is thick. Add figs. Boil until figs are transparent. The mixture may be taken up and put in jars now; or let sit overnight in syrup and next morning place cold figs in jars. Bring syrup to a boil then pour hot syrup over figs and seal. If overnight method is used, place jars, with figs in them (top on) in pan of hot water to heat figs before adding hot syrup. The overnight method makes the figs plump up more, but both methods taste the same. Makes 16 pints.

Mrs. C. D. Wilson

FIG PRESERVES II

8 pounds figs

5 heaping teaspoons alum dissolved in 5 quarts water

Remove stems from figs. Soak for one hour in alum mixture. Cook to rolling boil for three minutes:

5 pounds sugar
1 quart plus 1 cup water
4 lemons (sliced and seeded)
½ box whole cloves

¼ teaspoon salt
1 box cinnamon sticks
1 orange, sliced

Rinse figs twice and drain; then add to this mixture. Cook until figs are clear. Remove figs from syrup, cook syrup until desired thickness. Replace figs and boil a few minutes. Fill sterile jars, cover with hot paraffin. Makes 7 pints.

Mrs. J. F. Maury

OLD FASHIONED PEACH MARMALADE

Peel peaches, cook in just enough water to prevent burning. Mash cooked peaches thoroughly. Add one cup sugar for each cup of peaches plus one extra cup of sugar. Boil until mixture threads from a spoon like a goose web. Stir constantly to prevent sticking. Quick cooking gives the prettiest colored finished product. Pour in hot sterile fruit jars and seal.

Mrs. Mac Greer

CURRIED FRUIT

1 large can pears
1 large can pineapple
1 large can peaches
1 large bottle cherries

1 cup light brown sugar
½ cup butter
2½ teaspoon curry powder

Drain fruit well and mix together in baking dish. Melt sugar, butter and curry powder together and pour over fruit. Bake, uncovered in 300° oven for one hour. Serve as a relish.

Mrs. William T. Porter

231

GRANDMOTHER'S BREAD AND BUTTER PICKLES

6 quarts medium cucumbers, 6 onions, sliced
   sliced 1 cup salt

Combine and let stand three hours. Drain.

1½ quarts vinegar 1 tablespoon celery seed
6 cups sugar ⅓-¼ teaspoon Cayenne
½ cup mustard seed

Combine seasonings and vinegar and boil. Add cucumbers and onions. Heat to simmering. Be careful to avoid boiling as that softens pickles. Pack while hot in sterile jars and seal immediately.

Mrs. Mac B. Greer

GREEN TOMATO PICKLE

1 peck very green tomatoes 8 large green bell peppers
½ peck white onions 1 cup salt

Slice tomatoes and onions very thin, cut peppers in strips, and pour salt over all. Let stand overnight in china or porcelain container.

5 tablespoons flour 4 tablespoons dry mustard
4 cups sugar 2 quarts vinegar
4 tablespoons tumeric 4 teaspoons mixed pickling spice
½ cup celery seed   (tied, loosely, in 4 small thin
½ cup white mustard seed   bags)

Mix these ingredients and boil five minutes. Add tomato mixture that has been thoroughly squeezed out of brine. Cook about five to ten minutes longer. Pack in pint or half pint sterile jars. Flavor improves with a little age.

Miss Alice B. Frazer

232

MY FAVORITES

233

MY FAVORITES

Dessert Review

DESSERTS AND SAUCES

FROZEN BUTTERMILK CREAM

1½ quarts buttermilk	1 pint coffee cream
2½ cups sugar	1 tablespoon vanilla
1 pint whipping cream	juice of 5 lemons

Mix together and freeze in ice cream freezer. If you don't like buttermilk, try this anyway. (You can't tell this is made with buttermilk.)

Mrs. Marion S. Adams, Jr.

CRANBERRY ICE

2 cups cranberries	½ cup water
1½ cups cold water	juice of 1 lemon
1 cup sugar	(more sugar if desired)
1 teaspoon unflavored gelatin	

Cook cranberries in 1½ cups of water until skins pop; add sugar and cook until sugar dissolves. Add gelatin softened in cold water. Cool and add lemon juice. Freeze in refrigerator for four or five hours, stirring several times. Serves six to eight.

Mrs. S. R. Stephenson, Jr.

RASPBERRY SHERBET I

2 cups sugar	1½ quarts milk
juice of 8 lemons	1 can evaporated milk
grated rind of 3 lemons	1 package frozen raspberries

Dissolve sugar in lemon juice, add rind, milk and evaporated milk. Stir in thawed raspberries. Freeze in electric ice cream freezer. Yields 3 quarts.

Mrs. W. H. March, Jr.

RASPBERRY SHERBET II

2 egg whites
¼ cup sugar
1 small can frozen orange juice
   (thawed)
juice of 2 lemons

1 package frozen raspberries
   (thawed)
2 orange juice cans water
1 can crushed pineapple

Beat egg whites, add sugar. Add orange juice, lemon juice and water. Mix all together, add crushed pineapple. Put in plastic container in freezing unit, stirring once or twice as it hardens.

Mrs. John M. Morrissette, Sr.

STRAWBERRY SHERBET

4 cups fresh, ripe strawberries
   or 1 pack frozen

2 cups sugar
2 cups buttermilk

Rinse, drain and hull strawberries. Add sugar to berries and mash. Stir in buttermilk. Pour into two refrigerator trays. Freeze until firm. Break into chunks, beat with electric beater until smooth and refreeze. Serves 10.

Mrs. J. Tyler Turner, Jr.

FRESH FIG ICE CREAM

1 pint cream
1 pint milk
6 eggs, separated
1 cup sugar

1 quart fresh figs, peeled and
   mashed
2 tablespoons sherry
few drops vanilla

Scald cream and milk together. Beat egg yolks and sugar until light. Beat egg whites until stiff. Pour hot milk over sugar and egg yolks, stirring constantly. Add egg whites, mix thoroughly and add sherry and vanilla. Lastly, add mashed figs and freeze.

Mrs. N. D. Pitman

BANANA ICE CREAM

6 eggs	1 quart milk, scalded
2 cups sugar	1 tablespoon vanilla
1 tablespoon flour	1 pint whipping or coffee cream
pinch of salt	8 bananas, mashed very fine

Beat eggs. Mix sugar, flour and salt, add to eggs. Add scalded milk to egg mixture. Cook in double boiler, stirring constantly, until mixture coats a silver spoon. Cool. Add vanilla, cream and bananas. Freeze in ice cream freezer.

Mrs. Marion S. Adams, Jr.

PEACH ICE CREAM

6 eggs	10 peaches
1 tablespoon flour	1 tablespoon vanilla
2 cups sugar	1 pint whipping cream
pinch of salt	1 pint coffee cream
1 quart milk, scalded	

Beat eggs. Mix flour, sugar and salt and add to eggs. Gradually pour scalded milk over this. Cook in double boiler, stirring constantly, until mixture coats a silver spoon. Set aside to cool. Mash peaches or buzz in blender and add to custard mixture. Add vanilla and creams. Taste for sweetness, which varies with flavor of peaches. Freeze in ice cream freezer.

Mrs. Marion S. Adams, Jr.

HOME-MADE PEACH ICE CREAM

1 medium basket of peaches	1 pint whipping cream
sugar	½ cup sugar
3 tablespoons lemon juice	

Peel peaches, mash thoroughly, add lemon juice and sugar. Fold whipped cream into peaches. Pour into glass or ice trays and put in freezer. When partially frozen along edges, stir thoroughly and refreeze completely. This is an old recipe and that is why it is so vague. Just taste for sweetness as you go along.

Mrs. R. P. Lester

CHOCOLATE ICE CREAM

2 squares unsweetened chocolate   1 cup cold water
1⅓ cups (15 ounces) sweetened   2 cups heavy cream
     condensed milk

Melt chocolate in double boiler top. Add condensed milk and stir over rapidly boiling water five to ten minutes, or until thick. Remove from heat. Gradually add water and cream, mixing well. Cool. Freeze in two quart freezer. Remove dasher, pack in ice and ice cream salt for one hour or more after freezing. Yield: 1¼ qts.

Mrs. Norman A. Nicolson

VANILLA ICE CREAM FOR FREEZER

1 quart milk   1 tablespoon flour
1 cup cream   3-4 teaspoons vanilla
3 egg yolks   fresh fruit, if desired
1 cup sugar

Scald milk and cream. Beat together egg yolks, sugar and flour and add to milk. Cook custard till it coats a silver spoon. Cool in refrigerator. When cool, add vanilla and begin churning in ice cream freezer. Fresh fruit, such as peaches may be added to this recipe. Yield: one quart.

Mrs. Wilson Gaillard, Jr.

OLD TIME HOME-MADE ICE CREAM

5 eggs   2 large cans evaporated milk
2½ cups sugar   at least 4 tablespoons vanilla
½ gallon milk   (or more to taste)
2 cans condensed milk

Make custard of eggs, sugar and milk. Heat very slowly until mixture coats a spoon. Remove and cool thoroughly. Add evaporated milk, condensed milk and vanilla. Freeze in electric freezer. Recipe can be halved to make two refrigerator ice trays full.

Mrs. J. Tyler Turner, Jr.

CUSTARD ICE CREAM

5 or 6 large eggs   1 large can evaporated milk
1¾ cups sugar   1 pint whipping cream
1 quart milk   1 large kitchen spoonful vanilla

Beat eggs and sugar, add milk, cook in double boiler until mixture coats a spoon. Cool; add evaporated milk, whipping cream and vanilla. Freeze in one gallon electric ice cream freezer.

Mrs. S. A. Barrett

RUM SAUCE

2 eggs   1 cup whipping cream
1 cup confectioner's sugar   5 teaspoons rum

Beat eggs and add sugar gradually. Continue beating. Whip cream very stiff, add rum and continue beating. Fold whipped cream into egg mixture. Will keep for hours in refrigerator.

Mrs. Frank Webb

WONDERFUL CHOCOLATE SYRUP

⅓ cup cocoa   ⅛ teaspoon salt
1 cup sugar   1 tablespoon butter
2 tablespoons light corn syrup   vanilla
½ cup cold water

Combine cocoa, sugar, corn syrup, water and salt in saucepan. Bring to a full boil and cook ten minutes, timing from beginning of full boil. Stir only to keep from boiling over, not too much. Remove from fire, add butter and vanilla, stir. The longer this stands the thicker and better it will be.

Mrs. V. M. Dukes

CHOCOLATE SAUCE

1 large can evaporated milk   3 squares bitter chocolate
2 cups sugar   1 teaspoon vanilla

Combine all ingredients, except vanilla. Cook in double boiler fifteen minutes, stirring occasionally. Remove from heat, add vanilla, beat briskly with hand beater. Serve hot or cold. Keeps well.

Mrs. Tyler Turner

FOAMY SAUCE

1 egg, separated	½ cup whipping cream, whipped
¾ cup confectioner's sugar	1 tablespoon vanilla

Mix egg yolk and sugar, beating until light. Add stiffly beaten egg white and fold in whipped cream. Add vanilla. Delicious with gingerbread.

Mrs. Marion S. Adams, Sr.

BOILED CUSTARD SAUCE

3 egg yolks, beaten	2 cups milk, scalded
¼ cup sugar	1½ teaspoons vanilla
pinch of salt	

Cook over hot water until sauce begins to thicken.

Mrs. Selwyn Turner, Jr.

MOCHA FUDGE SAUCE

3 squares unsweetened chocolate	¼ cup butter
2 cups confectioner's sugar	3 teaspoons instant coffee
2 small cans evaporated milk	½ teaspoon vanilla

Place all ingredients, except vanilla, in double boiler top. Cover and heat over boiling water. When chocolate melts, stir until blended. Cook for thirty minutes, stirring occasionally. Add vanilla. Heat before serving. Makes one pint.

Mrs. Jack Gallalee

BUTTERSCOTCH SAUCE

¼ cup butter	2 egg yolks
2 cups dark brown sugar	1 large can evaporated milk

Cream butter and sugar, add egg yolks and milk. Cook in double boiler top until thickened. Makes three cups and keeps well.

Mrs. Tyler Turner

JANE REMBERT'S FAT MAN'S DELIGHT

1 package Famous chocolate wafers	1 cup nut meats
margarine or butter	1 whole egg
1 cup confectioner's sugar	2 tablespoons bourbon
1 stick margarine or butter	whipping cream
	shaved chocolate

240

Line nine inch pie pan with crust made with wafer crumbs and enough butter or margarine to hold together. Combine, sugar, butter stick, nuts, egg and bourbon. Pour into pie crust. Top with whipped cream and shaved chocolate.

Mrs. Horace T. Spottswood

BISCUIT TORTONI I

2 cups milk	1½ cups slivered almonds
¾ cup sugar	1 tablespoon vanilla
9 egg yolks	1 tablespoon sherry
1½ cups ground macaroons	1 pint cream, whipped

Scald milk and sugar. Pour over egg yolks, beaten until light. Return to double boiler and cook until thickened. Cool. Add macaroons, almonds, vanilla and sherry. Fold in whipped cream. Freeze.

Mrs. Marion S. Adams, Sr.

BISCUIT TORTONI II

1 egg white	¼ cup sugar
dash of salt	¾ cup fine macaroon crumbs
1 cup heavy cream	

Beat egg white with salt until stiff. Without washing beater, beat cream, gradually adding sugar. Beat until stiff. Fold in beaten egg white and one-half cup macaroon crumbs. Turn into custard cups, sprinkle with remaining macaroon crumbs and freeze until firm. (These should be wrapped for freezer if they are to remain in freezer for long.)

Mrs. W. B. Taylor, Jr.

SHERRY TORTONI

½ pound marshmallows	1 pint heavy cream
⅔ cup sherry	finely chopped almonds

Melt marshmallows in sherry in double boiler top. Cool. Whip cream and fold into marshmallows. Put into eight double thickness paper dessert cups set in muffin pans. Sprinkle with almonds and top with cherry, if desired. Freeze, then wrap individually in foil and return to freezer. Let stand at room temperature fifteen to twenty minutes before serving.

Mrs. W. B. Erickson, Jr.

CHIFFON DELIGHT

1 orange chiffon cake
1 package vanilla pudding
   (not instant)

1 can crushed pineapple
   (2½ cups)
1 pint whipping cream

Cut cake into four layers. Mix pudding, pineapple and juice in saucepan. Cook until thick. Cool. Fold mixture into whipped cream. Spread between cake layers, on sides and top of cake. Serve no sooner than the following day. Serves 12.

Mrs. John McGehee

SHERRY ALMOND CREAM DESSERT

4 eggs, separated
6 tablespoons sugar
¾ to 1 cup sherry wine
1 pint whipping cream

2 layers sponge cake
almonds
bittersweet chocolate

Whip egg yolks until light, add sugar and sherry (about ¾ cup). Refrigerate. Whip egg whites and add to above mixture. Whip cream and fold into mixture. Take two layers of sponge cake and sprinkle with remaining sherry. Place one layer on serving plate and cover with custard mixture. Add second layer. Toast almonds and sliver on top of cake. Grate chocolate to cover the whole cake. Refrigerate. Serves 12.

Mrs. Grover Taylor

CHOCOLATE ANGEL CAKE

7 5¢ almond Hershey bars
4 ounces chocolate chips
14 large marshmallows, cut
5 eggs, separated
1½ angel food cakes

¼ cup sugar
1 teaspoon vanilla
whipped cream
coconut

Melt chocolate bars and chocolate chips together with marshmallows. Add well-beaten egg yolks, stirring constantly. Allow to cool. Break cake into small pieces. Beat egg whites until stiff, with sugar and vanilla. Fold chocolate mixture into egg whites and add cake chunks to mixture. Let stand at least twenty-four hours in refrigerator. Cut in squares and top with whipped cream and then coconut.

Mrs. Walter Ogburn

ANGEL FOOD AND CHOCOLATE CHIP DESSERT

2 eggs, separated	1 tablespoon sugar
2 tablespoons sugar	1 cup whipping cream
1 teaspoon vanilla	1 large angel food cake
1 package (6 ounces) semi-sweet	chopped nuts or coconut
chocolate chips	additional whipping cream

Beat egg yolks with two tablespoons sugar and vanilla. Melt chocolate over warm water. Beat egg whites until stiff with one tablespoonful sugar. Stir egg mixture into egg whites. Fold in chocolate and one cup whipped cream. Break angel cake into pieces. Put one-half of broken cake into nine inch pan and pour one half of chocolate mixture over them. Add remaining cake pieces and chocolate. Press down lightly. Refrigerate overnight. Before serving sprinkle top with chopped nuts or coconut and top each square with a dab of whipped cream. Serves 12-16.

Mrs. Ernest Brown

FLORIDA SNOWBALL

1 envelope plain gelatin	1 large angel cake
¼ cup cold water	1 pint whipping cream
½ cup boiling water	juice of 2 lemons
¼ cup sugar	½ cup grated coconut
1½ cups orange juice	

Soften gelatin in cold water, add boiling water to dissolve. Add sugar and juice. Cool, let stand until nearly set. In the meantime remove crusts from cake and pull apart in small pieces. Line large bowl with wax paper. Whip one cup of cream, fold into set gelatin mixture. Place a layer of gelatin and cream mixture in mold, add a layer of cake, more gelatin mixture followed by cake until bowl is full, using last of gelatin mixture. Set in refrigerator overnight. To serve, unmold and cover with second cup of whipped cream and sprinkle with coconut. Serve in wedges. Serves 10 to 12.

Mrs. J. E. Brown

LEMON DELIGHT

¾ cup sugar	1 tablespoon grated lemon peel
¾ cup lemon juice	¾ cup sugar
6 eggs, separated	dash of salt
1½ envelopes plain gelatin	1 angel food cake
¼ cup cold water	½ pint whipping cream

243

Combine ¾ cup sugar, lemon juice, and egg yolks in double boiler top. Cook to custard consistency. Soak gelatin in water, add to lemon mixture, and stir until dissolved. When cool, add grated lemon peel. Beat egg whites until fluffy, gradually add ¾ cup sugar, and beat until stiff. Add a dash of salt and fold into custard mixture. Remove all crust from cake and break cake into bite size pieces. Lightly mix lemon mixture and cake, pour into oiled angel cake pan and refrigerate. Just before serving, remove from pan and cover with whipped cream.

Mrs. John Moss

LITTLE LEMON PUDDINGS

1 cup sugar	5 tablespoons lemon juice
¼ cup flour	grated peel of 1 lemon
½ teaspoon salt	1½ cups milk, scalded
2 tablespoons melted butter or margarine	3 egg yolks, well beaten
	3 egg whites, stiffly beaten

Combine sugar, flour, salt and butter. Add lemon juice and peeling. Gradually add milk to egg yolks. Add lemon mixture. Fold in egg whites. Pour into greased custard cups and place in pan with an inch of hot water. Bake in 325° oven 45 minutes. When baked, each dessert will have custard on bottom, sponge cake on top. This may also be baked in greased shallow baking dish. Serves 8.

Mrs. Tom Cowan

ORANGE FLUFF

1 cup water	juice and pulp of 1 orange
1 cup sugar	2 tablespoons lemon juice
1½ tablespoons (1½ envelopes) gelatin	1 pint whipping cream
½ cup cold water	½ pound marshmallows, small lady fingers

Boil water and sugar twenty minutes. Soak gelatin in cold water and dissolve in syrup. Cool until mixture begins to congeal. Whip like cream, add whipped cream and marshmallows. Line two greased loaf pans with lady fingers, leaving space between. Pour half full with mixture. Add another layer of lady fingers. Cover with remaining gelatin mixture. Refrigerate. This light dessert is very good after a heavy meal. Serves 12.

Mrs. Ann Donald

CHOCOLATE TORTE ROYAL

2 egg whites	¼ teaspoon cinnamon
¼ teaspoon salt	¼ teaspoon instant coffee
½ teaspoon vinegar	½ cup ground nuts
½ cup sugar	

Beat egg whites with salt and vinegar to soft peaks. Blend in sugar, cinnamon, coffee and nuts, gradually. Beat until stiff peaks form. Put on brown paper on a cookie sheet. Shape like a pie shell with high sides. Bake in 275° oven for one hour. Turn off heat and dry shell in oven for two hours.

FILLING:

1 (6 ounce) package chocolate bits	1 cup heavy cream
	¼ teaspoon cinnamon
2 egg yolks, beaten	¼ cup sugar
¼ cup water	¼ teaspoon instant coffee

Melt chocolate over hot water, cool slightly and spread two tablespoonfuls over bottom of cooled shell. Add egg yolks and water to rest of chocolate, blend well. Chill until thick. Whip cream with cinnamon, sugar and coffee. Beat until stiff. Spread half over chocolate in shell. Fold remaining whip cream mixture into remaining chocolate mixture. Spread over top of torte. Decorate with pecan halves or cut up pecans. Chill several hours or overnight.

Mrs. Glenn Cobb

SCHAUM TORTE

1 cup sugar	1 teaspoon vanilla
4 egg whites at room temperature	1 cup whipping cream
1 teaspoon vinegar	1 quart strawberries

Draw two circles of eight inch layer pan on smooth brown paper and place on baking sheet. Set oven at 300° about ten minutes before baking. Sift sugar, beat egg whites and add sugar in five portions, beating well each time. Beat in vinegar and vanilla. Spoon meringue on circles keeping mixture ¼ inch from edge. Spread to uniform thickness. Keep oven door open slightly and bake thirty minutes. Turn off oven and let meringue dry out in oven for thirty minutes. Remove from oven and carefully remove from paper. Place one layer on serving plate, spread with whipped cream then with strawberries. Top with second torte and spread with remaining cream. Serve at once. Serves 8. Although meringues may be made day ahead, strawberries and cream should not be added until shortly before serving.

Mrs. Walter Adler

COCONUT TORTE

1 cup graham cracker crumbs	1 cup sugar
½ cup snowflake coconut	1 teaspoon vanilla
½ cup chopped salted cashew	½ cup whipping cream
nuts	1 tablespoon confectioner's sugar
pinch of salt	1 teaspoon grated lemon peel
4 egg whites	¼ cup snowflake coconut

Combine graham cracker crumbs, one-half cup coconut and nuts. Add salt to egg whites and beat to form stiff peaks. Gradually add sugar, beating until stiff peaks form. Add vanilla and fold into graham cracker mixture. Pour into greased nine inch baking pan and bake in 325° oven forty-five to fifty minutes. Cool. Whip cream, add confectioner's sugar, lemon peel and coconut. Spread over torte. Cut into pie shaped pieces. Serves 6—8.

Mrs. Marion Adams, Jr.

LADY FINGER TORTE

4 packages lady fingers	1 tablespoon instant coffee
milk	⅔ cup toasted almonds
1 to 3 tablespoons rum	½ pint whipping cream
½ pound butter	4 tablespoons confectioner's
2 cups confectioner's sugar	sugar
2 eggs	1 tablespoon rum
8 ounces chocolate chips	

Dip split lady fingers in milk flavored with rum or vanilla. Line bottom and sides of nine inch spring form cake pan with lady fingers. For chocolate mixture, cream butter and sugar, add eggs, melted chocolate chips, coffee and almonds. Fill pan with alternate layers of chocolate mixture and lady fingers. Chill for at least four hours. Whip cream, add 4 tablespoons confectioner's sugar and one tablespoon rum. Unmold and spread cream on top. Decorate with chocolate chips.

Mrs. Rae M. Crowe

CHOCOLATE ICEBOX PUDDING

2 tablespoons milk	1 teaspoon vanilla
2 packages German sweet chocolate	6 tablespoons sugar lady fingers
6 eggs, separated	

Melt chocolate with two tablespoons milk. Add hot chocolate to beaten egg yolks. Add vanilla. Beat egg whites until stiff, add sugar, and beat. Fold into chocolate mixture. Line bowl with lady fingers. Pour layer of chocolate, layer of lady fingers on top and repeat. Refrigerate at least six hours, preferably overnight. Serve as is or topped with whipped cream. Nuts may be added to mixture if desired.

Mrs. Selwyn Turner, Sr.

LEMON TORTE

4 egg whites	3 tablespoons fresh lemon juice
1 cup sugar	1 tablespoon grated lemon rind
½ teaspoon vanilla	¾ cup whipping cream
4 egg yolks	2 teaspoons vanilla
¾ cup sugar	

Beat egg whites until stiff. Gradually add one cup sugar and one-half teaspoon vanilla. Divide the mixture in half. Spread each part on a circle of brown paper, about the size of a pie pan, bake one hour in 250° oven. Beat egg yolks, add sugar, lemon juice and rind. Cook in double boiler top until thick, stirring occasionally. Whip cream and add to lemon mixture, add vanilla. Peel brown paper from one meringue and place meringue on serving dish, spread with half the filling. Place other meringue on top and spread with remaining filling. Refrigerate.

Mrs. George R. Irvine, Jr.

LEMON DESSERT

3 eggs, separated	¼ cup butter, softened
juice of two lemons	2 tablespoons sugar
grated rind of one lemon	⅛ teaspoon salt
4 tablespoons sugar	½ pint whipping cream
about 24 vanilla wafers	

Add beaten egg yolks, lemon juice and rind to four tablespoonfuls sugar. Cook in double boiler until mixture coats a spoon. Combine crushed vanilla wafer crumbs and butter and line nine inch pie pan with this mixture. Beat egg whites with salt, until stiff. Whip cream with two tablespoonsful sugar. When lemon mixture is cool, fold egg whites and whipping cream into custard. Freeze.

Mrs. Dupree Hays

LEMON MOUSSE

¾ cup rolled vanilla wafers   ¼ cup lemon juice
2 egg yolks   ½ teaspoon grated rind
1 tablespoon flour   ⅛ teaspoon salt
⅓ cup sugar

Sprinkle half the crumbs into wax paper lined tray in freezing unit. Beat yolks, add flour and sugar. When well blended add juice, rind and salt. Cook in double boiler, stirring constantly until thick and creamy. Cool and add milk mixture.

MILK MIXTURE:

2 egg whites   ⅔ cup chilled evaporated
2 tablespoons sugar   milk, whipped

Add sugar to whites and beat until creamy. Add whipped milk and combine with cooked yolk mixture. Pour into crumb lined tray. Cover with rest of crumbs. Freeze about five hours.

Mrs. Jack Friend, Jr.

SWEDISH CREAM

2⅓ cups heavy cream   1 pint commercial sour cream
1 cup sugar   1 teaspoon vanilla
1 envelope plain gelatin   fruit

Mix cream, sugar and gelatin together. Heat gently and stir until gelatin is completely dissolved. Cool until slightly thickened. Fold in sour cream and vanilla. Chill until firm. Spoon into serving dishes and top with sweetened berries or fruit.

Mrs. Newland Knight

NUT CRISP

7 premium crackers   3 egg whites
1 cup sugar   1 teaspoon almond extract
1 teaspoon baking powder   1 cup chopped nuts

Roll crackers until thin. Add sugar, baking powder and nuts to crackers. Beat egg whites with almond extract until stiff. Fold cracker mixture into egg whites. Bake in 350° or 375° oven for thirty-five minutes in greased pan. Serve topped with ice cream and caramel sauce. Serves 9.

Mrs. Franklin King

PINEAPPLE REFRIGERATOR DESSERT

½ cup butter
1½ cups confectioner's
   sugar, sifted
2 eggs, well beaten
½ pound vanilla wafers

½ cup (or more) crushed
   pineapple
½ pint whipping cream
½ cup chopped nuts

Cream butter with sugar, add eggs, beat with beater until light. Roll wafers into crumbs, put half in 8 x 8 inch pan. Cover with cream mixture, next pineapple. Cover with sweetened whipped cream into which the nuts have been folded. Cover with remaining crumbs, refrigerate overnight.

Mrs. James Irby

DELIGHT

½ pound marshmallows
1 can (No. 2) crushed pineapple
1 pint whipping cream

1 cup broken pecans
2 cups red grapes, halved

Cut marshmallows in small pieces or use tidbits. Mix with crushed pineapple. Let stand for six hours or until marshmallows dissolve. Add whipped cream, nuts and grapes. Chill. Serves 12.

Mrs. Norman Hutchings, Jr.

STRAWBERRY MARLOW

1 cup strawberries
1 tablespoon sugar
2 tablespoons orange juice

20 marshmallows
½ cup water
1 cup whipped cream

Soak strawberries, sugar, and orange juice for one-half hour. Melt marshmallows in water over hot water. Whip marshmallows into strawberry mixture, cool. Fold in whipped cream and place mixture in ice trays in refrigerator to set. Serves 4.

Mrs. N. M. McInnis

CHOCOLATE MINT ROLL

1½ cups whipping cream
¼ cup sugar
green food coloring

⅛ teaspoon mint extract
1 package thin chocolate wafers
semi-sweet chocolate

Whip cream until just stiff, sweeten with sugar, add a few drops of green food coloring and mint extract. (A drop or two more mint for stronger flavor.) Spread chocolate wafers with cream and stack together, using full package of wafers. Frost outside with remaining mint cream. Garnish with shaved semi sweet chocolate, chill for several hours. To serve, slice diagonally. Serves 10.

Mrs. Robert Meador

CHOCOLATE COOKIE CREAM LOAF

1 cup heavy cream
1 tablespoon sugar
1 tablespoon cocoa

½ teaspoon vanilla
20 chocolate mint wafers
3 tablespoons pecans, chopped

Whip the cream until slightly thickened. Add sugar and cocoa gradually, beating constantly until stiff enough to hold peaks. Add vanilla while beating. Spread whipped cream on chocolate cookies, using about two-thirds of the mixture. Stack cookies covered with cream in a row, standing them on edge like a loaf of sliced bread. Spread the remaining cocoa cream over the top and sides and sprinkle with nuts. Refrigerate the roll until firm. To serve cut the loaf diagonally to get a striped effect. Serves 6.

Mrs. Mac Greer

PEPPERMINT DELIGHT

1 cup heavy cream
½ cup finely crushed peppermint
candy

14 snipped marshmallows
1 cup fine chocolate wafer
crumbs

Whip cream until stiff, gently fold in candy, marshmallows. Sprinkle one-half cup wafer crumbs into six sherbet glasses. Add cream mixture, top with remaining crumbs. Refrigerate twenty-four hours.

Mrs. R. Denny Wright

FUDGE BATTER PUDDING

3 tablespoons melted margarine
1 cup sugar
1 teaspoon vanilla
1 cup sifted flour
8 teaspoons cocoa

1 teaspoon baking powder
¾ teaspoon salt
½ cup milk
½ cup chopped nuts
1⅔ cups boiling water

Mix margarine, ½ cup sugar and vanilla together. Sift flour, 3 teaspoons cocoa, baking powder and ½ teaspoon salt together and add alternately with milk to first mixture. Mix well and stir in nuts. Mix together ½ cup sugar, 5 teaspoons cocoa, ¼ teaspoon salt and boiling water in a 10 x 6 x 2 inch baking pan or dish. Drop batter by teaspoonfuls on top. Bake in 350° oven forty to forty-five minutes. Serve warm.

Mrs. Frank Webb

BRANDIED CHOCOLATE POT DE CRÈME

1 cup evaporated milk
3 egg yolks
⅛ teaspoon salt
2 tablespoons sugar

1 (6 ounce) package semi-sweet
   chocolate pieces
1 tablespoon brandy
heavy cream

Scald milk. Beat egg yolks with salt and sugar until thick. Slowly add scalded milk, stirring rapidly. Cook over low heat, stirring constantly until mixture just begins to thicken, about three minutes. Remove from heat and add chocolate pieces, stirring until melted and smooth. Stir in brandy and spoon into pot de crème or custard cups. Serve with a dab of whipped cream atop each.

Mrs. R. L. Byrd

FIG MOUSSE

1 cup sour cream
1 cup cream, whipped
2½ cups mashed figs (peeled)

confectioner's sugar to taste
3-4 tablespoons rum

Mix all ingredients. (This can be frozen.)

Mrs. J. H. Friend

CRÈME DE MENTHE FRAPPE DESSERT

16 marshmallows
⅔ cup crème de menthe

1 pint whipping cream

Melt marshmallows over hot water. Add crème de menthe and dissolve. (Electric mixer speeds this.) Cool. Beat whipping cream stiff. Fold crème de menthe mixture into cream. Turn into sherbet glasses or serving dish and refrigerate several hours before serving. Serves eight.

Mrs. George Shedd

CHOCOLATE VELVET

8 ounces sweet chocolate	½ teaspoon vanilla
1½ cups milk	¼ teaspoon almond extract
1½ envelopes gelatin	1 cup whipping cream
½ cup cold water	2 teaspoons instant coffee
½ cup sugar	¾ cup whipping cream
⅛ teaspoon salt	¼ teaspoon vanilla
½ cup light cream	3 tablespoons sugar

Cut chocolate into pieces and scald with milk in double boiler until chocolate melts. Soften gelatin in cold water. Beat chocolate and milk with rotary beater. Add softened gelatin, ½ cup sugar and salt. Stir until dissolved. Add light cream, ½ teaspoon vanilla, almond extract, and one cup whipped cream. Mix until smooth. Chill in five cup ring mold until firm. Sprinkle instant coffee over ¾ cup whipping cream. When most of coffee is dissolved add ¼ teaspoon vanilla and whip cream stiff, adding 3 tablespoons sugar as you beat. Unmold dessert. Frost with coffee flavored whipped cream. Garnish with shaved bitter chocolate. (Mold can be prepared a day or two in advance.) Serves 8.

Mrs. Robert Byrd

LEMON MOUSSE SUPREME

1 envelope gelatin	⅓ cup sugar
2 tablespoons water	3 egg whites, beaten stiff
6 tablespoons lemon juice	⅓ cup sugar
3 egg yolks	grated rind of 3 lemons

Soften gelatin in water, add lemon juice and stir mixture over boiling water until gelatin dissolves. Beat egg yolks until they are very light, adding ⅓ cup sugar to them. Add the gelatin mixture to the yolks and sugar. Beat egg whites, adding ⅓ cup sugar until they are very stiff and add lemon rind. Fold meringue into yolk mixture. Chill in refrigerator. Serve with raspberry sauce. Serves eight.

RASPBERRY SAUCE:

2 jars currant jelly (8 ounce jars)
1 teaspoon cornstarch

1 (10 ounce) package frozen raspberries

Melt jelly over low heat and add corn starch dissolved in raspberry juice to thicken. Blenderize raspberries and combine with jelly. Chill.

Mrs. Barbara Cowan Butler

COFFEE MOUSSE

2 envelopes gelatin
½ cup water
1 cup confectioner's sugar
1 cup milk

4 teaspoons instant coffee
1 tablespoon rum
2 egg whites, beaten stiff
2 cups heavy cream, whipped

Sprinkle gelatin on cold water to soften. Stir together sugar, milk and instant coffee in top of double boiler over boiling water. Cook until just hot. Add softened gelatin and stir until dissolved. Set aside to cool to consistency of unbeaten egg white. Add rum and beat until light. Fold in beaten egg white and then whipped cream. Chill in mold in refrigerator. Serve with sauce. Serves ten.

SAUCE:

2 egg yolks
¾ cup confectioner's sugar
⅓ cup heavy rum

1 cup heavy cream, whipped
slivered toasted almonds

Beat egg yolks and sugar until creamy and light in color. Add rum and fold with a spoon. Fold in whipped cream. Pour over unmolded mousse and top with almonds.

Mrs. Barbara Cowan Butler

MOTHER'S MAPLE MOUSSE

3 eggs, separated
⅔ cup maple syrup
1 teaspoon vanilla

½ pint cream
½ cup chopped nuts

Over low heat, cook egg yolks and syrup to custard consistency. Add vanilla and refrigerate. When cold, fold in stiffly beaten egg whites and whipped cream. According to preference, fold in or top with chopped nuts. Serves 6.

Mrs. Horace Spottswood

MOUSSE DE MENTHE

Prepare two packages lemon flavored gelatin, substituting crème de menthe for ¾ cup water. Chill until mixture mounds, whip frothy, fold in two cups whipped cream, chill in five cup mold. Serves 8.

Mrs. Norman Hutchings, Jr.

CHOCOLATE MOUSSE

1 quart milk	2 cups sugar
2 envelopes gelatin	dash of salt
3 (1 ounce) squares unsweetened chocolate	2 teaspoons vanilla
	1 pint whipping cream

Divide milk into two pints. Soak gelatin in one fourth cup cold milk. Dissolve gelatin in remainder of this pint of milk, heated. Dissolve chocolate in the other pint of milk, heated. Strain into dissolved gelatin and milk and stir well. Add sugar and salt. Strain entire mixture again and refrigerate to thicken. When nearly stiff, beat briskly until very light. Whip cream with vanilla until stiff and fold into first mixture. Refrigerate until serving time.

Mrs. Richard Murray

ORANGE PUDDING

3 eggs, separated	1 dozen lady fingers
¼ cup sugar	½ cup coconut
juice of 4 oranges	

Beat egg yolks slightly, add sugar (increasing amount a little if still sour), and orange juice. Cook until mixture begins to thicken, boiling hard and stirring constantly. Sprinkle coconut over split lady fingers and line bottom of one quart baking dish with ladyfingers. Pour custard into baking dish and let stand in refrigerator overnight. Using egg whites and one-fourth cup sugar make a meringue, spread over custard and brown in 350° oven before serving.

Mrs. Basil McNeely

CARAMEL CUSTARD

⅞ cup sugar (¾ cup plus 2 tablespoons)	¼ teaspoon salt
½ cup water	3 cups milk
4 eggs	1 teaspoon vanilla
	whipping cream, if desired

254

Start oven ten minutes before baking, set at 325°. Grease a six cup casserole. Heat an aluminum skillet. Sift one-half cup sugar gradually into hot skillet, shaking pan vigorously. Continue to heat and stir with a wooden spoon until sugar melts and takes on a pale golden amber color. Remove from heat at once and cautiously add water, then two tablespoonfuls sugar. Return to heat and boil down gently to exactly one half cup syrup. This amount is important for caramel sauce to be of right consistency. If caramel boils down more than this, add hot water to make one-half cup. Pour caramel syrup into casserole. Beat eggs slightly, stir in remaining one-fourth cup sugar, salt, milk, and vanilla. Strain carefully over caramel into casserole. Set casserole in pan and pour three cups hot water in pan. Bake thirty-five to forty minutes or until custard tests done. (By inserting silver knife into custard, if knife comes out clean, custard is done.) Remove immediately to rack to cool. To serve, spoon custard into serving dishes with some of caramel sauce from bottom over each serving. Top with whipped cream, if desired.

Mrs. Hunter Boulo

BASIC BOILED CUSTARD

1 tablespoon flour
1 cup sugar
5 whole eggs

1 quart sweet milk
vanilla to taste

Mix flour with sugar. Beat eggs well, mix with cold milk, add sugar mixture and stir until dissolved. Place in top of double boiler and cook until thickened. Remove from heat, stir in vanilla and pour into lightly greased custard cups to set. (Festive with a bit of bourbon poured in center of each before serving.) Serves 6 to 8.

Mrs. Ernest L. Brown

CHARLOTTE RUSSE

1 cup milk
1 envelope gelatin
2 egg yolks
slightly less than ½ cup sugar

1 pint whipping cream
1 teaspoon vanilla
1 dozen lady fingers

Pour ¼ cup milk over gelatin. Combine eggs and sugar. Heat remainder of milk. Pour a small amount of heated milk over gelatin. Add remaining heated milk to egg and sugar mixture. Cook this custard over a very low fire, stirring constantly. While doing this, set gelatin in a pan of warm water. Put gelatin into custard. Strain into bowl. Chill until edges thicken slightly. Line serving bowl with lady fingers. Whip ½ pint cream at a time, not stiff. Lift cream off as it whips and add to custard. Add vanilla. Refrigerate. Serves 9. Can be made day ahead

Mrs. Gaylord Lyon

OLD FASHIONED CHARLOTTE RUSSE

1 cup milk	1 pint whipping cream
½ cup cold milk	4 egg whites
1 envelope gelatin	2 teaspoons vanilla or sherry
½ cup sugar	2 packages lady fingers
4 egg yolks	

Mix egg yolks with sugar and milk. Cook in double boiler top to a soft custard. Add gelatin (which has soaked in one-half cup cold milk and melted over hot water) to the hot custard. Cool and add whipped cream and stiffly beaten egg whites. Mix in vanilla or sherry. Line bowl with lady fingers, fill with mixture and refrigerate. May use sherbet glasses instead of large bowl.

Mrs. S. A. Barrett

FRESH FRUIT COMPOTE

canteloupe	½ pound fresh cherries,
watermelon	pitted
honeydew melon	½ fresh pineapple

Make enough melon balls to fill a quart jar. Add cherries and pineapple meat. Marinate in following sauce in refrigerator.
MINT SAUCE:

1 cup sugar	6 sprigs mint leaves,
½ cup water	chopped

Combine and cook over low heat until sugar dissolves. Stir, crushing mint with back of spoon, while cooking. Cool, pour through strainer over fruit.

Mrs. Frank B. Frazer

ORANGE CHIFFON ALMOND DESSERT

Slice orange chiffon cake and cover with following sauce.
ALMOND SAUCE:

1 stick butter	2 teaspoons almond
1 cup sugar	extract
¼ cup water	

256

Combine first three ingredients and stir over low heat until sugar dissolves. Remove from heat and add almond extract. Spoon over cake slices and run under broiler until edges are lightly browned. Serve topped with peach ice cream and fresh peaches, whipped cream, or vanilla ice cream sprinkled with toasted almond slivers.

Mrs. Frank B. Frazer

MY FAVORITES

MY FAVORITES

Cakes
and
Icings

CAKES AND ICINGS

ENGLISH TEA CAKE

½ cup butter	2 cups cake flour
1 cup sugar	2½ teaspoons baking powder
2 eggs, beaten	⅔ cup milk
1 teaspoon vanilla	

Cream butter and sugar, add beaten eggs, then vanilla. Sift flour with baking powder. Stir in flour, alternately with milk. Pour batter into two nine inch greased cake pans.

TOPPING:

| 3 tablespoons sugar | 1 teaspoon nutmeg |
| 1 teaspoon cinnamon | ½ cup chopped nuts |

Mix together and sprinkle over top of cake. Place in oven at 375°. Bake 25 to 30 minutes. Delicious served warm.

Mrs. Tom Cowan

GERMAN SWEET CHOCOLATE CAKE

1 4-ounce bar German	1 cup buttermilk
sweet chocolate	2½ cups cake flour
4 eggs, separated	1 teaspoon baking soda
1 cup margarine	1 teaspoon vanilla
2 cups sugar	

Dissolve chocolate in ½ cup boiling water. Beat egg whites until stiff. Cream margarine and sugar together, add well beaten egg yolks. Alternate additions of ¾ cup buttermilk and flour. Dissolve soda in remaining milk

259

and add pinch of salt to chocolate. Combine mixtures, add vanilla and fold in egg whites. Bake in three 9 inch layers in 350° oven. Remove from oven before cake springs back to finger touch. (about 30-40 minutes)
Icing:

Cook together until thick, stirring constantly:

1 cup coffee cream	4 egg yolks
¾ cup chopped nuts	1½ cups sugar
½ cup coconut	1 stick margarine

Add 1 teaspoon vanilla and spread between layers and on top of cake.

Mrs. C. E. Jones

CARROT CAKE

2 cups sugar	1 teaspoon salt
4 eggs	2 teaspoons soda
1 cup Wesson oil	2½ cups grated carrots
2 cups all purpose flour	1 teaspoon vanilla

Cream together sugar, eggs and oil. Add dry ingredients, carrots and vanilla. Pour into greased and floured cake pans. Bake in 325° oven thirty to forty-five minutes. Makes two large or three small layers.

FILLING:

1 8 ounce package cream cheese, softened	1 stick margarine, softened
1 pound confectioner's sugar	1 cup chopped nuts

Mix all ingredients well. Will frost three layers.

Mrs. W. P. Davidson, Jr.

RUM BABA

½ cup milk	½ cup sugar
1 yeast cake	¾ cup apricot juice
2 egg yolks	1 teaspoon lemon juice
1 cup sugar	1 large jigger rum
1 whole egg	vanilla ice cream
¼ cup lukewarm, melted butter	black pitted cherries
1¾ cups flour (about)	

Scald milk, cool to lukewarm, add yeast cake and let dissolve. Beat egg yolks until thick. Slowly add one cup sugar, beat in vigorously. Add whole

260

egg and melted butter. Add yeast mixture, then flour for thick batter. Set in a warm place and let rise three and a half hours. Fill a large ring mold, barely half full, and let mixture rise. Bake in 350° oven until a toothpick comes out clean, cool on rack. Boil sugar, apricot juice, lemon juice and rum for ten minutes; pour carefully over cake. Let season three or four hours. Pour a bit more run over the top, fill center with ice cream and top with black cherries.

Mrs. Frank Sauer

QUEEN ELIZABETH CAKE

Make batter of:

1½ cups sifted flour	¼ cup butter
1 teaspoon baking powder	¾ cup sugar
¼ teaspoon salt	1 egg

Cook one cup dates in one cup hot water. Mix ¾ teaspoon soda into cooked dates and stir all into batter. Preheat oven to 325° and bake forty-five minutes. While cake bakes mix topping:

5 tablespoons butter	½ cup brown sugar
3 tablespoons evaporated milk	¾ cup pecans

When cake is done spread topping evenly on top of cake. Slide under broiler, four inches from top, and broil two minutes.

Mrs. Frank Webb

COCONUT CAKE

1 cup butter	pinch of salt
2 cups sugar	6 large or 8 small egg whites
¾ cup cold water	1 coconut
3 teaspoons baking powder	white icing
3 cups sifted flour	

Cream butter and sugar thoroughly. Add cold water and mix well until sugar is completely dissolved. Sift in dry ingredients and mix well. Fold in egg whites. Bake in three nine inch pans, greased and floured, in 350° oven. When done, allow to cool, remove from pans, brush off loose brown crumbs and sprinkle with several teaspoons of coconut milk. Make fluffy white icing, using coconut milk in place of water called for in recipe. Sprinkle freshly grated coconut over top and sides of iced cake.

Mrs. C. D. Wilson

NUTMEG AND COCONUT CAKE

½ cup butter 1 tablespoon nutmeg
1½ cups sugar 1 teaspoon baking powder
3 eggs 1 teaspoon soda
2 cups flour 1 cup buttermilk

Cream butter and sugar together, add eggs by beating in one at a time. Sift flour with nutmeg and baking powder. Dissolve soda in buttermilk and add flour and milk, a little at a time. Add vanilla and bake in greased 9 x 13 inch pan in 350° oven, about thirty minutes.

Spread the following filling on hot cake:

6 tablespoons melted butter ¼ cup cream (top of milk)
1 cup shredded coconut ½ cup brown sugar
1 cup pecans

Cut into squares and serve with whipped cream on each square.

Mrs. Walter Ogburn

GINGERBREAD

1 egg ¼ teaspoon nutmeg
⅓ cup brown sugar ¼ teaspoon baking powder
⅓ cup molasses 1¼ cups flour
⅓ cup Wesson oil 1 teaspoon baking soda
1 teaspoon ginger ¾ teaspoon cinnamon
¼ teaspoon ground cloves ½ cup hot coffee

Beat egg lightly and add to sugar, molasses and shortening. Then add dry ingredients which have been mixed and sifted together. Mix well and add hot coffee. Bake in greased and floured 8 x 8 inch pan 30-40 minutes in 350° oven. Makes 8 large pieces or 12 small.

Mrs. C. D. Wilson

PECAN COFFEE CAKE

1 egg 1 teaspoon soda
½ cup white sugar 1 cup flour
½ cup brown sugar 1 cup sour cream
1 teaspoon cinnamon ½ cup broken pecans

Beat egg. Mix sugars, cinnamon and soda with flour. Add alternately with sour cream, beating after each addition. Pour into 8½ x 11 inch pan, sprinkle pecans on top. Bake in 350° oven thirty to forty minutes.

Mrs. Edward Converse

DARK FRUIT CAKE

1 pound butter	1 pound walnuts
2 cups sugar	(or blanched almonds)
12 eggs, separated	1 pound pecans
1 glass jelly	1 pound white raisins
1 cup grape juice	½ pound citron
1 cup molasses	½ pound cherries
1 teaspoon cinnamon	½ pound pineapple
1 teaspoon nutmeg	3 heaping teaspoons
1 teaspoon cloves	baking powder
1 teaspoon allspice	1 pound flour

Cream butter and sugar. Beat egg yolks until very light, add to butter and sugar. Fold in stiffly beaten egg whites, jelly, grape juice, molasses and all remaining ingredients cinnamon through pecans. Dredge all fruits with flour and add. Mix baking power with remaining flour and add. Bake in 325° oven about four hours.

Mrs. Frank Terrell

NUT CAKE (100 YEAR OLD FAMILY RECEIPT)

4 cups nut meats (pecans)	1 tablespoon cinnamon
1 pound raisins	1 tablespoon allspice
flour	1 tablespoon nutmeg
2 cups sugar	1 teaspoon ground cloves
1 cup butter	½ cup milk
6 eggs	2 wine glasses sherry or brandy
3½ cups plain flour	2 teaspoons baking powder

Lightly flour nuts and raisins, set aside. Cream sugar and butter together until fluffy, break eggs in, one at a time and beat on low speed. Sift together flour and spices, add to butter mixture alternately with milk. Add fruit and blend by hand. Add wine and baking powder. Bake in greased and paper lined tube pan. Bake in 250° oven for one hour, turn oven temperature to 300° and bake an additional hour.

Mrs. S. O. Starke

SPICE CAKE

2 cups sugar	1 teaspoon cloves
1 stick butter	1 heaping teaspoon cinnamon
3 eggs, separated	1 cup buttermilk
½ teaspoon salt	1 teaspoon soda
2 cups flour	1 teaspoon vanilla

Cream sugar and butter, add egg yolks. Sift together flour, cloves, cinnamon and add, alternately, with buttermilk mixed with soda, to creamed mixture. Do not use electric mixer anymore. Fold in stiffly beaten egg whites and vanilla. Grease bottoms, but not sides of three layer cake pans. Bake in 350° oven for approximately twenty minutes.

Icing:

3 cups sugar	¾ teaspoon soda
1½ cups buttermilk	2¼ sticks butter or margarine

Cook until thick, approximately one hour. Cool a minute, then beat with electric mixer until spreading consistency. Add a little vanilla. If icing gets too hard, place pot in pan of boiling water to soften.

Mrs. J. Tyler Turner

ORANGE DATE-NUT CAKE

1 cup butter	4 cups sifted flour
2 cups sugar	¼ teaspoon salt
4 eggs	2 tablespoons grated orange rind
1 teaspoon baking soda	1 pound dates, cut up and floured
1⅓ cups buttermilk	1 cup broken pecan meats

Cream butter and sugar well, beat in eggs, one at a time. Dissolve soda in buttermilk. To butter mixture, add flour sifted with salt in three parts, alternately with buttermilk. Beat after each addition until smooth. Lastly, add orange rind, dates and nuts. Bake in large tube pan in 325° oven for an hour and a half. When cake is done, pour over it the following sauce:

2 cups sugar	2 tablespoons grated orange rind
1 cup orange juice	¼ teaspoon salt

Stir slowly and heat until sugar is dissolved. Pour slowly over cake, allowing cake to absorb sauce. Cool completely before removing from pan.

Mrs. Albert Reynolds, Jr.

CINNAMON CAKE

½ cup butter
⅔ cup sugar
2 eggs, beaten
1½ cups flour
1 teaspoon baking soda
1 teaspoon baking powder

1 tablespoon cinnamon
1 cup buttermilk
½ cup sugar
1 cup butter
1 tablespoon cinnamon

Cream butter and sugar, add eggs. Add sifted dry ingredients alternately with buttermilk, stirring well after each addition. Pour this mixture into greased cake pan. In a saucepan combine one-half cup sugar, one cup butter and a tablespoonful cinnamon. Cook until sugar melts. Place cake in preheated 350° oven. Add syrup at regular intervals by spooning onto cake as it bakes, about fifty minutes. Delicious with coffee.

Mrs. T. E. McCown

AUTUMN BUTTER PECAN CAKE

1 pound butter
2¼ cups sugar
6 whole eggs
4 cups flour
1 teaspoon baking powder

1 small bottle lemon extract
(1½ ounces)
juice of 1 lemon
1 pound chopped white raisins
2 cups chopped pecans

Cream butter and sugar well, beat in eggs, one at a time. Add three cups flour sifted with baking powder, a little at a time. Add lemon extract and lemon juice. Lastly, add raisins and nuts mixed with the remaining flour. Bake in well greased tube cake pan in slow oven (300°-325°) approximately two hours. Wrapped in saran wrap, this cake keeps beautifully.

Mrs. H. W. Thurber, Jr.

WHITE FRUIT CAKE

½ pound margarine
1 cup sugar
6 eggs
1¾ cups flour
½ teaspoon baking powder
small pinch of salt

3 ounces good wine
1 tablespoon vanilla
1 pound each light raisins,
candied cherries, pineapple
1 pound chopped pecans

Cream margarine and sugar, add beaten eggs, mix. Sift one cup flour, baking powder and salt, add to egg mixture, alternating with liquid. Sift

265

¾ cup flour over nuts and fruit, mix, add batter and mix well. Bake in several loaf pans (or one large), well greased and lined with waxed paper. Cover with brown paper cut to fit pan. Place shallow pan of water on lower shelf of oven. Bake in 300°-350° oven for one to two hours, depending on size of pan. Remove brown paper fifteen minutes before cake is done.

Mrs. J. H. Friend, Sr.

PRUNE CAKE

¾ cup butter
1 cup sugar
3 eggs, separated
3 tablespoons soured cream
(coffee cream that has soured)
1 teaspoon soda

2 tablespoons hot water
1 cup prunes (cooked, chopped and mashed)
1½ cups flour
1 teaspoon allspice
1 teaspoon cinnamon
1 teaspoon nutmeg

Cream butter and sugar together. Add well beaten egg yolks, cream and soda which has been dissolved in hot water. Mix in prunes, add flour and spices sifted together. Fold in stiffly beaten egg whites and bake in one layer in 300° oven.

ICING:

1 whole egg
½ cup sugar
⅓ cup soured cream
½ cup stewed prunes, mashed

butter the size of an egg
½ cup raisins
1 cup chopped pecans

Mix all ingredients except pecans and boil two minutes only. Add pecans and smear on cake.

Mrs. Carl Hardin

JAM CAKE

1 cup butter
2 cups sugar
5 eggs, beaten
3 cups flour
1½ teaspoons cloves
½ teaspoon cinnamon
¼ teaspoon salt

1½ teaspoons allspice
1 teaspoon soda
1 cup buttermilk
1 cup nut meats
1 cup raisins
1 cup blackberry jam

Cream butter and sugar, add beaten eggs. Sift flour, spices and salt together. Dissolve soda in buttermilk and add milk and flour alternately to sugar and eggs. Lightly dredge nuts and raisins with flour and add to other mixtures. Add jam. Stir well and bake for forty minutes in two nine-inch pans. Ice with caramel icing or any icing of your choice.

Mrs. J. F. Maury, Jr.

CHEESE CAKE

½ cup melted butter
2 cups fine Zweiback crumbs
¼ cup sugar
2 teaspoons cinnamon
1 tablespoon gelatin
½ cup water
3 eggs, separated
½ cup sugar

½ cup water
2 cups cream cheese
    (2 8 ounce packages)
3 tablespoons lemon juice
1 tablespoon grated lemon rind
¼ teaspoon salt
½ pint whipping cream

Blend butter, crumbs, ¼ cup sugar and cinnamon. Line spring form cake pan with three-fourths of this mixture. Soften gelatin in water. Cook egg yolks, ½ cup sugar and ½ cup water in double boiler until thick. Add gelatin, beat into cheese with lemon juice, rind and salt. Chill, then beat well. Fold in stiffly beaten egg whites and whipped cream. Pour into cake pan and top with remaining crumbs. Chill at least eight hours.

Mrs. N. A. Nicolson

ELIZABETH'S CHEESE CAKE

1½ cups graham cracker crumbs
⅓ cup granulated sugar
½ teaspoon cinnamon
½ stick butter, melted
4 (3 ounce) packages cream
    cheese
4 egg yolks

½ cup sugar
½ teaspoon grated lemon rind
1 teaspoon vanilla
1 pint commercial sour cream
3 tablespoons sugar
1 teaspoon vanilla

Mix graham cracker crumbs, ⅓ cup sugar, cinnamon and melted butter and pat into greased spring form cake pan for crust. Beat egg yolks until thick, add sugar and blend. Add lemon rind and cheese, one package at a time, using slow speed on mixer. Add vanilla. Beat until smooth. Pour into crust and bake in 375° oven for thirty minutes or until top is lightly browned. Cool on cake rack for twenty minutes. Mix sour cream, 3 table-

267

spoons sugar and vanilla and spread on cake, sprinkle lightly with cinnamon. Bake seven minutes in 325° oven. Cool on rack and refrigerate for at least twenty-four hours before serving.

Mrs. Willis Brown

PINEAPPLE UPSIDE DOWN CAKE

2 tablespoons butter	¾ cup sugar
2 tablespoons pineapple juice	4 tablespoons pineapple juice
1 cup brown sugar	1 cup flour
pineapple slices	2 teaspoons baking powder
red cherries	sweetened whipped cream
2 eggs, separated	

In ten inch iron skillet combine butter, pineapple juice and brown sugar. Simmer slowly for two minutes. Arrange pineapple slices in bottom of pan, placing a cherry in the center of each. Seperate eggs, beat yolks, add sugar, 4 tablespoons pineapple juice, flour and baking powder. Add stiffly beaten egg whites. Pour into skillet and bake in 350° oven for 40-45 minutes. Serves with sweetened whipped cream.

Mrs. James Duffy, Jr.

FLORA DORA PIE

1 cake layer	¾ cup sugar
1 small can crushed pineapple	2 tablespoons cornstarch
3 well beaten egg yolks	1 tablespoon butter
juice of 1 lemon	

Combine all ingredients in top of double boiler. Stir constantly and remove from heat when pasty. Spread on *one* layer of cake previously baked. Over this spread meringue, using 2 tablespoons sugar to each egg white. Run in 350° oven to brown, about 20 minutes.

Mrs. John M. Morrissette, Sr.

SOUR CREAM CAKE

2 sticks butter	3 cups sifted flour
3 cups sugar	¼ teaspoon soda
6 eggs, separated	1 teaspoon lemon extract
½ pint commercial sour cream	1 teaspoon vanilla extract

Cream butter and sugar. Add egg yolks, one at a time, beating well after each addition. Add sour cream, flour and soda. Fold in beaten egg whites (stiff, but not dry), lemon extract and vanilla. Bake in greased, lightly floured tube pan in 325° oven an hour and a half or until well done.

Mrs. James Bledsoe

LANE CAKE

LAYERS:

1 cup butter	½ cup homogenized milk
2 cups sugar	½ cup evaporated milk
3¼ cups flour	1 teaspoon vanilla
¾ teaspoon salt	8 egg whites
3½ teaspoons baking powder	

Cream butter and sugar thoroughly. Sift flour, salt and baking powder three times. Add small amounts of flour to creamed mixture alternately with milk, beating until smooth after each addition. Add flavoring. Beat egg whites until fluffy, but not dry, and fold in. Grease three nine-inch layer cake pans lightly and line bottoms with waxed paper. Bake in preheated 350° oven 25-30 minutes or until cake springs back when tested.

FILLING:

8 egg yolks	2 cups grated coconut
1 cup sugar	1 cup chopped white raisins
1 stick butter	½ cup whiskey
1 cup chopped pecans	

Beat egg yolks until light. Gradually add sugar and softened butter and beat well. Cook in top of double boiler until slightly thickened, stirring constantly. While the above is being prepared combine nuts, coconut, raisins and whiskey and let soak. Fold into the thickened mixture. Alternate layers of cake and filling. After assembling cake in layers with filling, ice cake with your favorite white icing.

Mrs. George R. Irvine, Jr.

DATE CAKE

1 package dates, pitted	1 cup sugar
1 cup water	1 egg
1 teaspoon soda	1 cup flour
1 stick margarine	1 cup chopped pecans

269

Boil dates in water for three minutes. Add soda and cool. Cream margarine, sugar and egg, beat in dates. Add flour and nuts. Bake in greased and floured loaf pan about forty-five minutes in 375° oven. This cake is very moist and keeps well.

Mrs. W. B. Erickson, Jr.

AUNT HATTIE'S CAKE

1 cup butter	½ teaspoon soda
2 cups sugar	1 teaspoon vanilla
4 eggs	3 cups sifted flour
1 cup buttermilk	

Cream butter and sugar, add eggs, then milk in which soda has been dissolved. Add vanilla and lastly add flour, mixing well. Bake in three layer cake pans or tube cake pan in moderate oven.

Mrs. Tom Horst, Sr.

PLAIN CAKE MUFFINS

½ cup shortening	2 teaspoons baking powder
1 cup sugar	¼ teaspoon salt
3 eggs	½ cup milk
2 cups flour	

Cream shortening and sugar, add eggs, one at a time, beating well after each addition. Sift together flour, baking powder and salt and add to sugar mixture alternately with milk. Bake in greased muffin tins in 350° oven for twenty minutes. Yield: about two dozen muffins.

Mrs. Clyde Draughon

GRANDMOTHER'S DEVIL'S FOOD CAKE

2 squares chocolate	1 small teaspoon soda
½ cup boiling water	2 cups flour
1½ cups sugar	2 eggs, separated
½ cup butter	½ teaspoon baking powder
½ cup sour milk	1 teaspoon vanilla

Melt chocolate in boiling water. Cream sugar and butter together. Mix sour milk and soda. Add milk mixture alternately with flour (reserving ¼ cup) to creamed butter and sugar, beat well. Add chocolate and beat again. Add beaten egg yolks, stirring well. Beat egg whites. Sift in remaining flour with the baking powder and fold into batter with egg whites. Fold in vanilla. Bake in lined layer cake pans in 350° oven thirty to forty minutes. Frost with boiled chocolate icing.

Mrs. Mac Greer

YELLOW CAKE

1 cup butter	1 teaspoon vanilla
2 cups sugar	3 cups cake flour
4 eggs, separated	3 teaspoons baking powder
1 cup milk	¼ teaspoon salt

Cream butter well, add sugar and continue creaming until light and creamy. Add egg yolks, one at a time, beating well after each addition. Add milk and vanilla alternately; sift in dry ingredients. Fold in egg whites. Bake in 350° oven one hour and fifteen minutes. The three layer cake pans should first be greased and the bottoms lined with waxed paper.

Mrs. E. Sumner Greer

ANGEL FOOD CAKE

12 egg whites (13-14 if eggs are small)	1 cup cake flour, sifted 3 times
1 teaspoon cream of tartar	1 cup sugar
	1 teaspoon vanilla

Beat eggs and add cream of tartar before whites become real stiff. Beat hard. Fold in flour and sugar, add vanilla. Pour into greased tube pan and bake in 325° oven until cake slightly breaks from sides of pan.

Mrs. T. L. Griffin

CHOCOLATE NUT TORTE

1 sponge cake (baked in two layers)	⅓ cup cold milk
2 cups milk	1 cup butter or margarine
½ cup sugar	1 cup confectioner's sugar
½ cup flour	2 teaspoons vanilla
¼ cup cocoa	1½ cups chopped walnuts or pecans

Split each sponge cake layer in half, resulting in four layers. Heat two cups milk. Combine sugar, flour, cocoa and ⅓ cup cold milk. Add to hot milk and cook over hot water until thick, stirring constantly. Remove from heat.

Cover and cool at room temperature. Thoroughly cream butter and confectioner's sugar. Add to cooled mixture, beat smooth. Spread frosting generously between layers, on top and sides of cake and decorate with nuts. Serves 16.

Mrs. J. W. Hartman

CHOCOLATE FUDGE CAKE

1 cup butter	1 teaspoon soda
2 cups sugar	2 tablespoons water
5 eggs	1 large box confectioner's sugar
2½ cups flour	7 tablespoons butter
½ cup cocoa	6 tablespoons cocoa
1 cup buttermilk	5-6 tablespoons cream

Cream butter and sugar thoroughly. Add eggs, one at a time, beating well after each addition. Sift flour and cocoa together and add alternately with buttermilk, beating smooth after each addition. Add the soda, dissolved in water. Turn mixture into three greased and floured layer cake pans and bake in 350° oven about thirty minutes, or until cake springs back when tested. Cool. Sift confectioner's sugar with cocoa. Cream butter with small amount of sugar mixture. Gradually add remaining sugar and blend in cream. Stir to spreading consistency. Spread over layers & top of cake.

Mrs. G. R. Irvine, Jr.

CARAMEL CAKE

¾ stick butter	2 teaspoons baking powder
2 cups brown sugar	1 teaspoon soda
2 egg yolks	1 cup sour milk
2½ cups flour	2 egg whites

Cream butter, sugar and egg yolks. Add dry ingredients alternately with milk. Beat egg whites and fold into batter. Pour into greased pan and bake forty minutes in 375° oven.

Mrs. Rae Crowe

EXCELLENT SPONGE CAKE

2 cups flour	10 eggs, separated
2 cups sugar	1 teaspoon almond extract

Sift flour several times, sift sugar twice. Beat egg yolks and whites separately until very light, add one cup of sugar to each, beat each thoroughly.

272

Combine, add almond extract, fold in flour very gently and bake in 325°-350° oven for one hour.

Mrs. Potter Yeend

CHOCOLATE CAKE

1 stick butter	½ cup cocoa
1¾ cups sugar	1 cup buttermilk
2 whole eggs	1 level teaspoon soda
1 egg white	¼ cup hot water
2 cups sifted cake flour	1½ teaspoons vanilla

Cream butter, adding sugar gradually. Add eggs, one at a time, beating well after each addition. Sift flour three times with soda and cocoa. Add dry ingredients, alternating with liquid and mixing well. Pour into greased cake pans and bake in 375° oven twenty-five to thirty-five minutes. Ice with: ICING:

2 cups sugar	⅔ cup water
⅛ cup flour	1 stick butter
½ cup cocoa	1 teaspoon vanilla

Combine all ingredients in saucepan, cook to 228°. Remove from fire and cool. When cool add vanilla and beat to spreading consistency.

Mrs. Tom Snevely

CHOCOLATE POUND CAKE

½ pound butter	½ teaspoon baking powder
½ cup shortening	½ teaspoon salt
3 cups sugar	4 heaping teaspoons cocoa
5 eggs	1 cup milk
3 cups flour	1 tablespoon vanilla

Cream butter, shortening and sugar together thoroughly. Add eggs. Add sifted dry ingredients alternately with milk. Add vanilla. Bake in well greased and floured tube cake pan in 325° oven for one hour and twenty minutes. Ice cake while hot with the following:

ICING: mix well,

⅔ stick butter, creamed	1 heaping tablespoon cocoa
⅔ box sifted confectioner's sugar, added gradually	1 teaspoon vanilla
	3 tablespoons hot coffee

Mrs. Doug Barfield

POUND CAKE I

3 sticks butter (or margarine)	1 teaspoon vanilla
1 box confectioner's sugar	1 teaspoon almond extract
6 eggs	1 teaspoon orange extract
3½ cups flour	

Cream butter and sugar. Break eggs in one at a time. Add flour slowly, mixing well. Add flavorings. Turn into greased and lightly floured pan and bake in 225° oven for two hours.

Mrs. C. E. Jones

POUND CAKE II

3 cups sugar	1 cup whipping cream
½ pound butter	2 teaspoons vanilla
6 eggs	1 teaspoon lemon extract
3 cups cake flour	

Cream sugar and butter thoroughly, add eggs, one at a time, beating well after each addition. Add flour, a little at a time, and a little cream until all is blended. Add flavoring. Put into cold oven, turn temperature to 350° and bake for one hour or until a light brown crust forms on top. Use a well greased and floured tube cake pan.

Miss Ann Hearin

GREGG STREET POUND CAKE

1¾ sticks soft margarine	10 eggs
¾ cup shortening	3 cups sifted plain flour
3 cups sifted sugar	1 tablespoon vanilla

Cream margarine and shortening together well with mixer. Add sugar, then well beaten eggs, three at a time. Add flour and vanilla. When all ingredients are well blended pour mixture into lightly greased tube cake pan. Preheat oven to 250° for ten minutes. Bake cake at 300° for one hour and fifty minutes. Do not open oven during baking period.

Mrs. Russell Terry

WHITE ICING

½ cup sugar	2 tablespoons water
¼ cup white karo	2 egg whites

Combine sugar, karo and water in saucepan, stir well. Boil rapidly until mixture spins a thread (238°). Beat egg whites stiff, slowly pour hot mixture over egg whites, beat to spreading consistency.

Mrs. E. Sumner Greer

CHOCOLATE FUDGE ICING

3 squares chocolate	1½ tablespoons corn syrup
2¼ cups sugar	pinch of salt
½ cup milk	2 teaspoons vanilla
¾ stick margarine	

Cut chocolate in small pieces. Place all ingredients, except vanilla in a saucepan. Bring slowly to a full, rolling boil, stirring constantly. Boil briskly, without stirring for one minute (1½ minutes on a very humid day) Don't overboil! Cool to lukewarm. Beat, adding vanilla, until thick enough to spread. Adequate for big layer cake. Longer beating makes good fudge.

Mrs. W. B. Erickson, Jr.

NEVER FAIL WHITE ICING

2 cups sugar	8 marshmallows, cut up
½ cup water	1 teaspoon vanilla
2 egg whites	

Combine sugar and water in a saucepan and place on stove, on cold burner. At the same time, put eggs in electric beater and turn beater on. When eggs are almost stiff, add marshmallows. Start beater again and start heat under sugar and water. As syrup first starts to boil, add six tablespoonfuls of syrup to the egg whites while they are beating. Turn beater off. Continue cooking syrup until it spins a thread (238°). Turn beater on, pour remaining syrup into egg mixture, add vanilla and beat until mixture holds stiff peaks. Do not overbeat.

Mrs. T. L. Griffin

LEMON BUTTER ICING

1 stick butter	5 tablespoons grated lemon rind
1 pound confectioner's sugar	¼ cup lemon juice

Cream butter and sugar well. Add grated lemon rind and juice. Spread on cool cake. This is sufficient for two nine inch layers.

Mrs. Leon McVay

NEVER FAIL CARAMEL ICING

2½ cups sugar   ¾ cup milk
1 egg, slightly beaten   1 teaspoon vanilla
1 stick butter

Melt one half cup sugar in iron skillet slowly until brown and runny. Mix egg, butter, and remaining sugar with milk in large saucepan. Cook over a low fire until butter melts. Turn heat to medium and add browned sugar. Cook to soft ball stage (238°). Remove from fire, cool slightly and add vanilla. Beat until spreading consistency. If icing gets too thick, add a little cream. Sufficient for a two layer cake.

Mrs. R. W. Ogburn

LEMON ICING FOR WHITE CAKE

2 tablespoons flour   6 egg yolks
pinch of salt   scant 1 tablespoon butter
2 cups sugar   1 teaspoon cream or
juice and rind of 1½ lemons   condensed milk

Stir flour, salt and sugar together. Add lemon juice and rind. Beat egg yolks until light, add to mixture and cook over double boiler until thick. Remove from heat, add butter and set aside to cool. When cool, add cream and beat to spreading consistency.

Mrs. George R. Irvine, Jr.

LEMON FILLING

3 tablespoons flour   grated rind of two lemons
1 cup sugar   3 egg yolks
1 heaping tablespoon butter 1 cup hot milk
juice of two lemons

Sift flour and sugar together, cream with butter. Add juice, rind, well beaten egg yolks and hot milk. Cook in double boiler until thick. Can be used as cake or pie filling.

Mrs. Ben M. Radcliff

MY FAVORITES

MY FAVORITES

Parade

of Pies

PIES

SUNDAE PIE

1 roll butterscotch-nut icebox cookie dough	3 tablespoons water ice cream (about 1½ quarts)
¾ cup semi-sweet chocolate pieces	3 egg whites pinch of salt
3 tablespoons white corn syrup	6 tablespoons sugar

In nine-inch pie pan make cookie pie crust, using less icebox cookie dough for thinner crust. Bake crust and refrigerate when cool. In double boiler, over hot, not boiling water, melt chocolate pieces with corn syrup and water. Beat with egg beater until smooth, remove from heat and refrigerate. At serving time heat oven to 500°. Fill chilled pie shell with ice cream, refrigerate. Beat egg whites with salt until soft peaks form when beater is raised. Add sugar slowly, continue beating until mixture holds stiff peaks. Pour chocolate, reserving two tablespoonfuls, over ice cream. Cover ice cream evenly with meringue, being sure that meringue touches edge of pie shell at all points. Drizzle remaining chocolate over meringue, cutting through several times to give marbled effect. Bake pie two minutes or until lightly browned. Baked pie may be frozen immediately and served up to three days later. Refrigerate one hour before serving.

Mrs. Jack Gallalee

APPLE PIE

6 large apples	1 unbaked pie crust
½-⅔ cup sugar	½ cup butter
½ teaspoon cinnamon	½ cup brown sugar
½ teaspoon nutmeg	1 cup flour
2 teaspoons flour	

279

Slice apples and mix with sugar, cinnamon, nutmeg and two teaspoonfuls flour. Pour into pie pan lined with unbaked pie crust. Cream butter and brown sugar with fork and add one cup flour—makes a crumb mixture. Sprinkle over pie. Bake in 450° oven for 15 minutes, reduce oven temperature to 350° and bake until done.

Mrs. G. R. Irvine, Jr.

APPLE CRISP

½ cup water
1½ teaspoons cinnamon
4 cups peeled apples

¾ cup flour
1 cup sugar
1 stick butter or margarine

Mix water and cinnamon, a little at a time. Slice apples in casserole dish and pour cinnamon and water over them. Mix flour, sugar and butter with hands until crumbly and sprinkle over top of apples. Bake one to one and a half hours in 350° oven. Four to six servings.

Mrs. Tom Taul

KATE'S APPLE PIE

1 cup sugar
½ teaspoon salt
1 teaspoon cinnamon
1 unbaked pastry shell

pastry strips
4-6 York apples, sliced thin
½ stick butter
juice of 1 lemon

Combine sugar, salt and cinnamon. Sprinkle about half of this mixture over pastry shell. Fill pan with apples, dot with butter, lemon juice and remainder of sugar mixture. Cover with pastry strips, criss cross, and bake in preheated 400° oven for ten minutes. Reduce heat to 300° and cook until done.

Mrs. Homer Alexander

NUTMEG BUTTERMILK PIE

½ cup margarine
⅔ cup sugar
3 eggs
3 tablespoons flour
½ teaspoon salt

½ teaspoon grated lemon rind
2 cups buttermilk
2 teaspoons vanilla
1 unbaked pie shell
ground nutmeg

280

Cream margarine and sugar until fluffy. Beat in eggs and add flour, mix well. Add salt, lemon rind, buttermilk and vanilla, mix well and pour into pie shell. Sprinkle with nutmeg and bake in 325° oven forty-five to fifty minutes.

Mrs. Marion Adams, Jr.

BUTTERSCOTCH PIE

1¼ cups dark brown sugar	3 egg yolks
1¼ cups milk	5 tablespoons butter
4 tablespoons flour rounded	1 teaspoon vanilla

Place sugar, milk and flour in double boiler top, stirring constantly until thickened. Add slightly beaten egg yolks and cook three minutes longer. Remove from fire, add butter. When cool, add vanilla. Pour into baked pie crust. Cover with meringue or whipped cream.

Mrs. C. K. Rutledge

MINCE MEAT PIE

1 jar mince meat	1 teaspoon vanilla
½ stick butter	1 unbaked pie shell
½ cup brown sugar	pastry strips

Combine mince meat, butter and brown sugar, stir well and cook five minutes. Add vanilla and pour into unbaked pie shell. Cover top with pastry strips and bake in 450° oven thirty minutes.

Mrs. E. Sumner Greer

PUMPKIN PIE

4 eggs	2 teaspoons cinnamon
1½ cups sugar (or to taste)	½ teaspoon nutmeg
1 cup milk	1 large can pumpkin
½ teaspoon salt	½ cup brandy or whiskey
1 teaspoon ginger	1 raw pastry shell

Beat eggs and sugar together until creamy. Add milk and salt. Add spices to pumpkin, add to sugar and eggs, adding brandy last. Pour into raw pastry shell and place in cold oven. Set at 400° and bake fifty minutes to an hour.

Mrs. Frank Terrell

ANGEL PIE

4 egg whites	3 tablespoons water
¼ teaspoon cream of tartar	grated rind of one lemon
1 cup sugar	½ cup sugar
4 egg yolks	1⅓ cups heavy cream
3 tablespoons lemon juice	mandarin orange sections

Beat egg whites until frothy, add cream of tartar and beat until stiff. Add sugar and beat until glossy. Grease nine inch pie pan with shortening, line pie pan with meringue. Bake in 275° oven for about an hour. To prepare custard beat egg yolks until lemon colored, add lemon juice with water and grated rind. Gradually add one-half cup sugar and cook in double boiler until thick. When crust and custard are cool beat whipping cream and cover crust with cream. Then cover with custard. Finally cover whole pie with whipped cream and refrigerate. Be sure to have pie air tight in container or aluminum foil in order to keep crust crisp. Garnish with orange sections before serving. Serves 8.

Mrs. John Moss

RICE CEREAL ICE CREAM PIE

1 stick butter	coffee ice cream
1 package dot sweet chocolate	grated chocolate
1½ cups confectioner's sugar	toasted nuts
3 cups crisp rice cereal	

Melt butter and chocolate together in double boiler top. Add sugar and cereal, stirring until well blended. Pour into greased pie plate and smooth evenly over pie plate. When ready to use, cover with ice cream, piling high. Sprinkle grated chocolate over top or toasted nuts. Serve like slices of pie. Freeze leftovers, if any.

Mrs. J. E. Brown, Jr.

HEAVENLY PIE

1 vanilla wafer pie crust	2 ounces whiskey
2 cups whipping cream	4 Heath candy bars
1 cup confectioner's sugar	

Prepare pie crust in a nine inch pan. Whip cream, adding sugar and whiskey. Pile this mixture in pie crust. Break candy bars and sprinkle over top. Chill.

Mrs. Herbert Cole

MARGUERITE GRINER'S GRASSHOPPER PIE

14 Famous chocolate wafers
2 tablespoons butter
24 large marshmallows
½ cup milk

4 tablespoons crème de menthe
2 tablespoons crème de cacao
½ cup whipping cream

Crumble chocolate wafers with butter for crust. Melt marshmallows in milk. Add liquers, fold in whipped cream. Pour into chocolate shell. Store in freezer at all times.

Mrs. Horace Spottswood

CHESS PIE

1½ cups sugar
½ cup water
1½ tablespoons cornmeal
1½ tablespoons flour

½ cup melted butter
6 egg yolks
1 teaspoon vanilla

Combine ingredients and pour into unbaked pie shell. Bake at 250° oven about one hour or until firm in the middle.

Mrs. Jack Gallalee

DEEP DISH PEACH PIE

1 pastry shell
½ cup sugar
½ cup orange juice
lemon juice
pinch of salt

dash of nutmeg
dash of mace
1 tablespoon cornstarch
5 cups peaches
2 tablespoons sherry

Make pastry, line deep baking dish and brown. Make syrup of sugar, orange juice, a little lemon juice and seasoning. Thicken with cornstarch. Add sliced peaches and cook until tender. Remove from fire, add sherry and pour into baked pastry shell. Run in oven for a few minutes.

Mrs. J. F. Maury

LEMON DELIGHT

PASTRY:

1 stick butter or margarine
1 cup flour

1 tablespoon sugar
pinch of salt

Let butter soften and cut into flour mixture with a pastry blender or fork. After thoroughly combined, line baking dish (10″ square or comparable

283

size) which is lightly greased with salad oil. Press out pastry with your fingers until bottom and sides are evenly covered. Bake in 350° oven twenty-five to thirty minutes. Watch carefully and remove from oven when evenly browned. Cool.

FILLING:

1 envelope gelatin	⅓ cup sugar
⅓ cup water	½ teaspoon lemon flavoring
4 egg yolks	½ pint whipping cream
½ cup sugar	2 teaspoons sugar
juice of 1 lemon and grated rind	½ teaspoon vanilla flavoring
2 egg whites	(or lemon again)

Dissolve gelatin in ⅓ cup water. Beat egg yolks thoroughly, until very thick. Add ½ cup sugar, juice and grated rind. Cook in double boiler (over barely boiling water), stirring constantly (with a wooden spoon if handy), and frequently scraping sides of pot with rubber scraper. This must be done to keep eggs from scrambling. Cook ten minutes, until good and thick. If yolks have been thoroughly beaten it takes only these few minutes. Remove from heat and add gelatin. Beat egg whites until very fluffy, add ⅓ cup sugar and ½ teaspoon lemon flavoring, beating until thoroughly blended. Fold into custard and spread over cooked pastry. Whip cream, adding two teaspoons sugar and ½ teaspoon flavoring and spread over top. This may be garnished with grated lemon or orange peel if desired. Refrigerate to jell.

Mrs. John Scott

RUM PIE

¼ cup sugar	1 envelope gelatin
¼ stick butter	½ cup cold water
16 honey graham crackers	1 pint whipping cream
6 egg yolks	¼ cup rum
1 scant cup sugar	bittersweet chocolate

Roll Honey Grahams very fine and add sugar and butter. Line pie shell with this mixture. Beat egg yolks until light, add sugar. Soak gelatin in water. When dissolved place over low flame, bring to boil and pour over sugar and egg mixture, stirring briskly. Whip cream and fold into mixture. Add rum, cool and pour into pie shell. Chill until firm. When ready to serve add shaved chocolate on top. Serves 6.

Mrs. Ed Baumhauer

FRUIT COBBLER

1 stick margarine	1 cup sugar
1 cup sugar	¾ cup flour
2 cups cut up apples, cherries	¾ cup milk
or peaches	2 teaspoons baking powder

Melt margarine in two quart casserole. Sprinkle one cup sugar over fruit, set aside. Mix sugar, flour, milk and baking powder. Add to margarine, add fruit last. Bake for one hour in 300° oven.

Mrs. Tyler Turner

STRAWBERRY ICE BOX PIE

½ pound marshmallows	¼ teaspoon salt
½ cup milk	1 baked 8 or 9 inch pie shell
1 cup heavy cream	1½ cups sliced strawberries
1 teaspoon vanilla	

Melt marshmallows in milk over hot water. Cool thoroughly, but do not allow to jell. Beat out lumps. Fold in whipped cream, vanilla and salt. Arrange strawberries and marshmallow cream mixture in layers in baked pie shell. Chill in refrigerator at least one hour before serving. Remove from refrigerator about twenty minutes before serving to take chill from crust. Any well drained fruit may be used instead of strawberries. (fresh, frozen or canned.)

Mrs. Franklin King

BLACK BOTTOM PIE

20 gingersnaps, crushed fine	1 teaspoon vanilla
½ cup melted butter	1 tablespoon gelatin
4 egg yolks	¼ cup cold water
1½ tablespoons cornstarch	2 tablespoons rum
2 cups milk	4 egg whites
1 cup sugar	½ teaspoon cream of tartar
pinch of salt	1 cup whipping cream
2 (2 ounce) squares unsweetened	½ square chocolate, shaved
chocolate, melted	

Preheat oven to 325°. Mix gingersnaps and butter together, press on bottom and sides of buttered nine inch pie pan. Bake ten minutes; cool. Lightly beat egg yolks and corn starch in double boiler top. Gradually add

285

milk, mixing steadily, add one half cup sugar and a pinch of salt. Place over hot water and cook; stirring frequently, until mixture coats a silver spoon. Measure one and a half cups of the custard mixture and add melted chocolate and vanilla, mixing until well blended. Cool slightly and pour into prepared pie plate; chill. Soften. gelatin in water and add to remaining custard, stirring until dissolved. If custard is too cool to dissolve gelatin, heat slightly over hot water. Cool slightly. Add rum. Beat egg whites with cream of tartar until stiff peaks form. Gradually add remaining sugar, a teaspoonful at a time, beating stiff. Fold into custard. Pour this over chocolate mixture in pie plate; chill. Serve covered with whipped cream and sprinkled with shaved chocolate. Cream need not be flavored.

Anne Goode

CHOCOLATE ANGEL PIE I

½ pound marshmallows
1 cup milk
⅛ teaspoon salt
2 (1 ounce) squares unsweetened
   chocolate, grated

1 cup whipping cream
½ cup walnuts, chopped
1 teaspoon vanilla
1 nine inch pie shell
¼ cup shredded coconut

Add marshmallows to milk and heat in double boiler until melted. Cool. Add salt, whipped cream, chocolate, chopped nuts and vanilla. Pour into pie shell. Sprinkle with coconut. Chill. To serve decorate with whipped cream, grated chocolate and nuts.

Miss Margaret Hixon

CHOCOLATE ANGEL PIE II

2 egg whites
⅛ teaspoon cream of tartar
½ cup sifted granulated sugar
½ cup chopped pecans
½ teaspoon vanilla

1 package Baker's German
   sweet chocolate
3 tablespoons water
1 teaspoon vanilla
1 cup heavy cream, whipped

Beat egg whites with a pinch of salt and cream of tartar, until foamy. Add sugar gradually until stiff peaks hold. Fold in nuts and vanilla. Spread in greased 9-inch pan. Build up sides ½ inch above pan. Bake in 300° oven for 50-55 minutes. Cool. Melt chocolate with water in double boiler. Cool until thickened. Add vanilla and fold in whipped cream. Pour mixture into meringue shell. Serves 6.

Mrs. Inman Ellis

CHOCOLATE RUM PIE

1 (6 ounce) package chocolate   1 tablespoon rum
   chips   1½ cups heavy cream
1 egg   1 pie crust
2 egg yolks   grated chocolate
2 egg whites

Melt chocolate. Add whole egg and egg yolks, one at a time. Beat egg whites until they stand in stiff peaks. Fold with rum into egg yolk mixture. Whip one cup heavy cream and fold into chocolate mixture. Put in pie crust, top with remaining whipped cream. Chocolate may be grated over all. Chill for at least two hours.

Helen Johnston

FUDGE PIE

2 squares chocolate   4 whole eggs
¼ pound butter   1 heaping tablespoon flour
1½ cups sugar   1 teaspoon vanilla
pinch of salt

Melt chocolate and butter together. Add sugar and salt to beaten eggs, add melted ingredients. Stir in flour, add vanilla. Bake in greased pie pan for twenty-five minutes in 350° oven, reduce oven temperature to 250° and bake fifteen to twenty minutes longer.

Mrs. Milton Scheaffer

CHOCOLATE PIE

2 squares unsweetened   ¾ cup sugar
   chocolate   ½ teaspoon vanilla
1 cup milk   1 baked pie shell
2 eggs   4 tablespoons sugar
2 tablespoons flour

In top of double boiler melt chocolate and add milk. Separate eggs. Combine yolks, flour and sugar. Add this mixture to chocolate and milk in double boiler. Cook, stirring constantly, until very thick and smooth. Add vanilla and pour into baked pie shell. Beat two egg whites until very stiff. Add 4 tablespoons sugar, beat in and spread over pie. Brown in 350° oven.

Mrs. William Rowell

FROZEN LEMON PIE

1 cup milk	2 egg whites
1 cup sugar	1 small can evaporated milk,
2 heaping tablespoons flour	whipped
2 egg yolks	butter
juice of 2 lemons	graham cracker or vanilla
grated rind of 1 lemon	wafer crumbs

Make a custard of milk, sugar, flour and egg yolks. Cool. When cool, add lemon juice and rind. Fold in stiffly beaten egg whites and whipped milk. Rub refrigerator tray with butter and sprinkle with crumbs. Pour in lemon mixture and freeze. Serves 12.

Mrs. Theo Middleton

LEMON MERINGUE PIE

1½ cups sugar	½ teaspoon grated lemon peel
3 tablespoons cornstarch	⅓ cup lemon juice
3 tablespoons all purpose flour	1 baked pie shell (9 inch)
⅛ teaspoon salt	3 egg whites
1½ cups hot water	1 teaspoon lemon juice
3 egg yolks, slightly beaten	6 tablespoons sugar
2 tablespoons butter	

Mix first four ingredients in saucepan. Gradually stir in hot water and bring to a boil, stirring constantly. Cook and stir 8 minutes. Stir small amount of hot mixture into egg yolks. Add this to first mixture and cook five minutes more. Add butter and lemon peel. Slowly add ⅓ cup lemon juice. Turn into prepared pie shell. Beat egg whites with 1 teaspoon lemon juice to form soft peaks. Slowly add sugar, beating to soft peaks. Spread over cooled filling. Bake in 250° oven for 12 minutes.

Mrs. John J. Damrich, III

PECAN TARTS

1 (3 ounce) cream cheese	1 tablespoon soft butter
½ cup butter	1 teaspoon vanilla
1 cup sifted flour	dash of salt
1 egg	⅔ cup chopped nuts
¾ cup brown sugar	

Let cheese and butter soften at room temperature. Blend together and stir in flour. Chill for one hour. Shape dough into 2 dozen one-inch balls. Press balls on bottom and sides of small muffin tins. Beat eggs, sugar, butter, vanilla and salt until smooth. Add nuts. Fill cups. Place a nut meat on top of each. Bake for 25 minutes in 325° oven.

Mrs. Jack Gallalee

PECAN PIE

3 eggs	pinch of salt
¾ cup sugar	1 teaspoon vanilla
1 cup brown corn syrup	1 cup pecans, broken
1 heaping tablespoon butter	1 unbaked pie shell

Beat eggs thoroughly. Add sugar and corn syrup. Add butter, salt, vanilla and pecans. Pour into unbaked pie shell and bake in 400° oven for 10 minutes. Reduce temperature to 300°-325° and bake almost an hour, or until filling no longer shakes.

Mrs. N. A. Nicolson

MARIE GRINER'S RUM CHIFFON PIE

½ cup sugar	½ cup cream, whipped
1 envelope gelatin	3 egg whites
¾ cup water	¼ teaspoon cream of tartar
½ teaspoon salt	6 tablespoons sugar
1¼ cups milk	1 baked pie shell
3 egg yolks, beaten	¼ teaspoon nutmeg
2 teaspoons rum flavoring	

Mix ½ cup sugar, gelatin, water, salt and milk. Cook over low heat until mixture begins to boil. Remove immediately. Pour this mixture slowly over egg yolks and rum flavoring, and cool until mixture thickens. Fold in whipped cream. Beat egg whites with cream of tartar until foamy. Gradually add sugar to egg whites and beat until stiff. Fold beaten egg whites into rum mixture. Fill pie shell and sprinkle with nutmeg. Refrigerate until set.

Mrs. Horace T. Spottswood

289

MAGIC LEMON ICEBOX PIE

1 cup finely crushed chocolate cookie crumbs	1 (15 ounce) can condensed milk
2 tablespoons sugar	½ cup fresh lemon juice
2 tablespoons melted butter	¼ teaspoon almond extract
2 eggs, separated	4 tablespoons sugar
1 tablespoon grated lemon rind	

Combine crumbs and two tablespoonfuls sugar and butter. Press one cup of this on well buttered oblong pan and chill, reserving remaining crumbs for top. Beat egg yolks until thick. Add milk, rind, juice and extract, mixing well until thick. Beat egg whites and gradually add remaining sugar. Beat until stiff. Fold into lemon mixture and pour into pan. Top with remaining crumbs. Freeze 4 to 6 hours or until firm.

Mrs. Mason Dillard

GERMAN BLUEBERRY PIE

⅔ cup sugar	3 eggs
pecan sandies	1 teaspoon vanilla
butter	1 pint blueberries (fresh)
1 (8 ounce) package cream cheese	

Crumble enough pecan sandies for pie crust. Blend these with just enough butter to hold crumbs together. Press this mixture into an 8-inch pie pan and set aside. Cream sugar with softened cream cheese. Add eggs one at a time to cream cheese mixture beating well after each addition. Add vanilla. Pour this mixture into pie shell. Sprinkle blueberries over the top. (this will seem like an excessive amount of blueberries, but use them all as they drop down into custard) Bake in 350° oven for 25 minutes. When cool, chill several hours or overnight.

Mrs. Selden Stephens

BLACKBERRY PIE

1 cup sugar	4½ cups fresh berries
5 tablespoons flour	pastry for two crust pie
½ teaspoon cinnamon	1½ tablespoons butter

Mix together sugar, flour, and cinnamon. Mix lightly through berries. Pour berries into pastry-lined pie pan and dot with butter. Cover with top crust.

290

Bake in 425° oven 35 to 45 minutes until crust is brown and juice begins to bubble through slits in crust. Serve warm.

Mrs. Franklin King

DEWBERRY PIE

2 unbaked pie crusts	juice of ½ lemon
4-5 cups dewberries	dash of nutmeg
1 cup sugar	2 tablespoons butter
2 tablespoons cornstarch	

Spread berries evenly in pie shell. Mix sugar and cornstarch and sprinkle over berries. Add lemon juice and nutmeg. Dot with butter. Cover with top crust. Dot crust with butter and sprinkle with sugar. Bake in 425° oven 15 minutes. Reduce temperature to 350° and continue baking 45 minutes.

Mrs. Jack Campbell

APRICOT TART

1 box (12-16 ounces) dried apricots	2 cups sifted flour
¾ cup sugar	1 teaspoon salt
1½ sticks butter	½ teaspoon soda
1 cup sugar	½ cup walnuts or pecans
	1 can coconut (angel flaked)

Cook apricots until tender. Add three-fourths cup sugar and cook until thick. Cool. Cream butter, gradually adding sugar, and mix well. Blend in flour, sifted with salt and soda. Add nuts and coconut. Press about two-thirds of flour mixture in bottom and around sides of 13 x 9 x 2 pan. Bake for ten minutes in 400° oven. Remove from oven. Spread apricots over half baked crust, and sprinkle with remaining crumbs (add a little dry flour to make crumbs). Return to 300° oven for 20 to 25 minutes, until golden brown.

Mrs. Marshall J. DeMouy

RASPBERRY TARTS

2 (8 ounce) packages cream cheese	2 cups flour
½ pound butter	raspberry jam

Mix cheese, butter and flour, and refrigerate overnight. Roll thin on floured board and cut into squares. Place a bit of raspberry jam on each square, fold over and crimp edges. Bake in 350° oven 30 to 40 minutes. Yields about 45 tarts.

Mrs. Leon McVay, Jr.

SHERRY CHIFFON PIE

1¼ cups graham cracker crumbs	1 envelope unflavored gelatin
¼ cup butter, melted	½ cup sherry
4 eggs yolks	2 egg whites, stiffly beaten
½ cup sugar	½ cup sugar
½ teaspoon salt	½ teaspoon almond flavoring
½ cup hot water	

Line pie plate with cracker crumbs mixed with butter. Heat in moderate oven 10 minutes. Cool. Mix slightly beaten yolks with ½ cup sugar, salt, and hot water. Cook in double boiler until mixture coats spoon. Soak gelatin in sherry for five minutes. Pour flavored gelatin into hot custard. When congealed, fold in egg whites to which have been added ½ cup sugar and almond flavoring. Pour into pie shell. Cover with whipped cream. Serves 8.

Mrs. M. B. Slaughter

FOOLPROOF PIE CRUST

1½ cups flour	⅓ cup butter or
2 tablespoons sugar	margarine

Mix flour, sugar and butter. Press into nine or six inch pie pan. Bake in 375° oven until slightly brown. Watch carefully so it doesn't burn.

Mrs. George McNally

PASTRY

2¼ cups flour	1 teaspoon salt
¾ cup Crisco	5 tablespoons cold water

Mix flour, shortening and salt thoroughly. Add cold water. Sufficient for two crusts.

Mrs. Randall Hollinger

PIE CRUST ICE BOX PIE

1 cup graham cracker crumbs	3 tablespoons sugar
¼ cup wheat germ	⅓ cup butter or margarine

Combine crumbs, wheat germ and sugar. Stir in melted butter. Pack mixture into a nine inch pie pan. Bake in 350° oven for eight minutes. Chill and fill. This has a slightly nutty flavor and is especially good for lemon ice box pie.

Mrs. Will G. Caffey

292

MY FAVORITES

MY FAVORITES

Cookies
and Candies

YUM-YUM LAND

COOKIES AND CANDIES

COOKIES

ALMOND ROLLS

⅔ cup ground almonds
½ cup butter
½ cup sugar

2 tablespoons milk
1 tablespoon flour
sifted confectioner's sugar

Combine all ingredients except confectioner's sugar. Heat, stirring mixture until of a mushy consistency. Drop by teaspoonfuls three inches apart. Bake one sheet at a time, in 350° oven. Remove from sheet, one at a time, and quickly roll around the handle of a wooden spoon. Dust with sugar.

Mrs. Harold Winn

PECAN COCOONS

1 cup butter or margarine
½ cup confectioner's sugar
2¼ cups sifted flour

¼ teaspoon salt
1 teaspoon vanilla
1 cup finely chopped pecans

Mix all ingredients and form into finger shaped cocoons. Bake about 15 minutes in 350° open. Roll in confectioner's sugar while hot. Cool, then roll again.

Mrs. J. Everett Sapp

ALMOND ICE BOX COOKIES

½ pound butter
½ pound brown sugar
1 egg
3 tablespoons baking powder

pinch of salt
1 tablespoon vanilla
¼ pound almonds, blanched
    and lightly toasted
3 cups flour

295

Cream butter and sugar well. Add egg and work in dry ingredients, sifted together. Add vanilla and floured nuts. Make into a roll and refrigerate several hours or overnight. Cut into thin slices and bake on greased cookie sheet in 350° oven until crisp.

Mrs. Marion S. Adams, Sr.

TEA CAKES

1 cup butter	1 teaspoon salt
2 cups sugar	3-5 cups flour
3 eggs	1 teaspoon soda
1 tablespoon milk	2 teaspoons cream of tartar
1 teaspoon cinnamon	chopped pecans
1 teaspoon nutmeg	

Cream butter and sugar. Add beaten eggs and mix well. Add milk. Add cinnamon and nutmeg. Sift remaining dry ingredients together, starting with two cups flour. Sift gradually into first mixture, adding flour as necessary. Roll out on floured board, adding pecans. Roll very thin. Cut into desired shapes. Bake on greased cookie sheet in 400° oven until brown. About 8 dozen cookies.

Mrs. Mabel Toulmin

BESSIE'S ICE WATER COOKIES

⅓ pound butter	1 tablespoon ice water
4 heaping teaspoons confectioner's sugar	1 teaspoon vanilla
	1 cup chopped nuts
2 cups cake flour	

Cream butter and sugar. Add flour, ice water and vanilla and blend well. Stir in nuts. Shape each tablespoonful of dough into a crescent. Bake on greased cookie sheet thirty minutes in 250° oven. Do not brown. Cool on wire rack, then roll in powdered sugar. Makes 2 dozen.

Mrs. James E. Brown, Jr.

MRS. UNGER'S COOKIES

1 stick (¼ pound) butter or margarine	2 cups flour
	¼ teaspoon salt
1 cup sugar	1 tablespoon milk
1 egg	2 teaspoons baking powder

Cream butter and sugar together. Add egg and mix thoroughly. Beat in flour and salt. Add milk if batter is too stiff for cookie press. Squeeze through press or roll out and cut into various shapes. Decorate with colored sugar, nuts, dots of jelly or fondant, colored and squeezed through tube. Bake in 350° oven for about 10 minutes.

Mrs. D. S. M. Unger

BUTTER COOKIES

½ pound butter	½ teaspoon almond flavoring
⅔ cup sugar	½ teaspoon vanilla flavoring
3 egg yolks	2½ cups sifted flour
2 tablespoons cream	

Cream together butter and sugar. Add beaten egg yolks, cream, flavorings and flour. Make a stiff dough. Chill in refrigerator. Roll thin and cut out. (The dough could be shaped into a roll, wrapped in waxed paper, and sliced after chilling.) Bake on cookie sheet in 350° oven for 12-15 minutes. Yield: about 3 dozen cookies.

Mrs. Wilmer Scott

GERMAN ICE BOX COOKIES

1 cup butter	2 teaspoons cream of tartar
1 box brown sugar	4½ cups flour
4 eggs	2 cups broken pecan meats
1 teaspoon soda	

Cream butter and sugar. Add eggs and mix well. Into butter mixture, sift dry ingredients, mixing well. Stir in pecans. Make into rolls about one and a half inches in diameter and refrigerate for at least forty-eight hours. Slice into quarter inch slices. Bake on ungreased cookie sheet in 350° oven for 15 to 20 minutes.

Mrs. J. C. Carrington

DATE BALLS

1¼ cups sifted flour	1 tablespoon milk
¼ teaspoon salt	1 teaspoon vanilla
½ cup butter	⅔ cup chopped dates
⅓ cup sifted confectioner's sugar	¾ cup chopped nuts
	confectioner's sugar

297

Sift flour and salt together twice. Cream butter and gradually add sugar. Add milk and vanilla and stir in sifted flour. Blend in dates and nuts. Roll into one inch balls. Place 3 inches apart on ungreased cookie sheet and bake for 20 minutes in 300° oven. Remove from oven when light brown and roll in confectioner's sugar while still warm. Makes about 3 dozen cookies.

Mrs. B. Franklin King, Jr.

COCONUT MACAROONS

1 can (3½ ounce) flaked coconut	3 egg whites
	3 tablespoons flour
¾ cup sugar	1 teaspoon almond extract

Mix coconut, sugar and unbeaten egg whites together in a medium saucepan. Cook over moderate heat, stirring constantly, until batter appears to be as thick as mashed potatoes. Do not let the mixture boil. This takes eight to ten minutes. A good test is to pull a path through the batter with a spoon, and when the path stays clear for a short while, the batter has reached correct thickness. Remove from heat. Stir in flour and almond extract. Drop little mounds of batter from a teaspoon onto greased, lightly floured cookie sheet. To give the macaroons better shape let them stand at room temperature about a half hour before baking. Preheat oven to very slow 300° and make 22 to 25 minutes, until macaroons are golden brown. Remove from cookie sheet immediately. Yield: about 18.

Mrs. Mac B. Greer

OATMEAL COOKIES I

2 sticks (½ pound) margarine	1 teaspoon salt
¾ cup brown sugar	1 teaspoon vanilla
¾ cup granulated sugar	2 cups oatmeal
2 eggs	1 cup chopped pecans
1½ cups flour	2 packages chocolate chips or
1 teaspoon soda	1 cup raisins

Cream margarine and sugars. Add eggs and beat well. Add sifted dry ingredients. Add vanilla, oats, nuts and chocolate or raisins. Drop by teaspoonfuls onto ungreased cookie sheet. Bake in 350° oven 12 to 15 minutes. Run spatula under each cookie and leave on tin until cool. Makes 3 dozen.

Mrs. Randall Hollinger

OATMEAL COOKIES II

1¼ cups sugar	1 teaspoon cinnamon
1 cup shortening	½ teaspoon salt
2 eggs, well beaten	2 cups oatmeal
4 tablespoons milk	½ cup chopped pecans
2 cups sifted flour	1 cup raisins
1 teaspoon baking soda	1 teaspoon vanilla

Cream sugar and shortening. Add beaten eggs, then milk and blend well. Stir in sifted dry ingredients and blend. Add oatmeal, nuts, raisins and vanilla and mix well. Drop by teaspoonfuls onto greased cookie sheet. Bake in 350° oven 12 to 15 minutes.

Mrs. Clyde Draughon

CHRISTMAS ROCKS

1 cup butter	1 teaspoon nutmeg
1 cup sugar	1 teaspoon cloves
6 eggs	2 quarts chopped pecans
3 cups flour	1 pound crystallized pineapple
1 teaspoon cinnamon	1 pound candied cherries
1 teaspoon allspice	1 cup whiskey

Cream butter and sugar thoroughly. Add eggs, one at a time, beating smooth after each addition. Sift flour and spices together and add gradually, beating well. Chop nuts, pineapple and cherries and roll in just enough flour to coat. Add to mixture. Add whiskey. Drop on greased cookie sheet by teaspoons and bake in 350° oven about 18 minutes.

Mrs. George R. Irvine, Jr.

DATE FLUFFS

4 egg whites	1 (8 ounce) package
1¼ cups sugar	pitted dates, chopped
1 teaspoon vinegar	1 cup chopped pecans

Beat egg whites until stiff, but not dry. Add slowly, while beating constantly, the sugar and then the vinegar. Fold in chopped dates and pecans. Drop on greased paper. Bake very slowly for about 45 minutes in 275° oven. (These may be made a day or two ahead and wrapped in waxed paper until time to use.) Put whipped cream on each puff and garnish with a cherry.

Mrs. Walter Ogburn, Jr.

299

ROCKS

5 eggs	1 teaspoon vanilla
1 cup butter	1 teaspoon nutmeg
1½ cups sugar	1 pound dates
1 teaspoon soda	1 cup nut meats
1 tablespoon warm water	1 cup fruit cake mix or
3½ cups sifted flour	cut crystallized fruit

Beat eggs together lightly. Cream butter, sugar and soda dissolved in water. Add flour, vanilla and nutmeg. Add dates, cut and floured, and nut meats. Add fruit cake mix or cut fruit. Drop in little cakes on greased cookie sheet. Garnish with pecan half or crystallized cherry. Bake in 350° oven. (Nice Christmas cookies which will keep for weeks in a tin)

Mrs. Walter Ogburn, Jr.

LEMON MERINGUE SQUARES

½ cup shortening	1 cup sifted all-purpose flour
½ cup sifted confectioner's sugar	½ cup granulated sugar
2 tablespoons grated lemon rind	1 tablespoon lemon juice
2 eggs, separated	½ cup finely chopped nut meats

Cream shortening and confectioner's sugar together until light and fluffy. Blend in lemon rind. Beat egg yolks until thick and light. Add to first mixture. Add flour slowly and mix until smooth. Spread and pat this stiff mixture in a thin, even layer in a greased 9x13x2-inch pan. Bake in 350° oven for 10 minutes. Meanwhile beat egg whites until fluffy. Add sugar gradually while beating. Beat until stiff, but not dry. Fold in lemon juice, a little at a time. Fold in nuts. Spread over baked layer. Return to oven and bake 25 minutes longer. Cool about 3 minutes and cut into about 48 squares.

Mrs. Leon McVay, Jr.

BUTTER CHEWS

¾ cup butter	3 eggs, separated
3 tablespoons sugar	1 cup chopped nuts
1½ cups flour	¾ cup shredded coconut
2¼ cups brown sugar	confectioner's sugar

Cream butter. Add sugar and beat well. Blend first mixture thoroughly with flour. Pat mixture into a greased pan (or two 8 x 8-inch pans). Bake for 15 minutes in 375° oven. Remove from oven. Add brown sugar to the beaten

300

egg yolks and blend well. Add nuts and coconut. Fold in beaten egg whites. Pour over the baked mixture and return to the oven for 25 minutes. Cut in 1 x 2-inch strips and dust with confectioner's sugar. Makes about 3 dozen.

Mrs. Yetta G. Samford, Jr.

MOM'S BROWNIES

½ stick margarine (⅛ pound)	½ cup flour
2 squares unsweetened chocolate	pinch of salt
2 eggs	1 teaspoon vanilla
1 cup sugar	1 cup chopped nut meats

Melt butter and chocolate together. In a bowl, beat eggs well and add sugar, flour and salt, mixing well. Add melted chocolate and margarine, mixing well. Add vanilla and nut meats. Bake in well greased 8 x 8-inch pan in 350° oven for 25-30 minutes.

Mrs. George P. Shedd

ALMOND FINGERS

1 sponge cake (baked in long pans)	cream (or substitute coffee, rum, sherry, vanilla, almond or melted chocolate)
1 cup sweet, unsalted butter	
1 egg yolk, beaten	ground toasted almonds
about 2½ cups powdered sugar	

Cut sponge cake in the shape of fingers. Ice with a mixture of all above ingredients except almonds. Roll in ground toasted almonds.

Mrs. T. P. Yeend

NUT FUDGIES

2 squares of bitter chocolate	½ cup sifted flour
½ cup margarine	¼ teaspoon salt
1 cup sugar	½ cup finely chopped nuts
2 eggs, beaten	1 teaspoon vanilla

Melt chocolate and margarine in double boiler. Remove from heat. Stir in sugar and eggs. Add flour, salt and vanilla. Pour in buttered pan and sprinkle nuts on top. Bake for about 10 minutes at 400°. This is so easy and good. Cook in long pan if you like them chewy.

Mrs. H. Browne Mercer

BROWN SUGAR SQUARES

2 eggs	¼ teaspoon salt
2 cups brown sugar	1 teaspoon vanilla
1 cup flour	1 cup chopped pecans
¼ teaspoon soda	

Line 8 x 13-inch pan with waxed paper and grease paper well. Beat eggs. Add sugar and cream together. Add sifted dry ingredients. Add vanilla and pecans. Bake 25-30 minutes in 275-300° oven. Makes 2 dozen medium squares.

Mrs. J. H. Friend

ORANGE SQUARES

2 cups sifted flour	1½ cups chopped nuts
2 cups brown sugar	½ stick butter (⅛ pound)
4 eggs, well beaten	½ box confectioner's sugar
1 tablespoon water	orange juice
1 pound chopped candied orange slices	grated orange rind

Mix flour and sugar. Add eggs and then water. Fold in chopped orange and nuts. Bake in shallow pan 40 to 45 minutes in 375° oven. While hot, ice with the following: Creamed butter and sugar combined with enough orange juice to thin and grated orange rind to taste.

Mrs. Rae Crowe

DATE STRIPS

3 eggs	1 cup flour
1 cup sugar	1 teaspoon salt
½ cup raisins	1 teaspoon soda
1 (7¼ ounce) box pitted dates	2 teaspoons vanilla
1 cup nut meats	3 tablespoons water

Beat eggs until light. Add sugar gradually and blend until light. Add raisins, dates and nuts. Sift dry ingredients together and add to egg mixture. Add vanilla and water. Bake in greased square pan in 325° oven for 30 minutes. While warm cut in strips and roll in powdered sugar.

Mrs. J. Everett Sapp

CANDY

SPICED CANDIED NUTS

1 cup sugar	2 tablespoons water
½ teaspoon cinnamon	1½ cups nut meats
¼ cup Pet milk	½ teaspoon vanilla

Mix sugar, cinnamon, milk and water together in saucepan, cooking to soft ball stage (234°). Remove from heat. Add nuts and vanilla. Stir until mixture can no longer be stirred. Turn out on waxed paper and separate into small pieces. Must be done quickly.

Mrs. Rae Crowe

SPICED NUTS

½ cup sugar	¼ teaspoon ground cloves
½ teaspoon salt	2 tablespoons water
1 teaspoon cinnamon	¼ pound nuts
¼ teaspoon nutmeg	

Mix together sugar, salt, spices and water. Boil to soft ball stage (238°). Add nuts, remove from fire, and stir until all turns to sugar. Pour onto platter or waxed paper. When cool, break apart.

Mrs. Celia Fowler

PENUCHE NUTS

1 cup brown sugar	½ cup white sugar
½ cup sour cream	1 teaspoon vanilla
(or canned Pet milk with	2½ cups nut meats
1 tablespoon lemon juice)	

Cook sugars and sour cream over low heat, stirring constantly until dissolved. Cook until a little dropped in water forms a rather stiff ball (246°). Remove from fire. Add vanilla and nuts. Stir until nuts are well coated. Pour onto very lightly greased surface and separate nuts.

Mrs. Marion S. Adams, Sr.

CANDIED PECANS

2 cups sugar	1 teaspoon vanilla
½ cup water	3 cups pecan halves
½ teaspoon salt	

303

Boil together the water, sugar and salt until syrup threads when dropped from spoon. Remove from fire and add vanilla. Stir until mixed, and then add 3 cups of pecan halves. Turn these over in the syrup, being careful not to break nuts, until the syrup hardens. Remove to platter. When cool enough to handle, separate each nut and place on plates or wax paper and cool.

CHOCOLATE PECANS

Same as above, mixing 1 tablespoon cocoa with dry sugar before adding water. Test by dropping in cold water. Should form soft ball.

PEPPERMINT PECANS

Color the syrup with red coloring and add a few drops of essence of peppermint.

Miss Margaret H. Hixon

KISSES

3 egg whites 1 teaspoon rum
1½ cups sugar 1½ cups shredded pecans
½ cup hot water 1 teaspoon grated orange rind

Beat egg whites stiff, but not dry. In saucepan combine sugar and hot water and cook to soft ball stage (238°). Beat slowly into egg whites. Add rum, pecans, and rind. Drop by spoonfuls, spaced onto cookie sheet covered with waxed paper. Bake in 350° oven until light tan.

Mrs. Frank Sauer

MORAVIAN MINTS

1 box confectioner's sugar 14 drops oil of peppermint
4 teaspoons water Gold Brick Sauce

Combine sugar with water and peppermint oil, stir until smooth and drop on a platter from the end of a spoon. Flatten top and chill in refrigerator. Drop a small amount of Gold Brick sauce in center of each mint and chill again. Pass after dinner with coffee.

Mrs. Frank B. Frazer

FANCY CANDY BALLS

2 pounds confectioner's sugar	1 stick margarine
1 can condensed milk	2 cans coconut
1 teaspoon vanilla	7 squares semisweet chocolate
1 quart pecans	½ block paraffin wax

Mix sugar, condensed milk, vanilla, pecans, margarine and coconut. Chill mixture. Roll into balls and chill hard. In double boiler melt chocolate and paraffin. Dip chilled balls in this mixture and place on waxed paper to dry and cool.

Mrs. V. L. Oberkirch

DELICIOUS FUDGE

4½ cups sugar	3 packages chocolate tidbits
1 large can evaporated milk	5 ounce jar marshmallow cream
2 sticks (½ pound) butter	3 cups pecans

Combine sugar and milk. Cook fourteen minutes. Add remaining ingredients. Pour into greased pan and refrigerate. Return to room temperature to cut in squares. This recipe makes two pounds of delicious creamy fudge. Keeps well.

Mrs. Harold Winn

FUDGE

3 cups sugar	2 tablespoons light corn syrup
⅓-½ cup cocoa	3 tablespoons butter
1½ cups milk or diluted canned cream	1 teaspoon vanilla
¼ teaspoon salt	1 cup chopped nuts

Mix sugar and cocoa together thoroughly. Add milk, salt and corn syrup. Boil slowly to soft ball stage (238°). Remove from fire, add butter and cool. Add vanilla and beat until smooth. Add nuts and pour into greased 8 x 8-inch pan.

Mrs. Richard Cunningham

FOOL PROOF FUDGE

½ cup cocoa	⅓ cup water
3 cups sugar	1 teaspoon vanilla
⅔ cup evaporated milk	3 tablespoons butter

Combine cocoa, sugar, milk and water. Bring to a slow boil, stirring occasionally. Cook until a small amount forms a soft ball in cold water (234°). Remove from heat. Add vanilla and butter as mixture cools. Beat until it thickens. Pour on a buttered pan or platter and cut in squares. Allow to set.

Mrs. Wallace S. Clark, II

CREAM CANDY

3 cups sugar	few drops mint or vanilla
½ stick butter or margarine	flavoring
1 cup water	food coloring

Combine sugar, butter and water in saucepan over medium heat. Without stirring bring to rapid boil and cook until candy thermometer reaches 260°. Pour immediately on well greased marble. Let stand until cool enough to handle. Pull until white and stiff (about ten to fifteen minutes). Add flavoring while pulling and color also, if desired. Place long pulled strips on marble and cut into small pieces with scissors. Let stand until it turns creamy. Pack in tin box.

Mrs. John Morrissette

MERINGUE KISSES

3 egg whites	pinch of salt
½ cup sugar	½ teaspoon flavoring

Beat egg whites until very fluffy. Slowly add sugar, salt and flavoring, continuing to beat until thoroughly blended and stiff enough to hold a peak. Drop from a spoon onto cookie sheet covered with brown paper, if bite size kisses are desired. If kisses are to be used as a base for a filling, shape with spoon and hollow out center to a shallow well. Bake in 225° oven for one hour, turn off oven heat and leave kisses in oven with door closed until oven has cooled.

Mrs. John M. Scott, Jr.

BROWN SUGAR CANDY

2 pounds light brown sugar	1 stick butter
½ pint whipping cream	3 cups nuts

306

Cook sugar, cream and butter, stirring until mixture boils and for six minutes after boiling point is reached. Remove from fire, beat, add nuts, pour onto buttered platter.

Mrs. Mark Lyons, III

DIVINITY I

3 cups sugar
½ cup water
¾ cup light Karo syrup

3 egg whites
1 teaspoon vanilla
pecan meats

Boil sugar, water and Karo until mixture forms a long thread (238°). Add hot syrup to stiffly beaten egg whites. Add vanilla and pecans. Drop by teaspoonfuls on waxed paper.

Mrs. Rae Crowe

DIVINITY II

2½ cups sugar
½ cup water
½ cup white corn syrup

1 teaspoon vinegar
2 egg whites
2 teaspoons vanilla

Mix sugar, water, corn syrup and vinegar. Boil to thin thread stage (238°). Beat egg whites stiff. Pour syrup slowly over egg whites, stirring constantly. Add vanilla and beat until stiff. Drop by spoonfuls onto waxed paper. A cup of nut meats and (or) artificial coloring may be added after the flavoring, if desired.

Mrs. Robert Weinacker

ENGLISH TOFFEE

½ cup pecans
1½ cups vanilla wafers, ground
1½ squares bitter chocolate
½ cup butter

1 cup confectioner's sugar
3 eggs, separated
whipped cream or ice cream

Mix pecans and ground wafers. Melt chocolate. Cream butter, sugar and egg yolks, well beaten. Add chocolate and stiffly beaten egg whites by folding into creamed mixture. Spread half the crumbs in the bottom of an 8 x 10-inch pan and add filling. Top with remaining crumbs and chill overnight. Serve with whipped cream or ice cream.

Mrs. Robert Meador

307

PATIENCE CANDY

3 cups sugar	1 tablespoon butter
1½ cups milk	1 cup walnuts

Melt one cup sugar in iron skillet, stirring constantly. Mix remaining sugar with milk and boil while sugar is melting. Add melted sugar to milk mixture stirring constantly and boil to soft ball stage (238°). Beat and add nuts.

Mrs. Richard Overby

CARAMEL CANDY

1 cup light cream	scant ¼ stick butter or margarine
3 cups sugar	1 cup chopped pecans

In heavy saucepan, melt one cup of sugar to a light brown. Simultaneously, mix two cups sugar with cream and bring to a boil. Pour cream mixture into caramelized sugar and cook to soft ball stage (238°). Remove from fire and add butter. Let stand without stirring about fifteen minutes, or until cool. Then stir until thick and creamy. Add nuts and pour onto buttered pan.

Mrs. George R. Irvine, Jr.

PRALINES

1 box light brown sugar	1½ teaspoons vanilla
½ cup water	pecans
1 generous tablespoon butter	

Combine sugar and water in saucepan and cook to soft ball stage (238°), stirring constantly. Remove from fire. Add butter and vanilla. Beat until creamy. Add pecans (whole pecans are prettiest). Pour out on waxed paper. They look like they won't harden, but they will if mixture was cooked to soft ball stage.

Mrs. V. L. Oberkirch

MY FAVORITES

MY FAVORITES

QUICK AND EASY

EASY COFFEE SNACK

Cut crust from bread, spread thinly with applebutter. Place cooked sausage on bread, roll up and secure with toothpick. Bake in hot oven until toasted.

Mrs. Graham Willoughby

COCONUT TOAST

Mix six tablespoons confectioner's sugar, a few drops vanilla and one tablespoon milk to make thin icing. Spread on both sides of eight slices of bread. Broil on one side, turn and sprinkle with grated coconut, broil until coconut is golden.

Mrs. Kenneth Granger

SAUSAGE ROLL

1 pound highly seasoned pork sausage

1 small box Old Tyme biscuit mix

Roll out sausage into one long, flat piece. Make biscuit dough according to package directions. Roll out into one long flat piece slightly larger than sausage roll. Lay sausage on top of biscuit and roll up like a jelly roll. Wrap in freezer paper and freeze. To serve, cut into thin slices and bake in 400°-450° oven for several minutes. Can also be run under broiler following baking. Makes about 36 individual rolls.

Mrs. W. B. Taylor

311

CHEESE SNAPPIES

1 roll (6 ounce) Kraft   1 cup flour
   nippy cheese   ½ teaspoon cayenne
½ cup butter or margarine paprika

Mix cheese, butter and flour with cayenne until combined. Shape into two rolls, 1½ inches in diameter. Wrap in waxed paper, chill overnight. Slice ¼ inch thick, sprinkle with paprika. Bake on greased cookie sheet, a few inches apart for 5-10 minutes in 400° oven. Makes 36.

Mrs. J. Tyler Turner

CUCUMBER SOUP

2 cucumbers, peeled, seeded 1 cup sour cream
   and chopped   1 tablespoon lemon juice
1 envelope (1⅞ ounces)   green food coloring
   cream of leek soup mix chopped chives
2½ cups milk

In blender, buzz cucumbers, soup mix, milk, ¾ cup sour cream, lemon juice and food coloring. Chill for several hours, until icy cold. Serve with a dab of sour cream and a sprinkling of chives.

Mrs. Marshall J. DeMouy

EASY VICHYSSOISE

2 tablespoons minced onions pepper to taste
1 cup light cream   ¼ cup instant potato powder
2 cups milk   1 can condensed cream of
½ teaspoon salt   chicken soup

Add onion to cream, let stand ten minutes. Combine milk, salt and pepper, scald. Stir in instant mashed potatoes and cook over low heat, stirring until smooth and slightly thickened. Combine with cream mixture and soup, cool. Pour into blender or electric mixer bowl, blend until smooth and creamy. Chill well. Serve cold with chopped chives. Serves 6.

Mrs. Leon McVay, Jr.

BRIDE'S CHEESE SOUFFLÉ

1 cup mushroom soup   6 eggs, separated
1 cup shredded cheese

312

QUICK AND EASY

Heat soup slowly, stirring until smooth. Add cheese and cook stirring constantly until cheese melts. Beat egg yolks and add to cheese mixture, cool. Beat egg whites stiff. Fold whites into mixture carefully, but thoroughly. Pour into ungreased two quart casserole and bake for one hour in 300° oven, or until souffle is puffed and done in center. Serves 6.

Mrs. Robert L. Byrd, Jr.

QUICK CHEESE SOUFFLÉ

1 can Campbell's Cheddar cheese soup	½ teaspoon dry mustard
	¼ teaspoon salt
1 teaspoon Worcestershire	4 eggs, separated
	½ cup grated cheese

Heat soup over hot water with Worcestershire, mustard and salt. When smooth, remove from heat and cool. Beat egg yolks light and lemon colored, add to cheese mixture. Beat egg whites stiff, but not dry, fold into cheese mixture. Pour into greased six cup casserole, place in a pan of hot water and bake on bottom rack of 400° oven for ten minutes. Reduce heat to 350° and bake thirty minutes longer.

Mrs. Dewitt King
Mobile Country Club

CHEESE SOUFFLÉ

5 bread slices	salt to taste
4 eggs, beaten	½ pound grated New York
2 cups milk	State cheese
1 teaspoon prepared mustard	

Butter bread on both sides, cut in quarters. To beaten eggs add milk, mustard, salt and cheese, pour over bread. Bake in pan of water in 350° oven for fifty minutes. This is foolproof, won't fail and can be reheated. Serves 12.

Mrs. A. P. Ogburn

SCALLOPED OYSTERS

Preparation time—10 minutes
Cooking time—50 minutes
Amounts of ingredients must be determined by number to be served. Line the bottom of a casserole with a layer of well drained oysters. Sprinkle with salt, pepper, chopped parsley and, if desired, a few drops of Worcestershire.

313

Cover with layer of crushed saltine crackers, dot liberally with butter. Repeat layers until casserole contains sufficient amount to serve, ending with cracker crumbs and butter. Pour over a small amount of coffee cream or half and half. Bake in moderate (350°-375°) oven for forty to fifty minutes.

Mrs. Tom Horst

EASY FRIDAY CASSEROLE

Preparation time—15 minutes
Cooking time—45 minutes

8-10 ounces noodles	1 can cream of mushroom soup
1 large can tuna fish	⅓ can milk
1 small green pepper, chopped	Cheddar cheese, grated
1 small onion, chopped	

Cook noodles until almost tender. In greased three quart baking dish alternate layers of noodles, tuna, chopped pepper and onion and soup mixed with milk. Top with cheese and cover. Bake in 325° oven about forty-five minutes. Serves 6-8.

Mrs. Walter Adler

CURRIED SHRIMP

Total preparation time—20 minutes

1 pound large shrimp, de-veined	1 tablespoon flour
2 tablespoons butter	1 teaspoon curry powder
1 tablespoon white onion,	¼ cup sauterne wine
chopped	½ cup cream

Sauté shrimp in butter for two or three minutes, add onion and sauté three to four minutes more. Sprinkle flour mixed with curry powder over the shrimp. Stir and cook three or four minutes until shrimp turn slightly pinkish. Stir in sauterne, then cream. Simmer for ten minutes and transfer to chafing dish. Serve with rice pilaff. This recipe doubles, triples and quadruples easily.

Mrs. Barbara Cowan Butler

314

MARIE GRINER'S BAKED SEAFOOD SALAD

Preparation time—10 minutes
Cooking time—40 minutes

1 cup cooked, cleaned shrimp	1 teaspoon Worcestershire
1 cup crabmeat	½ teaspoon salt
1 cup chopped celery	pepper to taste
¼ cup chopped onion	1 cup homemade mayonnaise
¾ cup chopped green pepper	buttered bread crumbs

Mix lightly, top with buttered bread crumbs, bake 30-40 minutes in 350°
oven. Serves 6. Better if allowed to stand 3-4 hours before baking.

Mrs. Horace Spottswood

MAYONNAISE BY BLENDER

Time—5 minutes

1 large egg	1½ tablespoons lemon juice
½ teaspoon dry mustard	1 cup chilled salad oil
½ teaspoon salt	

Combine egg, mustard, salt, lemon juice and one fourth cup oil in blender.
Blend on low speed. Uncover immediately and pour in remaining oil in a
steady, slow stream.

Mrs. Paul E. Sheldon

UNCOOKED HOLLANDAISE SAUCE

Preparation time—10 minutes

2 egg yolks	½ cup melted butter
¼ teaspoon salt	1½ tablespoons lemon juice
dash of cayenne pepper	

Beat egg yolks until thick and lemon colored in mixer. Add salt and pepper.
Add, while beating, three tablespoonsful melted butter, a little at a time.
Slowly add remaining butter, alternately with lemon juice. This sauce may
be stored in the refrigerator in a glass jar. To reheat, stir over lukewarm
water, not hot water.

Mrs. Frank B. Frazer

315

GEORGE MAJOR'S BARBECUE SAUCE FOR CHICKEN

2 sticks butter   1 large bottle Worcestershire

2 lemons   2 bottles A-I sauce

2 onions

Melt butter in saucepan, cut lemons in half and squeeze juice into melted butter. Cut onions into six slices, add lemon rinds and onions to mixture. Simmer twenty minutes. Add Worcestershire and A-1, simmering an additional five minutes. Use generously on chicken roasted on a barbecue pit.

Mrs. Gillette Burton

CRANBERRY SAUCE SALAD

Preparation time—10 minutes

Chilling time—6 hours

1 package strawberry gelatin   2 mashed bananas (sprinkle with

1½ cups boiling water   lemon juice to keep color)

1 can jellied cranberry sauce   ¼ cup black walnuts

Dissolve gelatin in boiling water. Mash cranberry sauce and mix into hot mixture. Chill until mixture begins to set and then stir in bananas and nuts.

Mrs. Carl Hardin

BANANA FLAMBÉ

Preparation time—5 minutes

Cooking time—15 minutes

6 firm bananas   butter

1 cup orange juice   ½ cup rum

½ cup brown sugar

Peel bananas and slice in half, lengthwise. Arrange in layers in buttered baking dish. Sprinkle each layer with orange juice and brown sugar. Dot with butter. Bake in 400° oven until fruit is softened—not too soft—about fifteen minutes. Warm rum. Place bananas in chafing dish, bring to table and add heated rum. Ignite and serve when flame dies down. Serves 6.

Mrs. Jere Austill, Jr.

316

BANANAS FOSTER

Time—10 minutes

1 banana	a dash of cinnamon
2 teaspoons brown sugar	1 teaspoon banana liquer
2 pats butter	rum

Cut banana in four pieces and cook in sugar and butter. When tender, sprinkle with cinnamon. Pour over liquer and rum. Ignite. Pretty in chafing dish.

Mrs. Frank Webb

ARTICHOKE HEARTS AND ASPARAGUS

Time—10 minutes

1 package frozen artichoke hearts	4 tablespoons melted butter
1 can (10½ ounce) asparagus points	1 tablespoon lemon juice

Cook artichoke hearts as directed. Heat asparagus, drain. Combine the two vegetables. Pour butter and lemon juice over mixture and season with pepper.

Mrs. H. C. Slaton, Jr.

OUTDOOR GREEN BEANS

Preparation time—5 minutes
Cooking time—45 minutes

¼ cup soft butter	2 packages frozen green beans
2 tablespoons onion soup mix	broiler foil

Cream butter and onion soup mix together. Place each pack of frozen beans on a fourteen inch square of foil. Divide onion butter mixture between the two. Seal packs and place on grill forty-five minutes to an hour. Serves 6.

Mrs. Wallace S. Clark, II

BRAISED CELERY

Cut celery into one inch pieces and boil in unsalted water until tender, but crunchy. Drain and sauté quickly in butter, seasoning with salt and white pepper as you shake in pan.

Mrs. Kenneth Hannon

317

RICE CASSEROLE

Preparation time—8 minutes
Cooking time—1 hour

1 stick butter	**1 can beef consomme**
¾ pound rice	**1 can water**
salt, to taste	**mushrooms**
1 can onion soup	

Brown rice in butter, add other ingredients. Bake in covered casserole in 250° oven for about one hour. Serves 10 to 12.

Mrs. Gaillard Guillot

MEAT LOAF

Preparation time—5 minutes
Cooking time—60 minutes

1 egg, slightly beaten	**1 package dry onion soup mix**
2 teaspoons salt	**2 pounds ground beef**
¾ cup water	**½ teaspoon thyme**
1 cup bread crumbs	**1 teaspoon Worcestershire**

Mix together and pat into greased pan. Place four strips of bacon over top. Bake one hour in 350° oven. Serves 8.

Mrs. William E. Drew, Jr.

WESTERN HAMBURGERS

Preparation time—20 minutes
Heating time—30 minutes

½ cup chopped onion	**2 small cans chopped mushrooms**
¼ cup chopped green pepper	**catsup**
¼ cup chopped celery	**prepared mustard**
1 pound ground beef	**Worcestershire**
1 cup grated cheese	**Tabasco**
¼ cup sweet relish	**salt and pepper**

Sauté onion, green pepper and celery. Brown beef. Mix all ingredients together, using enough mustard and catsup to moisten, but keeping mixture fairly stiff. Hollow out center of hamburger buns and fill with mixture.

318

Wrap individually in aluminum foil and heat in 350° oven until hot all the way through, about thirty minutes. They freeze well.

Mrs. Thomas M. Taul, Jr.

BEANS AND WIENERS

Preparation time—5 minutes
Cooking time—1 hour

2—1 pound cans pork and beans	2 tablespoons brown sugar
1 envelope onion soup mix	1 tablespoon prepared mustard
½ cup catsup	8-10 frankfurters, sliced
¼ cup water	

Combine all ingredients in two quart casserole. Bake in 350° oven for one hour. Serves 6.

Mrs. William E. Drew, Jr.

HAM CASSEROLE

Preparation time—10 minutes
Cooking time—40 minutes

1 ham steak	1 can mushroom soup
sliced onion	Parmesan cheese
sliced potato	

Place ham steak in bottom of casserole dish. Place sliced onion and potato on top of ham. Cover with mushroom soup and sprinkle generously with cheese. Bake in 350° oven until potato and onion are done and dish is hot through and through.

Mrs. Paul E. Sheldon

CHILI

2 pounds ground beef	salt and pepper to taste
olive oil	1 teaspoon camino seed
2 garlic cloves	pinch of sugar
1 tablespoon paprika	1 cup minced onion
2 teaspoons oregano	1 small can tomatoes
2 tablespoons chili powder	1-2 cups hot water or consommé
(or more)	2 cans red kidney beans

319

QUICK AND EASY

Brown ground beef in olive oil. Add garlic, oregano, salt and pepper, chili powder, camino seed and sugar. Cook for a few minutes, then add onion, tomatoes, consommé and kidney beans. Simmer an hour or two.

Mrs. P. L. Wilson

BAKED CHICKEN ROSEMARY

Preparation time—10 minutes
Cooking time—30 to 40 minutes

6 chicken breasts	3 teaspoons rosemary
(3 whole breasts)	6 small pats of butter
salt and pepper to taste	

Place chicken breasts in pan lined with aluminum foil. Salt and pepper chicken and sprinkle with crushed rosemary. Place a pat of butter on each breast. Bake, uncovered in 375° oven, thirty to forty minutes, depending on size and thickness of breasts.

Mrs. R. Bruce Worley

CHICKEN AND SOUR CREAM CASSEROLE

Preparation time—10 minutes
Baking time—50 minutes

1 chicken, cut in serving pieces	1 stick butter or margarine
1 small onion, thinly sliced	½ pint sour cream
salt and pepper	

Place uncooked chicken in buttered baking dish, cover with onion rings. Add salt and pepper to taste and sliced butter. Bake in 350° oven for thirty minutes. Remove from oven, add sour cream by pouring over chicken and mixing with melted butter. Bake for twenty minutes longer, basting occasionally. There will be enough sour cream gravy to serve on rice.

Mrs. William Porter

CHICKEN FLAMBÉ

Preparation time—10 minutes
Cooking time—1½ to 2 hours

4 chicken halves	paprika
¼ pound butter	tarragon
salt and pepper	⅓ cup cognac

320

Rub chicken well with butter, sprinkle with salt, pepper, paprika and tarragon. Place chicken in shallow pan and bake in 300° oven one and a half to two hours. Baste frequently, adding more butter as needed. When done, transfer to serving dish, heat cognac, pour over chicken and ignite at serving time.

Mrs. Vance E. Thompson, Jr.

CHICKEN LIVER RICE CASSEROLE

Preparation time—10 minutes
Cooking time—20 minutes

1 package Betty Crocker's Rice Province	1 pound chicken livers

Brown chicken livers well. Mix rice according to package directions, add livers and bake.

Mrs. Willis R. Brown

BAKED PORK CHOPS

Preparation time—5 minutes
Cooking time—45 minutes

Salt and pepper four thick chops and rub them well with thyme or oregano. Arrange chops in a baking dish, cover with milk or light cream and bake in 350° oven until tender. Sprinkle liberally with chopped parsley.

Mrs. M. B. McMurphy

EASY COCONUT MACAROONS

2 egg whites	¼ teaspoon vanilla
¼ cup sugar	2 cups moist shredded coconut
¾ cup sifted confectioner's sugar	dash of salt

Beat egg whites until frothy. Gradually add, while beating, sugar and confectioner's sugar. Continue beating until very stiff and glossy. Stir in vanilla, coconut and salt. Drop by teaspoonfuls onto lightly greased baking sheet. Bake in 325° oven for fifteen minutes or until set and lightly browned. Makes two dozen.

Mrs. H. W. Thurber, Jr.

SHERRY PIE

1 package small marshmallows	graham cracker pie crust baked
¾ cup sherry	without sugar
½ pint whipping cream	grated chocolate or cherries

Melt marshmallows in double boiler top with sherry. Cool for several hours. Beat and add whipped cream. Pour into baked pie shell and chill several hours. Decorate with grated chocolate or cherries.

Mrs. Russell Terry

LEMON SPONGE CAKE

Preparation time—5 minutes, cooking time—45 minutes

1 box yellow cake mix	3 teaspoons lemon extract
½ cup plus 2 tablespoons	4 eggs
salad oil	⅔ cup apricot nectar

Mix all ingredients, pour into greased and floured pan and bake in 350° over for forty-five minutes. Before removing cake from pan pour the following over all:

juice of 2½ lemons mixed with 1½ cups confectioner's sugar. Cool cake completely before removing from pan.

Mrs. John McGehee

QUICKIE LADY FINGER DESSERT

Line ice cube tray with split lady fingers. Spread sherry jelly on single lady fingers, then spread squares of vanilla ice cream on top of this. Spread jelly and lady fingers on top. Serve cold with boiled custard sauce over each individual serving.

Mrs. W. H. Armbrecht, Jr.

QUICK COBBLER

Preparation time—5 minutes, cooking time—1 hour

1 can prepared fruit for pie	1 small box (1 layer) cake mix
(apple, peach, cherry, etc.)	(white, yellow or spice)
1 stick margarine	

Pour fruit into one quart casserole dish. Sprinkle cake mix over fruit and cut margarine into slices over top. Bake in 350° oven for one hour. Serve plain or with ice cream or whipped cream.

Mrs. Russell Terry

322

CHERRIES JUBILEE

1 (No. 2) can bing cherries   vanilla ice cream
¼ cup cognac

Heat cherries in their juice in nickel, silver or porcelain chafing dish. Pour in one half of the cognac while cherries are heating, do not boil. When hot, dash with remaining cognac, ignite and serve over ice cream.

Mrs. Robert Byrd

PRALINE CAKE

1 yellow cake	2 eggs
½ cup butter	1 teaspoon vanilla
1 pound light brown sugar	1½ cups chopped pecans
2 tablespoons flour	

Melt butter in skillet. Mix brown sugar, flour and beaten eggs. Add this to butter in skillet and cook three minutes over low heat. Remove from heat and stir in vanilla and pecans. Spread evenly over two cake layers or sheet cake. Return cake to oven and bake at 400° for eight minutes.

Mrs. Gilbert Dukes, Jr.

BAKED GRAPEFRUIT

Cut grapefruit in half, cut out center, cut pods loose from shell. Pour one tablespoon sherry in center. Fill center and sprinkle entire top with brown sugar. Bake in oven until grapefruit begins to brown on edges and is very hot. (about fifteen minutes at 375°)

Mrs. Robert T. King

GELATIN POUND CAKE

Preparation time—5 minutes, cooking time—1 hour

1 package Duncan Hines yellow cake mix	1 package lemon gelatin
	⅔ cup water
4 eggs	⅔ cup Wesson Oil

Preheat oven to 325°. Mix all ingredients together as directed on package of cake mix. Bake in greased and floured tube pan for one hour in 325° oven. Oven must be preheated. Do not try to use another brand of cake mix as it will not work.

Mrs. Tom Horst, Jr.

323

MY FAVORITES

QUANTITY COOKING

QUANTITIES NEEDED TO SERVE TWENTY-FIVE

lettuce, large—5 heads
mayonnaise or salad dressing—
  1 pt.
coffee—¾ lb.
cookies—75
cream for coffee—1¼ pts.
cream to whip—1 pt.
  (1 tablespoon per person)
salted nuts—1 lb.
olives—1 qt.
small pickles—1 qt.
punch—1 gal.

rolls or biscuits—3½ dz.
small sandwiches—100
turkey—20 lbs.
butter—⅜ of lb.
small cakes—50
celery hearts—5 bunches
chicken, diced—4 to 4½ lbs.
chicken salad—4½ qts.
ice cream, brick—4 qts. (6 servings
  to brick)
ice cream, bulk—1 gal. (7 servings
  per qt.)

MISCELLANEOUS INFORMATION

50 slices pineapple in a #10 or a gal. can
40 pear halves in a #10 or a gal. can
50 peach halves in a #10 or a gal. can
2 large boxes Uncle Ben's Rice serves 50
22 lbs. boneless beef serves 50 or 60
12 lbs. ground beef for meat loaf serves 50 or 60
20 lbs. turkey serves 50 or 60
20 lbs. boneless stew meat with carrots, onions and potatoes serves 80
10 lbs. rolled, boneless ham serves 60
1½ gal. green beans serves 50
6 lb. sheet cake serves 96
4 packages Spice Cake baked in long pans serves 60 (cut in squares)
20 slices coconut cake in large cake
14 cans green limas serves 60
pies—6 wedges
1 lb. coffee—makes 50 cups
2 lbs. sugar—serves 50 people coffee
2 1 lb. cartons cottage cheese, fluffed with a fork, ½ pt. mayonnaise—
  serves 60
2 large heads lettuce under any fruit salad—serves 60

Mrs. Rencher

325

INDEX

331

332

GAME AND FOWL, See Chicken, Cornish Hen, Dove, Duck, Pheasant, Quail, Turkey, Venison.
Garden Crisp Salad, 66
Garlic Grits, 203
Gaspacho, 42
Gelatin Pound Cake, 323
George Major's Barbecue Sauce for Chicken, 316
German Blueberry Pie, 290
German Ice Box Cookies, 297
German Sweet Chocolate Cake, 259
Ginger Ale Salad, Frozen, 70
Gingerbread, 262
Glazed Roast Pork, 163
Grandmother's Bread and Butter Pickles, 232
Grandmother's Devils Food Cake, 270
Grandmother's Ground Roast Beef Patties, 156
Grapes and Doves, 122
Grapefruit, Baked, 323
  Ring, 72
  Salad, 72
  And Cherry Salad, 71
Grasshopper, 33
Grasshopper Pie, Marguerite Griner's, 283
Green Beans, 179
  Casserole, French, 179
  Dutch, 177
  Outdoor, 317
  Salad, I, 60
  Salad, II, 60
  with Onions, 178
  with Water Chestnuts in Sour Cream, 178
Green Noodle Chicken, 138
Green Pea Casserole, 189
Green Peas, 188
Green Peas and Mushrooms, 188
Green Pepper Steak, 147
Green Rice, 201
Green Tomato Pickle, 232
Green Tomato Relish, 228
Gregg Street Pound Cake, 273
Grilled Fish, 100
Gulf Shores Special Sauce, 50
Gumbo, Mrs. Edward Sledge, Sr's., 40
  Nanny's Never Fail Crab, 40
  Turkey and Oyster, 39

HAM
  and Broccoli Casserole, 167
  and Oyster Chafing Dish Specialty, 107
  and Pineapple Dish, 168
  Baked Slice of, 168
  Casserole, 319
  Fresh Roasted, 167
  Loaf, 170
    Cold, 169
    With Cherry Sauce, 169

Rounds, 13
Swedish Balls, 170
Tennessee, 168
Sauces for
  Brandied Cherry, 169
  Cherry, 169
  Mustard I, 46
  Mustard II, 47
  Orange, 45
  Raisin, 45
Hamburgers, Western, 318
Hamburgers with Barbeque Sauce, 157
Harvard Beets, 177
Heavenly Pie, 282
Hen, Cornish a la Francaise, 128
Hen, Cornish in Wine, 128
Hen, Cornish in Cherry Sauce, 129
Hens, Cornish—Stuffing for Twelve, 129
Herb Chicken, 131
Herb Rolls, 213
Herb Toasted Buns, 224
Hollandaise Sauce, 52
  Absolutely Perfect, 52
  Uncooked, 315
Home-made Doughnuts, 218
Home-made Peach Ice Cream, 237
Home-made Waffles, 217
Hominy Pie, 154
Honey Fruit Salad Dressing, 78
Horseradish Dressing, 82
Hot Appetizers, 22
Hot Chicken Salad, 139
Hot Crabmeat Puffs, 14
Hot Dog Sauce, 47
Hot Pickled Shrimp, 16
Hot Shrimp Sauce, 49
Hot Tamale Pie, 158
Hush Puppies, 212
Hyden Salad (Relish), 229

Ice Box Pie, Crust for, 292
  Magic Lemon, 290
  Strawberry, 285
Ice Box Pudding, Chocolate, 247
Ice Box Rolls, 215
Ice Box Waffles, 217
Ice Cream Pie, Rice Cereal, 282
ICE CREAM, 235
  Banana, 237
  Chocolate, 238
  Custard, 239
  Fresh Fig, 236
  Home-made Peach, 237
  Old Time Home-made, 238
  Peach, 237
  Sauces for, 239
  Vanilla, 238
Ices, 275, see Sherbets
  Cranberry, 235
  Frozen Buttermilk, 235
  Raspberry Sherbet I, 235
  Raspberry Sherbet II, 236

Salads *(Continued)*
Fresh Pineapple Salad Plate, 73
Fresh Broccoli or Spinach Salad, 61
Frozen Eyeopener, 64
Frozen Fruit Salad, 67
Frozen Ginger Ale Salad, 70
Frozen Tomato Salad I, 64
Frozen Tomato Salad II, 65
Fruit Salad and Dressing, 67
Garden Crisp Salad, 66
Grapefruit Ring, 72
Grapefruit Salad, 72
Green Bean Salad I, 60
Green Bean Salad II, 60
Hot Chicken, 139
Jellied Artichokes, 57
Lime Fruit Salad, 70
Lime Pineapple Molded Salad, 71
Lime Salad, 70
Mint Flavored Pear Salad, 73
Perfection Salad, 62
Sauterne Salad, 69
Seafood Canapé, 56
Spiced Peach Salad, 74
Summer Treat Chicken Mold, 75
Tomato Aspic, 63
Tomato Aspic Ring, 63
Tomato Aspic with Cream Cheese Filling, 63
Twenty-four Hour Salad, 68
Vegetable Aspic, 62
West Indies Salad, 71
SALAD DRESSINGS, 77
Bleu Cheese Dressing, 79
Cheese Croutons, 82
Cooked Fruit Salad Dressing, 77
Cooked Salad Dressing, 80
Cream Garlic Salad Dressing, 79
Dressing for Fruit Salad, 77
Faucon Dressing, 80
French Dressing without Garlic, 82
French Dressing with Garlic, 82
Honey Fruit Salad, 78
Horseradish, 82
Lime Salad, 77
Mayonnaise, 78
Mayonnaise II, 79
Mayonnaise by Blender, 315
Our House French, 81
Poppy Seed, 78
Roquefort Cream, 79
Sina Skinner's Salad, 81
Thousand Island, 81
Tomato Dressing, 80
Sally Lunn, 219
Salmon Egg Spread, 18
Salmon Mold, 102
Sandwich, Curry Ripe Olive, 26
Sandwich, Mushrooms, 24
Sardine, Paté, 18

Sardine Spread, 18

SAUCES
For Desserts:
Boiled Custard Sauce, 240
Butterscotch Sauce, 240
Chocolate Sauce, 239
Foamy Sauce, 240
Mocha Fudge Sauce, 240
Rum Sauce, 239
Wonderful Chocolate Syrup, 239
For Meats:
Barbecue Sauce I, 46
Barbecue Sauce II, 46
Barbecue Sauce for Fresh Pork, 47
Barbecue, George Major's for Chicken, 316
Barbecue for ribs, 47
Brandy Cherry, 169
Brown, 170
Canadian Bacon, 46
Cherry Sauce, 169
Chili I, 48
Chili II, 48
Cranberry Fresh, 45
Espagnole, 148
Horseradish, 174
Horseradish, 82
Hot Dog, 47
Marchand De Vin, 44
Marchand De Vin Sauce, 44
Mustard Sauce for Ham I, 46
Mustard Sauce for Ham II, 47
Orange Sauce for Ham or Lamb, 45
Raisin, 45
Steak Marinade, 44
For Seafood:
Boiled Shrimp, 49
Cold Boiled Salmon, 49
Gulf Shores Special, 50
Hot Shrimp, 49
Mushroom, 49
Oyster Rockefeller, 104
Shrimp Arnaud, 50
Shrimp Green Goddess, 50
Shrimp Remoulade I, 51
Shrimp Remoulade II, 51
Tartar, 48
For Vegetables:
Almond Cheese, 52
Chive, 51
Hollandaise, 52
Hollandaise, Absolutely Perfect, 51
Hollandaise, Uncooked, 315
Sausage Roll, 311
Sautéed Red Snapper Bombay, 98
Sauterne Salad, 69
Scalloped Oysters, 104
Scalloped Oysters, Quick, 313
Schaum Torte, 245
Scrambled Eggs with Cream Cheese, 204

A unique phenomenon occurs on the eastern shore of Mobile Bay. Natives of the area know the signs to watch for—in the moon, the tide, and the winds.

Shrimps, crabs, and fish race to the water's edge and the cry of JUBILEE! rings up and down the beach. With buckets, baskets and nets in tow, visitors and natives alike gather a bounty of fresh sea food.

Recipe Jubilee!
Mobile Junior League Publications
P.O. Box 7091, Mobile, Al 36607

Please send me _____ copies of **Recipe Jubilee!** at $11.95 plus $1.50 postage and handling per copy. Alabama residents add $.48, Mobile County residents $.84 sales tax per copy.

Enclosed is my check or money order for $ _____

Name _____

Address _____

City _____ State _____ Zip _____

☐ Check for FREE gift wrap.
Price subject to change.

Recipe Jubilee!
Mobile Junior League Publications
P.O. Box 7091, Mobile, Al 36607

Please send me _____ copies of **Recipe Jubilee!** at $11.95 plus $1.50 postage and handling per copy. Alabama residents add $.48, Mobile County residents $.84 sales tax per copy.

Enclosed is my check or money order for $ _____

Name _____

Address _____

City _____ State _____ Zip _____

☐ Check for FREE gift wrap.
Price subject to change.

Recipe Jubilee!
Mobile Junior League Publications
P.O. Box 7091, Mobile, Al 36607

Please send me _____ copies of **Recipe Jubilee!** at $11.95 plus $1.50 postage and handling per copy. Alabama residents add $.48, Mobile County residents $.84 sales tax per copy.

Enclosed is my check or money order for $ _____

Name _____

Address _____

City _____ State _____ Zip _____

☐ Check for FREE gift wrap.
Price subject to change.

Reorder Additional Copies